RUGBY LEAGUE COACH

Rugby League Coach

13 Game-Changing Conversations to Transform Your Coaching

Lee Addison

Copyright © 2025 by Lee Addison

All rights reserved.

No portion of this book may be reproduced in any form without written permission from the publisher or author, except as permitted by Australian copyright law.

This publication is designed to provide accurate and authoritative information in regard to the subject matter covered. It is sold with the understanding that neither the author nor the publisher is engaged in rendering legal, investment, accounting or other professional services. While the publisher and author have used their best efforts in preparing this book, they make no representations or warranties with respect to the accuracy or completeness of the contents of this book and specifically disclaim any implied warranties of merchantability or fitness for a particular purpose. No warranty may be created or extended by sales representatives or written sales materials. The advice and strategies contained herein may not be suitable for your situation. You should consult with a professional when appropriate. Neither the publisher nor the author shall be liable for any loss of profit or any other commercial damages, including but not limited to special, incidental, consequential, personal, or other damages.

Book Cover by Kathy Shanks, Turtle Publishing

First edition [2025]

Contents

Dedication	IX
Foreword by James Tedesco	XI
Author's Note	XVII
Introduction	XXIII
Part One	
13 Things Coaches Do Wrong	5
Part Two	
1. Coaching: More Than Just X's and O's	43
2. Change Management	63
3. Footy and Coaching Talk	83
4. What to Coach	111
5. How to Coach It	121
"His knowledge of the game is second to none" –	
6. How to Plan It	141
7. How to Manage It	159
8. Long-term Player Development	175
9. A Strength and Conditioning Overview	203
10. Recruitment and Watching Players	227

11. Analysing the Game	243
12. Look After Yourself, Coach	267
13. Coaching in the 21st Century	281

Part Three

    The Coach's Calling...   313

Dedication

To the memory of my mother, your smile will never be forgotten! To my new niece or nephew that will arrive in 2025 and to my Dad, my greatest ever supporter.

Foreword by James Tedesco

In the last decade or so, I have done lots of work with a coach who has helped me to ensure I have a clear mind going into games, something I have heard referred to as being 'in the zone' or 'flow' in other sports. Funnily enough, this is the same concept the St Gregory's College Rugby League coach introduced to me in my last year of High School in 2010!

In 2009, I only briefly played first grade for the college as I was still in Year 11. That year, I remember sitting on the bench for a National Schoolboy Cup game but never getting on the field. I was at the younger end of the group at only 16, so it seemed my chance to play regular first grade at the school would have to wait until I got to Year 12. There was also a fair bit of disappointment that we didn't do better that season, as our side contained many talented players.

Towards the end of 2009, we started hearing whispers around the school that we were about to get an experienced footy coach to take our first grade the following year. Traditionally, it was Physical Education teachers who tended to take our teams, but we hadn't won a championship for a long time, so we were now getting a coach who focused specifically on Rugby League.

We were told that this was happening to get us to win more. This created some excitement amongst the boys, even though we were losing some talent at the end of that school season. Alex McKinnon, Jack DeBelin and several other strong players were about to graduate, leaving Matt Groat - who would also be my future teammate at Wests Tigers – as the only New South Wales (NSW) and Australian Schoolboy representative on our books for 2010. We were looking a bit weaker in terms of playing squad for the following season.

2010 came, and our new coach was this big Pommy guy called Lee Addison! He'd been at Manly Sea Eagles and was now at Penrith Panthers. In our first meeting, he told us that *"every position in the team was up for grabs"*, or words to that effect. I jumped on this straight away because I was playing a lot of wing. In younger age groups, though, I had played a bit of fullback and occasionally at five-eighth, too, so I knew I could have a serious go at one of those positions.

In the first session, he got us to play each other to see what talent we had. It was a wet day, so we had been moved to the lower fields, which resembled the small fields you play on as kids, with longer grass and not much room to play. I went up to Lee and his Assistant Craig Bissell after the warm-up and asked if I could have a go at five-eighth. Lee said yes straight away, and (Lee tells this story not me) he was so impressed that it was my position to lose after that session.

I and several of the other boys were swamped during the pre-season months because we were also playing in SG Ball representative teams. I was at Wests Magpies, and we got to the semi-final of the comp that year, very narrowly losing to Sydney Roosters, who won the title the week after. David Nofoaluma – a future NRL wing - was playing fullback for us for most of that year whilst I – a future NRL fullback - played wing!

Lee appreciated that we were busy, so he kept the work we SG Ball boys did with the St Greg's team to a reasonable level. The players who didn't feature in SG Ball were getting put through their paces more than ever, though! There was a proper gym program set up, they were asked to come in for early morning sessions and they trained four days a week straight after school! The other SG Ball boys and I only had to do the team run each week. Lee called them the 13 v 13 sessions.

I remember training being intense and the season in general being a great time, but Lee was a strict coach and if I am honest, it was just what we needed that year. In one session we did 3 v 2's for an hour until we got them right! It was a shock to the system for many players, but the boys also knew it was moving us in the right direction.

Lee wasn't just cracking the whip on us; he wanted us to have fun while we were doing it. During the first school holidays, he had us in a camp at the school, staying in the boarding houses over a weekend. We SG Ball players got home from our game and Lee asked us to star in his home cut version of Channel 9 Cricket to simulate some 'KFC Classic Catches'! (He says he has a video of all these catches and threatened to release them if I didn't write nice things about him!) The day after, we had a light training run and then played cricket all afternoon. It was all recorded, with Lee and other teachers, including one of the Deputies, fully suited and booted and acting as Channel 9 commentators. We had great fun, and our school season was due to start a matter of weeks later.

We had a really good season, going undefeated during the week-to-week fixtures in our Sydney competition and also winning some National Schoolboy Cup games. This was a massive improvement on previous seasons. I played five-eighth in every game, and he also had me goal-kicking!

What Lee did for me that season was encourage me to back myself. He showed lots of confidence in me and allowed me to use my instincts on the field. Lee taught me things but emphasized that he didn't want to put any restrictions on me. Instead, he used to teach me to *"Let it Flow"*, which meant not to overanalyze things and relax and play my way. When he was going around the sheds before a game giving players instructions, he would only ever tell me those three words... 'Let It Flow'!

One instruction Lee did give me during training though was to not chip-kick to myself in our half! He had seen me trying it in training and felt he needed to reign that one in, but I wasn't giving it up without a fight! In a huge Schoolboy Cup game at Westfields High, we were 14-0 up with not long left to play, so I felt brave enough to do it. The chip came off perfectly, and I passed it to one of the lads who went in under the sticks. I turned to Lee, pointed to him and winked. In return, he pretended to be angry with me and pointed back!

In the Grand Final of our Sydney comp, we played Patrician Brothers Blacktown who were full of NRL contracted players while we only had one or two. We went in as huge underdogs. We were helped, however, by a great turnout from the school's boarders who gave us amazing support.

In the opening minutes of the Grand Final, I did what my coach said and backed my instincts when I saw space on the short side, and it worked - we went in for an early try! My halves partner, James Luff, was brilliant that night and all season, knowing instinctively knew what to do and when. He'd pass the ball to me cleanly, quickly and repeatedly early in the game but, later in each half, he would take a sharp turn off his right foot and ghost through the defence who thought he was passing to me again. He did this that night and scored right under the sticks, as did our full-back Sabir just before half-time. It was a lead we never lost, and we went on to win! The boarders went, wild and it was a massive moment for the school.

A few weeks later, I got picked for NSW Combined Catholic Colleges and, from there, Australian Schoolboys. I also signed my first contract at Wests. 2010 was a year of firsts! Groaty also got picked, so the pair of us were off to England. Lee's Dad came to watch us and say hello after one of the games!

A lot of the team, including myself and Groaty, left school at the end of 2010, but the lads won the comp in 2011 as well when nobody expected them to, so Lee's training obviously worked! Lee and I have always kept in touch, and he has always sent me a supportive message in the good times and the not-so-good times, too which means a lot.

He's a very smart coach who knows his footy. He also knows how to avoid overcomplicating the game for his players, which is very important and something many coaches don't yet understand. I spend lots of time as a professional ensuring that I keep my thoughts about the game and the role I have to play as simple as possible and free of mental clutter. When I was a teenager, Lee first taught me that and it worked.

Reading the football sections of this book has brought back so many memories of what Lee had us St Greg's boys so. If it worked for us, I know it will work for you.

James Tedesco is fullback and captain of the Sydney Roosters. He has played for Australia 13 times and for New South Wales 23 times, captaining both teams. He won the Dally M Medal as the NRL Player of the Year in 2019. He has also won the Dally M Captain of the Year in 2021 and Dally M Fullback of the Year award on four occasions, 2016, 2019, 2022 and 2024.

Author's Note

When was the last time you saw or read a book about coaching Rugby League? By that, I mean, when was the last time you found a book with tips on how to coach the sport, designed entirely as a guide to improving your coaching?

As I sit here writing, I've just typed 'Rugby League Coaching' into the search engine of one of the biggest book providers in the world. The only things I can find that go close to meeting the criteria on the first page of online offerings are:

- A 1982 'Coaching Rugby League' paperback by the British on-field and commentary box legend Ray French

- A 1988 book by former England coach Phil Larder

- A 1997 book on 'Conditioning for Rugby League' by another former England coach, John Kear.

When I tried Google, I found another old book, a fourth edition published in 1999 of 'Coaching Rugby League' by Peter D Corcoran, then of the Australian Rugby League.

Several stories have written about Rugby League coaches, and each has some coaching anecdotes and tips weaved within, but there is a distinct lack of books out there that talk directly to coaches. It is this void on your bookshelf that **'Rugby League Coach - 13 game-changing conversations to transform your coaching'** aims to fill.

If you're as passionate about coaching as I have been for the last 26 years, then I am very confident that you will enjoy reading this book. I possess a unique coaching resume in that I have coached players at every level of the game of Rugby League and had an extensive and distinctive range of experiences, some of them concurrently! I have also studied coaching academically and in a self-directed manner for that time.

I'm a coach who has won many games and a lot of competitions with my teams and helped many players to get to a place they never did before. I have produced and helped to develop a lot of players to a professional standard and have coached from grassroots to professional and World Cups.

I am a coach who has been lucky enough to work with some of the top coaches and to have helped some of the best players in the game, but also some of the freshest coaches and players to the sport, in countries as far apart in Rugby League ability and experience as they were geographically. I am a coach who has worked with players who were almost the finished article, others who had huge desires to become the finished article and some who were too young even to consider what their future might have in store.

I have also made mistakes along the way, be it in my desire to take on almost any coaching challenge without doing due diligence on whether the team and I were the right fit for each other or demanding too much of players who were not at the same level of motivation or ambition as each other or myself. Over the years, coaching delivery, conversations and messages have all been more refined with age, experience and (hopefully) wisdom. I still occasionally catch up with people who remember something from my coaching history that makes me wince a bit. In my defence, I am not aware of anyone who started selecting teams and coaching in their teens, continuing to work for over a quarter of a century in opposing hemispheres, with groups with a wide range of abilities who could say they have an unblemished record.

What I do know is that I have dedicated most of my life to helping coaches, players, clubs and schools become better versions of themselves and have done

AUTHOR'S NOTE

this for close to three decades and counting. I am extremely confident I can do the same for you as you (hopefully) power your way through this book.

This book includes some of the most important lessons, working models and philosophies from a coaching journey that has taken me worldwide and many players and teams to places they'd never been before. The lessons I have learned and any errors I made along the way are not in vain because I will share them with you, the reader, so that you don't fall into the same trap. The book is suitable for coaches at any level, from those doing the all-important grassroots work to those getting towards or at the top. All the way through, I am talking to you, the coach.

After the introduction, we will go through the **'13 Things Coaches Do Wrong'** in Part One. If you read them and think, *"shit – that's me!"* please don't give up coaching or get down on yourself! These things I outline are so common that I see them almost every time I visit a place where Rugby League training is being conducted, and this includes 'professional' coaching environments and so-called 'high performance' ones, too. I also made all these mistakes when I started coaching. I believe they are all part of and a result of the Rugby League 'eco-system' and certain historical influences, which I elaborate more on within these pages.

The '13 Things Coaches Do Wrong' is designed to get you thinking about your own coaching before we embark on thirteen chapters which form the ***'13 Game-Changing Conversations to Transform Your Coaching'*** – written to cover key areas of coaching practice that will, in essence, be 'How to do them right!' These chapters are a mix of 'theory', 'case study' or 'story' as, in my mind, there is little that is more frustrating than reading a technical book full of jargon that takes some deciphering. As a result, much of this book will include stories that support the advice offered. I have also tried to keep as much of the book as possible in 'story form' or in 'general chat' form. I want it to be readable, relatable and understandable, not to blow you away with scientific jargon that you have to 'google' to understand the meaning!

At the end of each of the main chapters in Part Two, you will see a summary of the key points highlighted, followed by words from those who have been with me on the journey. Some of them are well-known names, and all are very respected people in the sport. In Part Three right at the end of the book, I tell you more about my own journey as a person. Can you guess why there are '13 Things That Coaches Do Wrong' and (in Part Two) '13 Game-Changing Conversations to Transform Your Coaching' in a Rugby League coaching book? It's 13v13!

I'd love you to read it all front to back, but if you want to jump directly into the things you may be doing wrong as a coach or straight to the coaching advice or anything else that you like the look of, you certainly can! Please use the contents page to guide you around this book if you want to.

The philosophies, theories and approaches included in the book are for coaches and players and by direct association, they will relate to clubs, schools, emerging Rugby League territories and nations and similar organisations.

The theories, ideas and stories within these pages are relevant and applicable to many environments, both sporting and non-sporting. Many of the examples I use are from the sport I have coached for so long. I should, however, let it be known at this juncture that I have also been a Physical Education teacher, worked in Marketing departments and run various businesses too. Whatever your role in rugby league or sport in general, my hope is that this book provides you with some inspiration and guidance on your own personal journey or that of your club, school or similar organisation.

I have written and edited every word in this book (with contributions), and zero AI was used to compile it. The book has been largely self-published, so every effort has been made to ensure it is of the best quality. The places I have been tapping away on my keyboard include various locations around the cities of Logan and Brisbane (including my sofa and my office at home), the Queensland State Library, on a 27-hour train journey from Brisbane to Cairns, in Cairns itself, on the plane back from Cairns, plus Warialda and Sydney in New South Wales.

AUTHOR'S NOTE

Thanks to former Queensland Times, Courier Mail and Channel 7 journalist Chris Garry for giving the penultimate draft a thorough read and giving me pointers to make it better. Thank you to legendary League journalist Joel Gould, who has documented so much of my coaching journey for public consumption over the years. A huge thank you also to my little army of proofreaders including, Katie Murphy and Trent Williams from up here in Queensland, Peter Kolodziej and Leisa Proc down in Sydney and Chris Adasko over in the UK. May I also give another huge thank you to Kathy Shanks of Turtle Publishing for her work and counsel in the closing stages of this book project.

There have been many fellow coaches, officials and volunteers who have been an integral part of my coaching journey and therefore, the stories that are mentioned within these pages. Also, let's not forget the most important people in any coach's life – the players. Mentioning them all in the book was extremely difficult, so here I extend my heartfelt thanks to all of the staff and players over the years. So many of you are lifelong friends who mean an awful lot to me.

If you've picked it up to read and got this far, I'd love you to join me each Monday by listening to The Rugby League Coach Podcast wherever you get your pods. I give free coaching advice each week on that and also answer coaching questions for free. Feel free to email me at admin@rugbyleaguecoach.com.au to say hello, maybe ask a question that arises from you reading this book and tell me all about yourself.

I hope you enjoy reading it as much as I enjoyed writing it.

Lee Addison, 24th January 2025.

Introduction

It was a call I was not expecting at all because all the signs in the weeks leading up were that I was getting promoted at Penrith Panthers after 'Gus' had arrived at the club, not sacked!

"We're not going with the same coaches next year, Lee. We're bringing in new ones at all grades. It's a clean-out. Sorry mate." Said the man on the other end of the line.

With that phone call, taken on a dark, wintry Western Sydney night in June 2011, my time as a lower-grade coach at Penrith had come to an end. Instead of moving up the grades as I was told I would be, I was now on the coaching scrap heap as far as the professional game was concerned. I had left Manly Sea Eagles and Premiership winner Des Hasler to come to Penrith, an area that was a Rugby League hotbed, and now I had no club to go to. Was my coaching career over?

The 'Gus' in question was none other than Phil Gould of Channel 9 fame, one of the sharpest minds in the sport, the newly appointed General Manager of Football at Penrith Panthers and someone I still, to this day, admire for his football acumen. He has won first-grade premierships as a head coach, is the most successful New South Wales coach in Origin history and to me, reads the game and describes how it is unfolding in such a brilliant way. He also sorted Penrith out top-to-bottom and did a fantastic job in his time there.

Gus had arrived at the Panthers months earlier with a remit as a change agent and change things he did. Despite my team finishing highest out of all grades at the club that year (a group containing only two (soon to be) well-known first-grade players), I was gone via a phone call from one of his offsiders. I didn't even get a chance to meet Mr. Gould to state my claims and still haven't met him to this day. This was the second time I had been punted as a coach, but the first since I had been in Australia, and to get turfed out by an NRL club in what seemed unfair circumstances was a bitter pill to swallow. I was 32 years old and thought I was on the coaching scrap heap.

After a night or two feeling down, I comforted myself with the fact that I had a big Grand Final to prepare a team for a few weeks later. By night, I was working at the Panthers, but by day, I was in what was then a dream coaching job at St Gregory's College, a Sydney school with a huge history in Rugby League. It was a role that ultimately kickstarted a chain of other events that saw me enjoy some of the most amazing coaching experiences I have ever had, achieving some great successes in places beyond my wildest dreams, both in Australia and overseas. (More of all that, later).

It was our second consecutive Grand Final as we prepared to become the first back-to-back premiers from St Gregory's, a former powerhouse in the sport, since the 1990s. Our opponents, Patrician Brothers Blacktown, were now **the** powerhouse in this particular realm, and they were chock full of future professionals and man for man, a lot bigger and more powerful than every other team.

In winning the Grand Final against all odds and the same opponent a year earlier, I remember doing so much homework on them that I think me and the Greg's boys knew more about their team than they did! After all, Sun Tzu, the Chinese military general, said in the *'Art of War'* that *"If you know your enemy and know yourself, you need not fear the result of a hundred battles",* and I had just spent an off-season consuming as much of Sun Tzu's teachings in whatever format I could.

In August 2010, as we prepared for the school's first Grand Final appearance in a while, I didn't need to prepare the team for a hundred battles. Just one. A year on, I had taken the same approach ahead of the second Grand Final against

'Pats'. There was now no time to dwell on my culling from Penrith; we had a competition (or a battle) to win at Parramatta Stadium.

In terms of 'knowing my enemy', I had charted Pats as much as I could for the last year and a half, obtaining every video of them I could and every bit of information I could gather. Also, they were resplendent with several of the players from the side I had coached that year at Penrith Panthers! They chopped and changed their side a lot, but their game plan, under their coach who was in the Parramatta Eels coaching system, often stayed the same. They often barged through the middle of the field with their biggest players before moving the ball one way, then back to the middle, then moving the ball the other way, then back to the middle.

They had beaten virtually everyone in their path for the last couple of years, sometimes blowing their opposition off the park. My players seemed to live in a little fear of them and held them in the highest regard. Everyone in wider schoolboy Rugby League circles seemed to talk about how good they were, and many of their players were on the books of professional clubs such as Penrith, Parramatta and Sydney Roosters, whereas only one of mine at the time, Adam Elliott, went on to play in the NRL.

In winning the competition a year earlier, I had given the players every bit of information I felt was relevant. The key word is 'relevant' – no need to overwhelm them with things. It's not about what you tell them; it's about what they hear. And what they can use. Because every opposition team has an Achilles heel, but every one of my teams, including my sides at Greg's, didn't need to know too much about their own weaknesses at this time of the year. Why? I wanted them to feel they were the best players in the world and that they could achieve anything.

I showed the boys on video and taught them about the spaces that existed in the Pats defensive line. If, as we expected, their defence was to be spaced, their big men would tire if we played by probing 'away' from the play the ball, using our halves to give the ball to the forwards a good 12 to 16 metres wide of the ruck as much as possible. We practiced this relentlessly in training, with our reserve grade holding pads (so they could hit us hard) and defending in the same formation as we expected Pats to defend in. I also showed them this in team meetings, small groups or one-on-one sessions. They also got video previews that identified which opposition players struggled to tackle on one or sometimes both shoulders.

Rather than trying to get my much smaller side to beat them by engaging in a direct battle in the middle, we planned to make Pats chase after us. That meant that they did more passive tackles with their arms than front-on tackles with their shoulders throughout the game. Big men, after all, don't like moving sideways constantly and going to ground without being dominant and on their terms. Sun Tzu also offers support for this theory it seems, when he said, *"Outmanoeuvre the enemy before the first battle then fight to win."*

General Tzu also said, *"Your momentum must be overwhelming. Your timing must be exact – like the pulling of a trigger"*, so I always interpreted this as an instruction to make sure we always got quick play the balls and were aware of any chances that opened up, anywhere on the field and at any time. I have always coached with the philosophy that we should never let the opponent relax, either with or without the ball, and we should always do what the opponent doesn't want us to. They wanted us to try to take them on in midfield. No, thank you!

In the final we won in 2010, we had started the game so alert, fast and sharp that we scored the first try in the opening minutes down the short side where they were least expecting or wanting us to go. We also did the same at the start of the second half. In 2011, we scored early again but had done something very different in the opening exchanges. We moved the ball side to side so much that the opposition must have thought we must surely run out of room and go over the sidelines. But when they least expected us to move the ball again, we shifted it once more and went in for a four-pointer. It didn't become six, though, as the kick was missed.

Unlike in 2010, Pats weren't going to be shocked or overwhelmed by our mobility or speed. By any reasonable measure, we had less talent on the field than a year earlier, and we were smaller and visibly slower. One of my wings was nicknamed 'The Mattress' because he looked like he was running on one all the time because his legs were that long! Yet he had more pace than first appeared, and I assured him that we would create the space for him to run in. He was great under the high ball and at taking direct carries when we needed him to, so he was often a first name on the team sheet.

I was hoping to control the game in the first half like we did almost twelve months earlier, but it was clear very early on that this would not be happening the second time around. Pats were bigger, stronger, and more in sync than a year before. They were also focused and angry because in the three times we had played them in the last 18 months, we had won twice and only lost one game against them. Even that loss was by only two points when I called on my team to chance their arm to win rather than kick a penalty goal to secure a draw. I selfishly did that because a draw wasn't enough to satisfy me, and if we lost, it was only Round One, and it wouldn't impact our premiership chances, so I thought, *"Let's have a crack!"* I cannot find advice from Sun Tzu to support that one, though, and I did tell you earlier I had made mistakes.

The rest of the half at Parramatta Stadium felt like an onslaught from our angry opponents and after some relentless pressure, we succumbed, and it was actually Pats who went in 8-4 ahead at halftime. We had something to think about in the sheds and I had to come up with the words to make sure the Greg's lads could come up with the goods in the second half.

The scoreboard is only ever one side of the story. A team can be behind on the scoreboard but actually ahead in the game in terms of how things are unfolding on the field. I was (mostly) confident that our opponents were starting to get tired in defence. In all the games in which we had played them, we had always hit them with the shock treatment at the start of each half, scoring quick points so that they had to chase us both on the field and the scoreboard.

In that halftime break, and indeed in any pre-match or halftime discussion, there is no room in my dressing room for any doubt. There is also no room for negativity and even the negatives in our performance are attacked positively. We focus heavily on what we can do and don't dwell at all on what we can't or haven't done well. I focus on speaking calmly and giving them what they need to win the game. (Mostly!)

What we needed, in addition to a fast start with the ball, was a monumental effort in defence against a team that was so much bigger than us. Conventional wisdom suggested that they were bound to break through eventually if they kept coming at us. I asked the Greg's boys to dig deep, calling on some collective memories we had shared together in an attempt to inspire.

In the second half, we got our fast start again with the ball, scoring a try when a very high kick of ours (never let the opponent relax) was dropped by their normally unflappable fullback and we pounced to draw level before taking the lead thanks to the easy conversion, score 10-8.

Then from the resultant kick-off came the play that (ultimately) was to win us back-to-back Grand Finals. When Pats least expected us to, we sneaked down the short side in our own half and our left centre ended up making a break before giving the ball that would send The Mattress on his way to the try line for his second score of the match! Kick missed 14-8 to us.

We didn't know it then, but they were to be the last points we would score, and we had to see out a further 24 minutes of the 30 minutes a side match. Using Sun Tzu's advice of, *"When you surround an army, leave an outlet free"* we left our defensive flanks spacious so that the opposition would get excited and go away from their game plan by trying to push passes wider. We would slide as a unit and scramble like mad to push them to the sidelines in the hope of either tackling them, knocking them over the sideline or forcing them into mistakes. If they did happen to score, the kick would be from so far wide that their odds of slotting home the goal narrowed. It was a risky strategy, but you have to risk it to get the biscuit after all.

Pats scored on our right edge with about a quarter of the game to go, and we faced a fight to hold on to our 14-12 lead. The only people who thought we were going to hold on in the stadium that day were our players and coaches. The onslaught was overwhelming. But our players didn't just think they would hold on; they knew they were going to.

Everyone who doubted us failed to understand what playing in this jersey and for this team meant to the players, nor did they understand the 'brotherhood' that existed and the work that had gone into this side. It felt like every last drop of energy was left on the field that day to keep the opposition scoreless for the rest of the game. It also felt that the accumulated strength from 18 months of work that was focused on changing every habit of the football team had paid off in those moments. The job that needed doing, both in offence and defence, was so well known to the players that it was ingrained in them. They knew what they needed to do instinctively when under the severest pressure, and they knew that the man on their left and the man on their right would never let them down.

That 2011 Grand Final win was the second I had enjoyed as a coach in Australia, the first being a year earlier in 2010. The gentleman who called me to tell me that Gus didn't want me was in attendance and spoke highly of our discipline and standards in the game. We also made the statewide Catholic Schools final later that year but narrowly lost to Pats on this occasion.

Between 2010 and 2021, I won thirteen competitions with my various teams and finished runner-up in five. The premierships ranged from schoolboy tournaments to men's, regional competitions and international (world) tournaments. I was also a successful Head Coach of one of the oldest representative sides in Australia, an Assistant Coach during a very successful World Cup campaign and Head Coach of an Emerging Nation during those years. During that time, I coached the vast majority of the 100-plus players I have coached that went on to play NRL, Super League, State League in New South Wales and Queensland or lower divisions in England.

I do not think I have coached any side as intensely as I did that St Gregory's side in 2011. After winning the competition in 2010, it became clear the school leadership was very happy with that but wasn't too worried either way about whether we would win or lose in the next few years. They wanted us to win, but not at all costs. That meant no recruitment of talented students was allowed, nor was any training or too many games during school time. All the things many of our competitors at Pats and neighboring dedicated Sports High Schools were doing, such as training as part of the timetable or attracting local talent, we couldn't do.

Knowing that we only had what we had, I started work mere days after the 2010 season, studying our performances in depth to find all the weaknesses we had and to try and eradicate them for the following year.

One thing I noticed was that when my team were tackling bigger players (seemingly all the time), their bodies appeared to be 'collapsing' a little under the weight of the larger attacker. To counter this, I put the squad through a specific strength program in the gym, where half of each session was focused on 'core' strength. In other words, strengthening the area from the knees up to the bottom of the chest using lots of Swiss ball exercises. We also focused on a huge lift in our core skill and decision-making performance levels by putting more ball through their hands in training than they had ever done before, setting high targets for success, and not moving on to the next tasks unless those targets were met.

I knew that if I could prepare the 2011 Greg's side to win a competition and get to a Grand Final in another, then if I ever got to run my own program from top to bottom, including junior development and the chance to recruit and coach during lesson time rather than always being in a classroom, the sky was the limit.

The ultimate goal for any serious Rugby League school is the National Schoolboy Cup. As many predicted would one day happen, Patrician Brothers Blacktown went on to become the national champions in 2012. This championship had traditionally been dominated by the Sydney schools, but even then, I sensed something was changing as the Queensland schools were starting to emerge victorious more regularly. As of early 2025, Queensland schools had won nine of the last fifteen championships. Most of the ones from North of the border were won by Keebra Park and Palm Beach Currumbin from the South East Queensland (SEQ) region. The balance of power was shifting, and I could see this emerging in 2012 during my final year at Greg's. After three very enjoyable years there, I got a call (out of the blue) from Mr Mick Hornby, the Deputy Principal (DP) of a school in SEQ.

INTRODUCTION

Was the school Keebra Park, Wavell or Palm Beach Currumbin?
No.

It was a school called Ipswich State High, and they were a little-known college of knowledge with a senior team in the third division of the game in SEQ. In 2012, they had finished third in it. This was the only division they had ever played in, too.

I had gone from the private, palatial and very wealthy surrounds of the big fee-paying St Gregory's to a school where some families struggled to pay a couple of hundred dollars for learning resources. In terms of Rugby League, Ipswich State High just wasn't on the map. Everyone thought I was mad.

I had a great meeting with Mick, and he was clear that he was giving me free rein to run the program how I wanted. Unlike anything previously, I was in complete control of my own coaching destiny and the destiny of every player and coach in the program. It was also a timetabled subject at the school but had been used primarily as a method to control student behaviour.

If we wanted to invite students to the program that was fine, but we also had to raise the money to do it as there was no pot of gold to tap into. Mick had the drive to help with finding sponsorships to fund the program, so I had a kindred spirit who was willing to go all the way with me in building it. If I were the coach, he was the CEO and the Principal, Simon, was the Chairman!

I decided that this was going to be a Rugby League school very was much moulded in my coaching vision from now on. Getting this school where I wanted it to be would take some very heavy lifting. It became clear I would need to put in place a huge coach development program as well as a player development program, so I wrote one for both players and coaches and updated it every year.

What followed was a huge success story. I stayed at Ipswich for five years. Of the 51 games we played, we won 43, drew 2 and lost 6. We never lost back-to-back games, and we only ever lost one home game. We shot up in no time to the premier division and finished second in it in 2015, 2016 and 2017. We also had a powerhouse junior development program, and several players went on to sign professional contracts. By the time I left, Ipswich was well and truly on the map, and we had collected plenty of lower division and lower grade championship wins along the way.

For season 2018, I left to join Mick Hornby when he became Principal at a school a 40-minute drive away from Ipswich. And, in a case of history repeating, it was a third-division Rugby League school, and they had hardly won any games for a long-time. They too, had only ever played in that division.

I used the same model and approaches in an attempt to get Mabel Park State High School up the ladder in record time. Only this time, it took three years, not two. Mabel Park arrived in the top division for the first time in their history in 2021 and won several lower-division titles on the way there.

Ipswich went on to win their first national title in 2022. Mabel Park finished third in the top division in 2023, too. Both Ipswich and Mabel Park are now powerhouse Rugby League schools, and both schools' female sides won the Schoolgirls National Title in the first two years it existed. Nobody had heard of Mabel Park in footy circles five years previously, nor Ipswich ten years previously. Now, many people in the game are well aware as to who they are.

This book contains the full details of how I prepare and coach my teams as well as how I set up those championship-winning programs. It also includes the things I learned prior, working under and alongside some of the best coaches in the game - with plenty of associated stories of course.

Most coaches in our world, when they get a coaching job, get tapped on the shoulder by the committee who say *"Well done! You've got the coaching job"* and that's it! You're left to sink or swim. I was when I started, so my aim with this book is to help you navigate some of the trickier coaching waters. I have been on that road many, many times before and I understand what you are going through.

The next section of this book is titled the *'13 Things Coaches Do Wrong'* and it is absolutely designed to get you thinking about your own coaching. Remember, don't get upset if you do these things because I used to do them too! The rest of the book has been designed to then give you some answers!

Part One

13 Things Coaches Do Wrong

13 Things Coaches Do Wrong

Currently, I mentor hundreds of coaches around the world. I go through the '13 Things Coaches Do Wrong' with them and, there's not a coach I have met yet who gets less than six of them wrong! Talking about these with the coaches allows me to assess where they are at in their journey and in their thoughts with regard to how they approach their coaching. By reproducing these here, with explanations, I am inviting you to assess yourself as a coaching practitioner.

Now we will go into each of these in detail, either giving you some answers within these examples or there will be a reference as to where you can find answers within the rest of this book!

1 – Setting no or few disciplinary standards

I have not interviewed any three-month-old children for this book, so based on absolutely zero research (although many adults seem to agree with me when I ask them), I firmly believe that the first thing babies work out when they come into the world is which parent will respond quickly to their cries, and which one won't!

As society has changed, younger people have made it clear they are not happy to be spoken to in a certain way. Gone are the days when you can shout, scream and rant uncontrollably at a player of any age in our current society, nor should you use derogatory names.

Where I firmly believe (again without any supportive evidence apart from what I have seen time after time after time) so many coaches, teachers and family members get things mixed up is that they believe this shift in emphasis in terms of 'how' we speak to the younger generation and being more careful about what we say also means we need to relax standards or feel we cannot enforce boundaries across the board. Boundaries that are universally accepted by all concerned.

An NRL coach was sacked from his position during 2024, and another coach, known for his approach to team discipline and standards, started pre-season for the following year with that same group of players. The day after the news broke of the old coach being sacked, I spoke with a very high-profile player agent (over lunch) about the issue. The agent has several players at the club in question, so I knew he would know EXACTLY why this coach had received his marching orders. I asked him why the coach got sacked, and the reply was:

"He let the lunatics run the asylum."

At the same lunch, the same agent also correctly told me which coach would get the job days before the media did.

Boundaries are key to lasting relationships and are essential for a coach and their team.

Have a look at **Chapter 1** for some examples of how to manage relationships with your squad and **Chapter 7** for how to manage a squad.

2 – Doing stretches without a pulse raiser first

There's no need to send you to another part of the book here; I'll tell you what not to do right now. DO NOT get your players to stretch in any way before they have done a pulse-raising activity. This helps to avoid the threat of injuring 'cold' muscles.

A pulse-raising activity can be defined as 'anything that gently raises the heart rate'. Do it for ***at least*** five minutes but also consult with your players as to how 'warm' they feel.

If you get your team doing stretches of any kind before warming the muscles with a pulse-raising activity, you are severely risking injuring one, or more, of your players.

3 – Trying to coach more technical content than can fit into four weeks of training

One of the big issues many coaches face, particularly those who do not coach at elite levels, is uncertainty about training attendance. A big consideration for coaches is trying to make sure that all players in the group get to learn all the technical things that are being taught. Otherwise, you'll have some players who know things that others don't.

One of the best ways to deal with this as a coach is to look at how much you are actually trying to teach your players. I say to coaches I mentor that if you can't teach what you want to in four weeks, you are probably trying to teach too much. For how to plan those four weeks of work, refer to **Chapter 6.**

4 – Giving players too many labels to remember

In the last decade, I did a study on a UK Super League team and their strategy of play. I had acquired their playbook, got access to all the footage of their league games and had access to their detailed training schedules. So, I just watched, studied and recorded. On repeat.

I went into this study with a ready hypothesis that the club was wasting its time doing too much 'set play' training on plays they were never going to remember and many that they probably would hardly use.

The playbook had forty-four (yes 44) set plays in it for the players to remember. Einstein would have had trouble remembering them all, never mind a group of players not known for their academic prowess. The effort taken for players to learn how to execute those plays was taking up an awful lot of training time.

I charted their season, and only three of their plays were used regularly; a further eight were used occasionally at various points throughout the year and never at the same time, whilst the other thirty-one either happened once or not at all. The players had clearly been given too much to remember, and an awful lot of training time would have been wasted.

These things still happen today at many levels of the game and the coach of that team is also still a professional coach to this day. See more about playing strategy and playbooks in **Chapter 3.**

5 – Doing stuff in training that doesn't relate to the game

Even as a player and then a young coach, when I started, I never understood why coaches did drills that had either very little game specificity or none at all. As a young player, I remember dreading the drill, which we called the 'Union Jack' in England, and which (I think) is colloquially known as the 'Corners Drill' in Australia. If you don't know what I am talking about, I apologise. But I'll also ask you to search *'Columbia MBA Rugby 4 Corners Passes'* on YouTube so you know what kind of drill I am talking about. Sorry if it's removed before you try.

I was often bamboozled by the drill, whether it was the one where you run in a square formation around the outside of the drill or the one where you all meet in the middle. If you are running outside the drill in an anticlockwise manner for example, some coaches wanted you to pass right to left from the right side of your body, but other coaches didn't and don't push through that rule.

For a moment, let's judge the efficacy of the 'right side of the body' pass intervention.

As you run in a straight line towards a corner of a square drill, your body is naturally running straight and you then have to pass a ball forward, towards something like the number 10 on a clock face, to a teammate who has timed their run from the cone you are running towards.

Are you confused yet?

This drill, regardless of which side of the body you pass from, does NOT replicate what happens in a game. You are practising forward passes!

Now, let's move to the one where all people move towards the centre of the drill. How do I write this one up?

Well, players from all four corners meet in the middle, and two of them from opposite ends of the drill have a ball in their hand. The coach instructs them to pass to the player on the right or left (who meets them in the middle from the opposite two cones).

Are you confused yet?

Needless to say, players often are, and some balls fly forward which is absolutely, not game specific. Other players crash into each other and inevitably look for some kind of shortcut to navigating this equivalent of a football minefield that is this drill.

Now let me be clear; these activities are great for getting players to think, for creating communication between players and for developing problem-solving skills. Using these activities in a part-time coaching environment, however (which most of you will be in), wastes lots of time on something that creates bad passing habits (forward) and does not specifically apply to the game.

In a part-time training environment, you have no time to waste on activities that develop skills not directly applicable to the sport.

6 – Focusing on drills rather than skills

Prior to launching rugbyleaguecoach.com.au, I did lots of filming! I got my own sessions filmed but also accumulated footage from different places and filmed other coaches at work before deciding what made the final cut.

One coach was desperate for me to film him. We will call him 'Super Coach' because he really rated himself as a coach! You know the type. They continually tell you how good they are, how much they know, how many drills they've got ...

He was the 'Coaching Director' of this particular club and was also the Assistant Coach of the A-grade team. The Head Coach of A grade that he was working under, was young, dynamic, up-to-date, and equally as qualified as his assistant and Coaching Director. He actually had more coaching experience at higher levels! He also had a very different way of doing things to Super Coach!

The session I filmed was a 'circuit' type affair and Super Coach had a station in the circuit. He had ten minutes to do his thing, and he had to do it four times as the groups moved around. We filmed each station in the circuit, of which there were also four.

Before the session, Super Coach briefed me on what the session entailed. Personally, I don't think I came down in the last shower, and I couldn't understand what in the world he had just described to me. I just assumed, because of his background, his confidence in his own ability and the respect so many people seemed to show him, that it was going to be something worth recording.

We went to his station first with the camera and it was a moment I remember clearly. He was over to the left as we filmed from the gantry. I stood next to my cameraman and said, *"I'm keen to watch this."* As I was watching, it occurred to me that Super Coach was taking an awfully long time to explain his drill. It seemed like a long five minutes at least. And then, when they started moving, the players looked confused, moving gingerly, looking at each other, asking questions of the coach and their teammates. This phase lasted what seemed like five minutes at the time. I remember thinking, *"What the heck is he trying to achieve here?"*

They managed to work it out eventually and I looked at my watch and there were only twenty-two seconds of the station remaining before players had to move on.

The head coach of the group blew his whistle and shouted, *"Next station"*. All three other groups moved swiftly to the next station, but Super Coach was still running his drill, berating the players, trying to correct them. He was clearly frustrated.

When the next lot of players arrived at his station, they had to stand around for about 20 to 30 seconds before the previous group moved off and then, of course, Super Coach had to fix the markers that had been messed up by the last group.

He started the next group late, and of course, they finished late. The Head Coach didn't go over to Super Coach to remind him to keep time at any point. He had too much respect for this self-appointed guru of Rugby League coaching.

What Super Coach doesn't seem to understand is that the skill you are trying to teach should be of paramount importance to the coach who is planning a drill and that the players should be able to focus almost exclusively on their skill development rather than trying to decipher how to navigate a drill that resembles a maze.

It's about the skill, not the drill. For more on how to coach, see Chapter 5. For more on what to coach, see Chapters 3 and 4.

7 – **Not practicing the promotion of bilateral learning**

Please forgive me for talking to you as a right-hander if you aren't one. In all explanations, we will talk about the right side as the 'dominant' side.

Before you go to bed tonight, try and brush your teeth with your left (non-dominant) hand. If you are anything like me, this will be harder than trying to ballet dance. You are good at brushing your teeth with your right hand because it is your dominant hand. You can brush them on autopilot even if you're half asleep. With your left hand, you'll likely have to concentrate like the day you first sat in the driver's seat of a car or if you opted to conduct medical surgery all of a sudden.

If, on the day you started to brush your teeth as an infant, you did the morning brush with your right hand and your evening brush with the left, you would indeed be an ambidextrous tooth brusher now. And you would have also learned the art of brushing them approximately three times faster.

This is the benefit of practising any skill on both sides of the body. Bilateral learning or bilateral transfer is thought to increase the efficiency and speed of performing bilateral tasks. It improves neural connections and communication between the left and right brain, and it increases a player's ability to adapt and transfer skills to other activities or sports.

So, the lesson is, in training, do everything in equal measure on both sides of the body. This is really a non-negotiable if you are serious about your coaching.

Whatever you do in training, you need to do equal times on both sides of the body, the field or both sides of an activity. If it can be measured, it needs to be programmed in. See more in Chapter 5.

8 – Treating conditioning and ball work as two separate things

Anyone who has been involved with Rugby League for a significant enough amount of time will realise that many training sessions over the years have been separated into 'fitness' or 'conditioning' work and then 'ball' work. This invariably involves players being asked to warm up and then partake in anything between 15 to 45 minutes (in most cases) of hard physical fitness work. After this often gruelling introduction to training then the players might be lucky to see a football. In pre-season, sometimes the ball isn't seen for months!

The less sophisticated versions of this hard physical work often will see different types of running that get the players so tired they can hardly breathe, walk or function correctly for a while. The more thought-out and considered versions of this are measured, timed and follow principle-led approaches.

For a moment, let's consider the 'principle-led' approaches that we should all be aware of as coaches. We don't necessarily need to be experts in the field, but a good over-arching knowledge of the concepts will allow you to plan appropriate activities or make sure you ask the right questions of and keep accountable the ones that are planning them for you.

These principles should thread through everything we ever do as athletes or coaches. If they don't, then we are leaving everything to chance and potentially not improving anything at all.

With no knowledge of sports science principles, you are simply leaving it to chance. If you are doing this work without rhyme or reason, you need to change it immediately. You could be harming your players!

I will put this in the simplest terms I can for you, the reader. I will be referring to these principles in **Chapter 6** of this book when I discuss planning sessions. If you found yourself intrigued by the conditioning minutiae being hinted at here and you want to learn more about this topic, please head to **Chapter 9**.

Work and rest ratios are often labelled in numerical form. For example, a 2:1 ratio would represent twice the amount of work than rest. The first number represents the duration of work (2) and the second (1) the duration of rest.

An exercise designed to improve higher endurance levels and increased cardio-vascular ability would have an equal or higher duration of work figure than the rest figure. For example, 1:1, 1.5:1, 2:1, 3:1 etc. These are the kinds of activities that get players tired over a prolonged period. They are the kind of drills that lead players to exhaustion, deep breathing and that burn in the legs that makes them feel that they can't control them anymore!

You can teach, practice skills AND condition your players at the same time and in a far more enjoyable way than the 'old school' methods.

9 – Coaching and judging the performance of players when they run against fresh air

While you are sat reading this book, please do me a favour. (If you are able)

1. Put the book down

2. Stand up!

3. Pretend you are a championship-level boxer and throw some 'shadow' punches (please don't punch anyone or anything!) Instead, just 'box' against fresh air for about 10 seconds

4. Sit down again

5. Grab the book again

6. Read on!

The chances are you threw some excellent punches! Depending on your age, you're probably picturing yourself as Muhammad Ali, Mike Tyson, the Klitschko brothers or Oleksandr Usyk right now! Depending on your ability (and age), there is a chance that you actually DID resemble one of those very famous and very successful boxers in your 10-second bout against......no one. Against fresh air!

Anyone looks good against fresh air!
(Note: Please don't try any of the next things at home!)

Imagine we put a light or heavy punching bag in front of you. You would all of a sudden have some resistance to work against, and it would move. If we put a heavier punch bag in front, you'd have even more resistance. Regardless of your fitness level, it will fatigue you more quickly than shadow boxing, and you'd have to pick and choose when and where you punched, getting your timing right.

Should I bother putting someone in front of you to avoid your punches and to punch you back? They will move their feet, too, so you might have to move yours.

Hopefully, imagining these phases of your most recent development as a potential world-class Boxer gave you some indication that there is a difference between training in front of fresh air, training with a controlled level of opposition and then actually competing against a walking, talking human being with their own brain!

Later in **Chapter 5,** you will learn how to navigate that in your training!

10 – Judging a session on what coaches say about it, not what the players learned

Formal coach education programs and resources can often confuse the reader or at least take some deciphering. Indeed, at the very start of my coaching journey, I took the time to study these formal documents in depth but learned quickly that regurgitating everything I had consumed was often confusing the players I coached and their physical efforts at carrying out what I had regurgitated were a physical manifestation of that confusion.

I was telling them lots, but it seemed they weren't necessarily hearing me.

So, I decided to do some research to find a formal coaching document that is typical of much of what circulates in our game before showing you how I have used that type of information in the past to make life easier for my players and to create better training outcomes. One of the coaches I have studied most, Brian Clough, purveyor of greatness in the round ball game, proudly stated in one of his own books, *"There is no room for confusion in my dressing room"*. When I read these simple yet powerful words a couple of decades ago from a very successful coach who did things his own way, I decided it would be a mantra I would follow, too. And I have never looked back!

It's not what you tell them; it's what they hear.

The formal coaching document

This is from an undated document titled *"Game Development Coach Education Volume One"*, written by staff at an NRL club.

The second page of this fourteen-page document says it is a:

"...resource (that) has been developed by a number of the games (sic) finest educators and will provide aspiring coaches with the framework in which to teach basic skills".

Page four of this resource states that:

"The skill you are aiming to teach has coaching points and it is now that you must teach each of these in stages. For example: Stop the drill, demonstrate and explain the 1st coaching point then have them perform that before you move on to the next point."

Also, on the same page, it says:

"Player must practise with correct skill technique before moving onto the next coaching point. The coach must evaluate and provide feedback to the players at this stage".

I use this manual here simply to give an example of the type of coaching instruction that is very common in our game but also, formal education programs everywhere in many sports.

The paragraphs highlighted on page four clearly state to the reader that, the *"coaching points"* have to be taught *"'In stages"* and that they have to be practised with *"correct skill technique before moving onto the next coaching point".*

Nothing in the fourteen-page manual suggests that the coach should simplify or synthesize the information to make it easier for players to understand. Indeed, nothing in all of the formal manuals I have ever read does such a thing.

All the instructions from this resource for 'Grip, Catch, Pass' amounted to 662 words, and it was two pages of the manual. I also counted twenty-six coaching points for gripping, catching and passing a football.

I also saw some interesting statements that, if taken literally, could see some very unique manoeuvres being performed. They included requests to put

"Thumbs on top, fingers spread underneath" the ball, which *"travels underneath your body, not around your body"*, apparently. The instruction is then to *"Weight the ball as it travels upwards towards the support runner's eyes."*

It is no wonder that coaches often get confused and yet also feel compelled to deliver as much as they can of what they consume from this kind of document. They want to be seen as up-to-date and relevant, and they also want to impress anybody who may be looking at them.

But it's not about what you tell the players; remember, it's about what they hear.

How Coach Addison teaches it

After studying countless coaching manuals particularly early in my coaching career, I knew that the simple act of catching and passing a ball had to be simplified. I would say I really refined this process in 2010 when I was coaching at St Gregory's.

Here, though, I now outline the coaching points I use to coach 'grip, pass, catch, carry' as I refer to it, when coaching a normal, short pass:

Clap, Grip, Tip, Flick.

The first thing you will notice there is that the twenty-six coaching instructions from the formal coaching document have now become four! There was also no reference to feet or hips here. These four coaching points are things that I explain quickly to players, adding that I want their hips square at all times.

To understand the four coaching points in context, it is key to know that these should be seen as major keywords that mean more to players after a quick explanation before commencing repetitions. Coaches literally often have to repeat the four words above more often than not, or at least two of them, namely 'clap' and 'tip' more often.

The 'clap' is a reminder to players to clap their hands and keep their thumbs together after that clap. I tell them I want targets to the side of the body rather than in front of their body. The clap is a very physical way of getting the hands together for that purpose. (Kids, in particular, love this)

'Grip' is something I can explain quickly to players and show them with a ball before they start. I am heavy on fingertip grip, rather than palms on the ball. The grip coaching call is something we often don't need to repeat much, based on experience, and why will be clearer soon.

The 'Tip' of the ball is the real key to success using this method. Imagine a Steeden ball when it is caught. If the ball arrives at the catcher upright, the word 'STEEDEN' written in bold capitals on the panels of the ball is a clear visual for the players. I tell them that, if the 'S is on the top' they need to tip the ball so that the 'N' replaces it at the top. If the players have a fingertip grip, they can do this easily, which is why I tend not to need to use the 'grip' call often. When they do this tip, their elbow will automatically come up, too, and I never mention foot placement because I want them to do this catch and pass quickly in practice, so their feet have no time to think of anything! I want them to focus on the ball, not their feet. Also, by tipping the ball and facing the person they are passing to, their hips start to open up that way anyway.

The last of the four coaching points asks the player to 'flick' the ball with their fingers and wrists towards their teammate, and, once again, if the player has a finger-tip grip, this is easier.

I have also used markers to write 'A' or '1' on each of the four panels of a ball right at the furthest point of it and then 'B' or '2' on the other side of the panels at the opposite point.

If this part got you interested, then make sure you read **Chapters 3 to 8**

11 – Doing the most complicated stuff at the end of the pre-season

I have never understood why so many 'old school' Rugby League practices prevented players from touching the ball until a few weeks out from the season start and on top of that, they start introducing the most complicated and convoluted moves and directional play on the eve of the campaign. When the elusive ball finally appears, sometimes as late as two weeks out from the start of competitive matches, coaches start to allow players to pass it a little bit and they will start some set construction activities saying, *"This is how we are going to play"*.

They will invariably start at the 'back' of the field, doing 'exit' sets, designed to get the team out of their own half. 99.99% (recurring) of the time, these exits are very simple, normally one 'scoot' or two from the play the ball (person at the back of the play the ball (dummy half) just grabs the ball and runs) followed by three 'hit ups' (each one pass from the dummy half to an oncoming player) before a kick.

As they move 'up' the field, towards the opposition try line, play becomes somewhat more complicated, with several players running different angles either with or without the ball and the ball will change hands more than once.

I still see this happen, quite a lot.

This is absolutely BONKERS!

Why would you leave the most complicated stuff that the players have to learn until as late as possible?
Don't. It's crazy!

12 – Doing the toughest session on a Tuesday during pre-season

Most Rugby League teams train on Tuesday and Thursday nights. The rest tend to train on Monday and Wednesday nights, or Wednesday and Friday nights. Only rarely do we have less or more than, a night's rest in between two training sessions in the world of Rugby League.

So, using a Tuesday – Thursday model as an example, this means, that if we train our players in a very hard manner on a Tuesday, they only have approximately 46 hours until the next session.

Here's why we need to reconsider that.

Delayed Onset of Muscle Soreness (DOMS) is muscle pain that happens after certain workouts. The pain regularly starts between 12 and 24hours after said workout and can last up to 3 days! Most people notice it on day two, which in our case, would be the day of our second training session of the week.

In pre-season, with no games at weekends, it can be a big reason why training numbers sometimes drop off on a Thursday, particularly when players work in a manual job or attend a school with PE lessons taking place often. Kids are also good at running around at break times.

So, it stands to reason that, towards the end of the week, energy levels (or perceived energy levels) start to drop in the individual, particularly if the session was superhard on a Tuesday.

Saving your physically toughest session for a Thursday in pre-season gives your players five nights' rest before the next Tuesday and can increase productivity in all sessions.

13 – Keeping players guessing about the team but not about training

Players like to either mentally prepare for what's coming in training or alternatively, they might want to know what's coming so they can pace themselves through the session, feign an injury or, in the most extreme cases, not turn up to training at all!

A common process in Rugby League is to have the toughest session on a Tuesday (see previous section for why you shouldn't always do that) and for a lighter session to take place on a Thursday. As a result, players instinctively realise that after a while and start voting with their feet at so many of our clubs. So, it pays to keep them guessing, when you get the inevitable question *"What are we doing in training today, coach?"*

But, quite frankly, I believe that's where the guessing games must stop. **When it comes to announcing playing squads for the weekend's game, I believe in absolute transparency. Be straight up with your players.**

Note that I stopped short of saying you should 'name your team as soon as possible'. If you're trying to elicit a better training outcome from some players, tell them. If you genuinely don't know your team yet, tell them. If you're waiting on the fitness of some players, tell them. If you're worried that if you name a squad early, all those not selected won't turn up to the game, potentially leaving you short of players if your chosen ones don't show up, tell them.

Key Points from This Chapter

The 13 Things Coaches Do Wrong are:

1 – Setting no or few disciplinary standards

Boundaries are key to lasting relationships and are essential for a coach and their team.

2 – Doing stretches without a pulse raiser first

If you do get your team doing stretches of any kind before warming the muscles with a pulse-raising activity, you are severely risking injuring one, or more, of your players.

3 - Trying to coach more technical content than can fit into four weeks of training

If you can't teach what you want to in four weeks, you are probably trying to coach too much

4 – Giving players too many labels to remember

They will not use, or forget, most of them

5 - Doing stuff in training that doesn't relate to the game

In a part-time training environment, you have no time to waste doing activities that develop skills not directly applicable to the sport.

6 - Focusing on drills rather than skills

It's about the skill, not the drill

7 - Not practicing the promotion of Bilateral Learning

Whatever you do in training, you need to do equal times on both sides of the field or activity. If it can be measured, it needs to be programmed in

8 - Treating conditioning and ball work as two separate things

You can teach, practice skills AND condition your players at the same time. It is a far more enjoyable way of doing things than the 'old school' methods.

9 - Coaching and judging the performance of players when they run against fresh air

Anyone looks good against fresh air

10 - Judging a session on what coaches say about it, not what the players learned

It's not what you tell them, it's what they hear

11 - Doing the most complicated stuff at the end of the pre-season

Don't leave the most complicated stuff that the players have to learn until as late as possible.

12 - Doing the toughest session on a Tuesday during pre-season

Saving your physically toughest session for a Thursday in pre-season gives your players five nights' rest before the next Tuesday and can increase productivity in all sessions.

13 - Keeping players guessing about the team but not about training

When it comes to announcing playing squads for the weekend's game, I believe in absolute transparency. Be straight up with your players.

Part Two

13 Game-Changing Conversations to Transform Your Coaching

1
Coaching: More Than Just X's and O's

Are you a dickhead or a good person?

Most Rugby League players would rather play under and for a good person, even if they're not necessarily the best technical and tactical coach, than for a dickhead or poor 'man-manager' who is good at the X's and O's.

Players don't care about how much you know until they know how much you care.

Have you noticed that coaches often get characterised as either 'good tactically' or as a 'good man manager'? My response to that is, why can't a coach be both? And does a good coach need to be an expert at the technical and tactical thing anyway?

One of the best coaches I have ever seen at the 'man management' business was Frank Endacott, the former New Zealand Warriors, Wigan Warriors and New Zealand national coach. His nickname was 'Happy Frank' – but he did have a severe streak in his coaching, too. Then Wigan Chairman Maurice Lindsay brought Frank in to make the team, in his words, 'happy' again after the team finished fourth in the ladder and failed at home in the first round of the 1999 finals to unfancied Castleford Tigers. Under Frank, the team finished top in season 2000, losing only three games throughout the regular season. Unfortunately, they lost their fourth and fifth games of the year in the finals – twice to St Helens, one in a Qualifying Semi-Final and the other on Grand Final day.

A few months into the 2001 season, Maurice dispensed with Frank's services and appointed Australian Stuart Raper to replace him. He didn't have to travel far to join Wigan – he was the Castleford coach who had knocked Wigan out in 1999 and brought his underdogs to the finals again in 2000, much to everyone's surprise. The rationale behind Raper's appointment from approximately 100 km away was that he was more of a technician. The appointment was validated when he also brought Wigan to the 2001 Grand Final (which they lost again). Still, they did win the 2002 Challenge Cup.

The late Maurice Lindsay was definitely in the camp that thought a coach was either 'good tactically' or a 'good man manager'. But a man who, ironically, is still thought of as a star in the town of St Helens (Wigan's main rivals) has, as recently as 2024, shown that you can be a great coach for many years even if the public is told and often believe that he's 'not great tactically'. One look at the replies on my Rugby League Coach Facebook page if I ever do a post about this big man and his coaching exploits is proof positive that there is a strong narrative out there that doesn't support claims that he is a superb tactician.

Australia, Queensland, Canberra Raiders, Souths Brisbane and St Helens legendary player Mal Meninga turned his hand to coaching in 1997. His 53%-win ratio over four years seemed to be enough for media and footy types to decide he'd had a poor start to his coaching career. (For the record, every coach since him has a lower win ratio than Meninga at the time of writing. Meninga left Canberra in 2001).

In late 2005, Meninga was appointed as Queensland State of Origin Coach. He is now regarded as the greatest and most successful coach in Origin history. That's all. The Maroons had unprecedented success under him, including eight series wins in a row and twenty victories from his thirty Origin games in charge. His record will never be matched. Ever. Meninga is rarely discussed as a coaching great. Not considered in the spheres of Craig Bellamy and Wayne Bennett. Bellamy is a brilliant NRL coach who struggled as a representative coach. Meninga is a brilliant representative coach who was (supposedly) an average NRL coach. Yet Bellamy is lauded as the greatest, and even when Meninga is lauded. it's with asterisks.

I posit this; Meninga is the most underrated coach in Rugby League history.

Meninga's achievements are attributed as a product of a playing group. The Smith's, the Lockyer's, the Cronk's, the Inglis's... yet few remember he also coached the Steve Bell's, Dallas Johnson's, Adam Mogg's, Neville Costigan's, Ben Hannant's. Players who need their full name written to know who they are.

After this success, he became coach of Australia in late 2015. He has won two World Cups with Australia and has also navigated a period where Australia are arguably at their weakest for generations, with defections galore to the island nations, New Zealand and even England from those who qualified to play for more than one nation.

This still wasn't (and isn't) enough for some people in the game, in the media, on the terraces and social media keyboard warriors, who still label Meninga as 'poor tactically'. These so-called self-appointed 'experts' should take a deeper dive into what coaching actually means before they throw their casual labels around.

I have been talking with several people associated with Australia since he was appointed. They include players I have coached in the past who are currently or were previously playing for him and the staff who are or were working with him.

Quite frankly, these conversations reveal that Mal Meninga is literally a world-class coach. And leader.

A friend of mine worked for Meninga during a recent Kangaroos tour and was inspired by the attention to detail Meninga had. My friend, who has seen the best and worst of many NRL coaches, was stunned at how strategic Meninga was, how he weaved narrative through every day, carefully mapped out amongst the playing group to create a series of moments for the team each week.

Each moment tied into themes all harking back to key Kangaroos values. For instance, Meninga used Surf Life Saving Clubs as a vessel to instill selflessness into the team. Surf Clubs are the bastion of Australian values and are run by volunteers. Every-day Aussies dedicating hours as the sun rises to save lives and doing so without payment, doing so because they care about their community, doing so because they want their children to understand sacrifice. Meninga organised two separate days for the Kangaroos to join Surf Clubs and participate in nippers activities and then stay for dinner with the Surf Club members. Kids with inked signatures on their arms still wet, screaming, *"I'm never washing again"*. Grown men explaining to multi-millionaire players how they simply don't think of not showing up for duties because it means so much to the community.

Players woke up the next day feeling grateful for their privilege. Feeling a desire to give back to the kids who idolise them. Feeling perspective.

My friend explained that Meninga, often seen as a strong leader but not a strong football coach, often derided as inspirational but not detailed, was exceptionally analytical throughout the tour. Fastidious to a fault. In the team room, every piece placed with precision. Meninga would have large posters, billboards, and photos printed daily to decorate the team room with unique messages. He would walk through the team room by himself, imagining how the players would feel, dissecting which piece of information they would digest first. And then redecorate if it wasn't exactly right.

Meninga doesn't pretend. Full stop. A man who knows who he is is a man who must be respected. His game plan simple, his messages simple, his delivery perfected.

He understands that players and staff need to be spoken to fairly, treated with respect and especially, with honesty. He understands that the discipline of his players is paramount, but he treats them like adults, like men. He recognises that by representing Australia after the regular season, his squad members have experienced months of intense games and training with their clubs. He treats the players accordingly. Those linked to him with Queensland said he was intuitively excellent regarding their needs.

What wasn't and isn't relaxed with Big Mal though, is discipline. And standards. We underestimate Mal Meninga at our peril. We underestimate any coaches that, for some reason, we don't think are 'technical' coaches, at our peril. That's because players value the type of coach they play under. It's something inherent in rugby league, probably because of its brutal nature as an invasion s port.

Coaching isn't all about X's and O's. If it was, then Meninga wouldn't have created a legacy in representative football that will never be matched. Ever.

If you're good with people, you can make a very good coach. But if you're just good technically and treat your players poorly, it's harder to turn that around.

Over six years before the publication of this book, I coached a young Mabel Park school team that I mentored several times a day, both in the gym and on the field. By young, I mean a team of year 11s playing in a competition meant for year 12s. 16 and 17-year-olds in an Under 18's league.

The impact of the COVID pandemic and the subsequent restrictions decimated the group. Many of the players who had joined the team from interstate or overseas had to return home and then remain in their original homes.

It never even crossed my mind to ask any of the players to stay to ride out the COVID wave. Players being happy and settled away from football is always my priority, and, in this case, if that meant the players being with their families in a distant location for a time, then I encouraged them to go.

At any level and in any circumstances, if you give players something akin to a leave pass from training for what seems like a genuine and personal issue they are dealing with away from the game, you can learn a lot about that person when the time arrives for them to return to work. If they value you for trusting them and caring for their welfare, they'll give you everything when they return to the training field. If they start asking for more and more or don't come back at all, it means they're the kind of player who will let the team down when they're needed the most. And you don't win championships with those types of players in your team.

When we had that pesky COVID outbreak, several of the boys were granted leave to go home and spend time with loved ones for obvious reasons, but some of them didn't come back. Every one of those who didn't, communicated with me and kept communications up with the team, including sending messages and good luck videos when we made that season's Grand Final.

Their absence left our team depleted, but such was our depth we still had plenty of players, yet our team was far weaker to all observers, and I think the players knew that too. It left us in that middle ground where, if we chose to work hard, we would get to a semi or final and maybe even win the competition if the stars aligned. If we didn't commit to work, then it could be a long season. It was such a fine margin that year.

Unlike the St Gregory's team of 2011, which was weaker than its predecessor, this Mabel Park side didn't have months to prepare from the end of the previous season for a premiership onslaught. Just as we thought our season was about to start, we were at full strength with all our troops before we got forced into lockdown and lost some members.

As a coach, sometimes you have squads where talent will keep them in the mix to win games all the time; other times, you have squads that no matter how much work they do, they will struggle. This squad post lockdown was now right, smack bang in the middle of that. Post-lockdown, nothing was going to get handed to them on a plate and they would go into games as underdogs on several occasions. It really was now up to them and their effort how far they progressed this particular season.

Once society returned to something resembling normality, our training standards were inconsistent and I didn't feel I had control of the group, nor that they were training like a team that was going to threaten the competition's best. During one week in the middle part of the year, two weeks before the start of the delayed season, I reached a breaking point with the team.

The day before, there was a training session that was fantastic, and I thought that, finally, the penny had dropped with the players, and this would be the norm from now on. We seemed to be in the 'zone', as I like to call it. I told the players after the session that their attendance and commitment had to stay at that level.

Our time in the zone lasted less than 24 hours! At our next session, some players were missing (either late or didn't arrive). In the circle at the start of the session, I noticed that some players were missing! I cancelled training immediately and told all players to attend an impromptu meeting in the hall.

In that meeting, I asked them to articulate what needed to change for us to be the best version of ourselves. I put it squarely on them and said that if I wasn't getting the 'buy-in' I needed, they could sit in meetings every day when they should be in the gym or on the field. I told them that if we did that, then they would go into Round One under-prepared and looking foolish.

The players, almost to a man, admitted that some people weren't pulling their weight. Also:

- A few individuals were made to realise by their teammates that their efforts were impacting others, not just themselves.

- There was a 'perceived hierarchy' in the group, and those who were meant to be role models weren't doing it very well, according to their teammates.

- They said they needed discipline, attendance, teamwork and work ethic to succeed.

What I didn't know or plan for after our cancelled session was that, overnight, the players contacted each other, either by phone or social media. The messages were clear - to rally around and start the next day with a fresh attitude. The following day's session was the best for a long, long time.

It was the start of a new era of focused training. It was thanks to a collective decision about what the boys all thought needed to change. Indeed, what mattered.

We got to a Grand Final that year but missed out on the trophy. Still a huge achievement. When they were 'up against a wall', these young men showed outstanding leadership qualities.

What matters in this sport are things like:

1. Constant commitment to your task

2. Mateship - doing it for your mates

3. Togetherness/shared endeavour

4. Team first (no ego's)

5. Working as hard as possible

6. Doing point 5 every time you train

You will notice there are no X's and O's, listed in the above. Different coaches will have different terms for the above, but essentially the message is very similar. I remember Ricky Stuart talking about *'"Want and Care"'* or essentially, *"How much does a player want it"* and *"How much does a player care?"*

Wayne Bennett's books over the years talk regularly about similar messages that, at face value, sound quite generic but actually mean so much. Des Hasler was huge on '1%ers' when I worked under him, and those are a lot easier to do if you have the desire, the want and the care to do them. I could go on and list several coaches from several eras and several sports.

I found it very interesting that, when given a chance to be honest with each other and share what they felt they were lacking, my team basically gave the answers that you'd also hear from seasoned campaigners. And the message coming from their peers was powerful. I was so proud of them.

Another thing that happened the day when I assembled the players in the hall was that I had reached my 'breaking point'. I didn't have a nervous breakdown, but my line had been crossed, and I wasn't copping this kind of effort from the players anymore. I wasn't walking past it, and I wasn't allowing it to continue.

When I think of Grand Final-winning teams of past years, it always seems to be the team that goes the extra mile for each other that reigns supreme. When you have two teams that do that, you end up with epic finals or memorable moments that turn a game. As I write, both Hasler and Stuart are still very adept at getting their team to beat fancied opposition despite their team having underdog status in most matches.

For over a century, our sport has been one of the most brutal, possibly up there with combat sports such as Boxing. As a result, when the players play, it doesn't pay to fill their heads with too many tactical or technical things. A player's 'fight or flight' response is on show, and survival instincts kick in. Let's face it; you're essentially carrying a ball against thirteen people who want to hurt you. Einstein, one of the most intelligent people this world has ever seen, would have trouble processing lots of information in such a brutal environment.

To me, knowing this kind of thing is one of the reasons that Wayne Bennett and Jack Gibson have been Premiership accumulators over the last half a century. Gibson once said, *"Kick it to the seagulls"* to half-back Peter Sterling in a tense Grand Final dressing room. A confused 'Sterlo' went out for the warm-up and saw all the seagulls camped out at one end of the Sydney Cricket Ground; he then knew exactly what his coach meant. Bennett, when his St George Illawarra team were down at halftime in the 2010 decider against the Roosters, apparently said little more than. *"Can you play like the Dragons in the second half, please?"*

In my own coaching career, there are examples I can use where I've channelled that kind of approach. As he told you in the Foreword, I used to just tell James Tedesco to *"Let it Flow"* before each game. What that meant was that I just wanted him to unleash what he had in his armoury on the opposition. I also wasn't going to fill his head with noise pre-match. His teammates got a lot more information from me pre-match. Another one, Matthew Groat (formerly of Wests Tigers), was a player with whom I had to push some other buttons. In a bid to get him fired up to play a game against opponents that included David Klemmer (future Kangaroo, New South Wales prop), I told Groaty that his opposite number, Klemmer, had bashed him around the park the last time they played each other. (Completely fabricated story, by the way) It would be enough for Matthew to go out and be the best forward on the field in a crunch game.

I had another player a few years later up in Queensland who could tear up the top opposition in the competition all on his own. I just unleashed him from the bench when the opposition forwards were tired, and he would create havoc. But could he defend? Not a chance. He didn't know where to stand half the time never mind follow a defensive structure. To that end, before each game, I'd remind him that he had to stand ten metres back when the opposition had a play the ball but that in attack, he could *"Do what the (insert expletive) he wanted"*. He appreciated that and flourished. He never scored less than two tries a game! To avoid him being the reason we leaked more than two, I told him to move around the defensive line, in the opposite direction to where he thought the ball would go. We had a great season too!

The key to coaching is simple instructions for players to carry out under pressure. Of course, there is an awful lot more to it than that, but it's a superb starting point and should thread through everything a coach delivers. One of the best managers ever to coach the round ball game (soccer) once said *"There's no room for confusion in my dressing room."* Also, more famously, when one of his players was going through all the potential permutations that could happen during a free kick in training, Brian Clough famously responded, *"I pay you to shoot, son"*.

Motivation and Mind Games

Mind games are something that many players and coaches use but frequently deny they do or ever have done. Motivation is something that can either be intrinsic or promoted/created by coaches and players. We have all heard the criticism of a coach who is struggling so much that they are 'failing to motivate the team', according to outsiders and pundits.

A team I used to coach a few years ago had excellent success overall under my watch, but one year after I left, they started slowly. They were struggling and sat at the bottom of the ladder without a win. Back then, I started looking for the reasons why they might be struggling. I discovered that they had started to create too much propaganda lauding themselves on social media before they truly deserved it. I believe that the players were falling for their own self-created hype.

The late Maurice Lindsay, the former Wigan Warriors Chairman I told you about earlier, used to teach me so much about this when I was a young coach who also worked in the media and marketing department there. He knew I had a desire to go deep into the coaching world, so he used to imbue me with tales of the Wigan glory days. This dovetailed with my work because I was responsible for a lot of the information that the Wigan club sent out day to day. He used to teach me that you should never give the opposition something to help them get motivated and never put a target on your own head. So, we used to talk the opposition up and talk ourselves down. That certainly stayed with me.

If you lose, say nothing. If you win, say even less.

Basically, my old team, in this instance, had been doing the exact opposite. They'd been talking themselves up about how they performed in training and doing it very much in the public arena. Making things even worse, they were doing this at the START of the season and on social media. They were posting more than Taylor Swift. I could imagine the fuel this was giving to all their opponents. A dominant team in previous years, their opponents will have prepared for a mammoth task when facing them and it would have been all the motivation they would have needed.

Silly, silly. Rule 101 of coaching if you ask me... don't put a target on your own head.

I've been the beneficiary of other coaches' or opposition players giving my team motivation by talking too much in public places. I remember once struggling a little bit for something to give my players before a local derby game where we were slight favourites. As I was walking to the meeting room to see the players, somebody handed me that day's local newspaper. Like a gift from the heavens, the headline and the story underneath in that day's local rag was to provide the perfect script for my team talk! I will not tell you the team I was coaching nor the opposition because I don't want to embarrass them.

On this day, the opposition coach spouted off to the local journalist about how good his squad was and how they were going to give us a really tough game because they fancied their chances. I duly read the contents of our local news source to my players and said no more after it. You could hear a pin drop on the bus going to the game. I also arranged for photocopies of the article to decorate our changing room wall above each player's locker area.

What followed was one of the most one-sided matches I have ever coached. My team were so fired up. The referee blew the full-time whistle (a few minutes early, I am sure, to give mercy) when we had reached 100 points, and the opposition had yet to score. I could not believe the motivation my team had been presented with and still can't to this day.

The prevalence of social media frequently grants your opposition the platform to provide you, every day, with the motivational fuel if you take some time to look for it! I see posts from players or clubs almost daily on Facebook, Instagram, TikTok and the like that I would love to show my team if I were a coach in the opposition dugout!

There's an old tale about Wayne Bennett falsifying some 'tip sheets' that he said were from his grand final coaching opponent Brian Smith in the early '90s. The old Master allegedly slipped them under his players' hotel room doors the night before the game. True, false, embellished or otherwise, what this teaches us is that nothing motivates a player more than how good his opponent thinks he/she is and how they think you have weaknesses. These preach to the base instincts that our game relies on so much.

Another coach trick you will have seen (sometimes without realising it) is the team sheet trick. Some coaches don't play any games at all with their team sheet; others sometimes do. One of the most famous tales of ducks and drakes in recent memory was the 2018 NRL Grand Final. Roosters coach Trent Robinson kept everyone guessing as to whether a partially fit Cooper Cronk was going to play. To cover this up in Rugby League is almost a miracle; it is a sport that leaks like a sieve!

Why is a team sheet so important? Well, as an opposition coach, if you know that a certain player is playing, you can look to either exploit the weaknesses or counter the strengths of that person. At the highest levels I have seen or worked at, players get information on what the halves do, which foot they kick with and where they favour to target their kicks. In terms of the powerful runners, players will find out what foot a key opposition player likes to step off or a hand they like to fend with. Then, all opposition players will be studied for defensive frailties, where they leave the line, if they are poor tacklers or have weaker shoulders to target.

Harry Siejka, a former Panthers, Warriors and Bradford Bulls player, is someone I have coached and coached against. When I coached against him and before I had even met him, I noticed from studying his footage that when he wanted to run the football, he stood closer to the ruck than if he had passing in mind, and my players used it to predict his movements. When I coached him, I told him I had found that, and he didn't even know that he did it! It was a subconscious act. According to some opponents, Immortal Andrew 'Joey' Johns always used to dig his toe into the ground seconds before he caught the ball to run straight at the defensive line. Barrie McDermott, the former Great Britain prop, has a glass eye due to an accident with an air rifle as a teenager and enjoyed a stellar career despite this disability. His issue was well known by opponents who often tried to exploit him on that side of his body in defence.

One team I coached against kept playing a certain two defenders on the same edge, so my team targeted all sets there. Both these players were/are ok in attack but the coach was crazily making them defend together. Both of them were very good at missing tackles and to put them on the same side and next to each other was like manna from heaven for opposition coaches. It's that obvious I don't understand why he never noticed. So, the team sheet was important ahead of that match!

If a coach doesn't brief the players and those in and around the squad to keep their words to themselves, then this stuff often leaks to the opposition. It can be the difference between a four-point win and a two-point loss. Many of your players will be friends with opponents for all sorts of reasons, so be careful because loose lips sink ships!

Much to the chagrin of administrators and public announcers everywhere, my attitude to team sheets in crunch scenarios has been varied; I'll be honest. Much to the chagrin of administrators and public announcers everywhere!

Once, I listed all 30 players in my squad for a Grand Final and it was in alphabetical order too. Other times, I have said a player was on the bench and then started them or I have genuinely had a different formation. I put a 15-year-old Alex Leapai in jumper 17 for his first-grade debut at school, but I always intended on starting him, and both he and I knew that. I just didn't want the opposition to plan on bashing him in the opening stages which is commonly known as the 'softening up' period, especially as there was reasonable media interest in the game. Several years earlier, at Ipswich, I planned on starting a young prop called Monson against Palm Beach Currumbin but didn't tell anyone, not even him, until the teams were just about to run out. I knew he would get nervous if I gave him too much notice! An ex-player of mine who is now a star in the NRL will tell you a similar story at the end of this chapter.

At Mabel Park, we played half a season with a half who also played at fullback in our defence. I also used him as my only half, which meant I played with four props starting on the field. The 6 and 7 jerseys didn't fit those extra props, so we had to just get players in jerseys that fit them. The opposition coach would not have had a cat in hell's chance of knowing what was going on.

There are no rules in Rugby League that say you have to have one fullback, two wingers, two centres, two in the halves, two props, a hooker, two second rows and a lock/loose forward. It has always baffled me when official governing body team sheets ask you to name someone in those positions. What if a team wants to play with thirteen props? Or thirteen half-backs?

As England Students coach, I once started with no hooker and used my second rows on each side to do the dummy half duties. It worked a treat and also allowed us to play a third prop at the start of the game. Countless times, my fullback has played as a half, giving me an extra prop. Having more than two props gives a team a great opportunity to get that all-important initiative that you need in the middle of the field.

On one occasion, my fullback had to play in number 12 because we'd left the number 1 jersey on the floor when we left on the team bus to go to the ground! Several times, I've coached props who cannot fit into jerseys 8 or 10, outside backs who cannot fit into jerseys 1 to 5, and I've even had a half that had to start the game in a substitute jersey as that was the only one that fit him.

I'm sure the opposition thought we were playing mind games!

Key Points from This Chapter

- They won't care how much you know until they know how much you care

- When the players play, it doesn't pay to fill their heads with too many tactical or technical things

- The key to coaching is the simplicity of instructions for players so they carry them out under pressure

- If you lose, say nothing. If you win, say even less. Don't put a target on your own head

- With social media these days, your opposition will be giving you fuel every day if you take some time to look for it

- Study opposition as much as you can

He prepared me for the NRL – by Ronaldo Mulitalo

I wouldn't be where I am now without Lee Addison coming into my life and having such a huge impact on me.

Sure, I have an amazing family and friendship group that have played such a big role in my career to date, and Lee is one of those friends now, but he was undoubtedly the piece in the jigsaw that I needed to complete the journey to the NRL. It was perfect timing for me when we first met.

My family lived in two garages in NZ until 2013. We had little but we got on with life and it was such a loving environment, even though the living conditions were tough. Mum knew that we had talent in our family and believed that my brother Lorenzo and I could do something in Rugby League. We had family in Queensland, in a place called Ipswich. Our cousins told us about the big academy that had started up at a place there, the Ipswich State High School.

We moved over to Australia and stayed with family and rocked up at Ipswich State High to enrol. I had no contract with a club or a scholarship at the school or anything, so we came off our own back to try and get one. It was massive for us and for any kid from New Zealand to get any kind of scholarship from a footy school in Australia. To get one would make us feel like we were halfway to cracking it in the game!

When we went to enrol, we were told the Head Coach of the program was away as the Assistant Coach of the United States of America at the World Cup and I knew they had done well at that tournament, so this was huge for us, too, to get coached by a different calibre of coach.

We met Lee when he got back, but we didn't see eye to eye! I have seen the error of my ways now with maturity but when I was fourteen, I was a handful. I was angry with the world, and I definitely rubbed my new coach up the wrong way! As I said, I felt I was halfway to making it in League! But Addison kept trying to tell me and other lads like me that we hadn't and that we needed to learn lots more, but we didn't want to hear that!

The big learning moment came for me when I was in Year 10, and our team in that age group was on its way to two Grand Finals, so some of us, still young and learning, were full of ourselves, especially me! Ahead of a big semi-final, I'd 'played up' a bit too much and was selfish in the lead-up, and Addison dropped me from the team just before we were due to get on the bus to go to the game! I was devasted. My mum often only heard my side of the story, and she was angry, too. My brother Lorenzo was playing, so I had to watch along with my mum as our team played outstanding football without me.

It taught me a huge lesson that I have never forgotten. I wasn't expendable. The team COULD win games and play exceptionally without me. The world didn't revolve around a fourteen-year-old Ronaldo Mulitalo.

Once the penny dropped, I started listening to this coach a lot more, and I got better as a player, quickly. I also learned that Lee was caring for me, he was showing me tough love. When I knuckled down a bit more after that, we won some silverware that season and something just clicked, on and off the field.

In the following school year, I qualified to play for school in the Langer Trophy, the top school competition in Queensland, but I was very young still. Addison showed faith in me, though, and fast-tracked me, putting me in first-grade training as soon as he could and allowing me to rub shoulders with the best players at the school for the rest of that year. After one session, I went home after the session and told Mum that one of the older boys had hit me too hard in training. She rang Lee, ready to complain about my treatment, and he then told her his side (the truth). I had been provoking the older lads constantly in training, so one of them just taught me a little lesson. As soon as she put the phone down, she turned her anger to me instead! That's the last time I did that!

At the time, it was the pinnacle for me as a footballer. From where I had been only 12 months prior to now training with the big boys, was a huge leap. To try and get into the first grade at the school the following year, as I was coming through the juniors, ensured that summer I couldn't think of anything else, and I wanted to do a huge pre-season. I wanted to make the first-grade squad in 2015 – I didn't care if I was the youngest.

To be able to make my debut for school first grade at 15 was huge for me. As young players coming through, we idolised the first graders at our school, and it made us want to compete at a higher level and to emulate them. It was a culture I wanted to embrace. It was a culture that Lee Addison had created from scratch.

The night before the school's round one game in the Langer Trophy, the school's first-ever match in the top division, Lee called me to say I was in. And starting. I was going to make my first-grade debut. He kept it a secret from everyone on purpose and only contacted me late so that I didn't put too much pressure on myself. It shows how much he knew the mindsets of his players; he judged it perfectly. I couldn't sleep that whole night! In my head, I felt like I was débuting in the NRL! If he'd told me seven days in advance, I think I'd have been hospitalised due to sleep deprivation and insanity!

It was very special for me and when I told my mum about it, she was very happy. That was all I wanted to do as a junior – play first grade for Ipswich State High School. I couldn't even believe I'd be turning up the next day, putting the boots on to play with the boys I had so much respect for. I had already planned who I would be watching the game with, but instead, they'd be watching me.

I had two great years in the first team for the school. I started on the wing for a few games before Lee switched me to fullback. A year, later he made me captain. I felt we were a brilliant coach and captain combination – he trusted me, and I trusted him. He used to leave some of the talks to the players to me, often telling me what he wanted included. He was growing me as a leader and as a person as well as a footballer. It was all a massive thing to be a part of and a hugely rewarding journey. I learned so much about myself as a person and as a player. I learned so much about my craft in those years as Lee used to break the game down for us so well and coached us individually a lot. We added so much to our toolbox and that's what he did for all of us until we finished up at school. He used to always say, *"Leave no stone unturned"* when it comes to preparation.

Video reviews with Lee were something else! I copped the good and bad of it, but I was more scared of the clips he'd show us of our training! Training was pretty hard, and we'd often go up against local A-grade sides in opposed sessions. He or his camera (or both) would be on a balcony at the top of the library next to the field during training, and I would be more nervous about these training sessions than games because I knew that whenever I did something wrong, I'd be starring on the video a day later!

All these lessons though and this style of coaching were all very good things. The best things, actually. Because when I got to the NRL, it was exactly like everything I'd done before at school, just more intense because of the calibre of players around me!

When I made my NRL debut, I found out minutes before due to an injury in the warmup. But it wasn't my first rodeo of the late call-up for a first-grade debut. Just a bigger version of it! At an NRL club, you're getting watched and videoed from every angle, and coaches are criticising every move, every left foot or right foot not in place and pulling you up on the way you're facing or carrying the ball. Thank God all of us boys learned how to deal with this in school under Lee before getting to the top level, where the scrutiny was bigger. Getting all this out of the way as a junior at school made it a lot easier to come into the top grade at Cronulla. He prepared me for the NRL.

If I have made Lee seem a bit too tough and a complete hard arse, that wasn't the intention. School holidays were brilliant because we would have a first-grade camp, and they were hilarious times. He wanted us to express ourselves and have as much fun with each other as we could, creating tasks for us that enabled us to do just that!

When I made the Queensland Schools rep side, the tournament came just after school holidays when our training wasn't happening, so Lee helped me train before we went to camp. He was standing there and timing me during his school holidays when he didn't need to. He made sure I could understand what the Queensland staff were asking me to do.

When I left school and went to Cronulla, I used to always call Lee at the school and tell him to *"Sign me back up. I want to come back home"*. He would always reply, *"Stick it out one more week 'Naldo"*. I was lucky enough that he wouldn't let me come back to school, even though I was still young enough to qualify for the first grade at the school. I always tell this story. He could have easily told me to come home and put me straight back in the first grade at school, but instead, he kept telling me to stick it out for 'one more week' and that was it. He even got an old player of his who lived in Cronulla to pick me up and take me out for a round of golf when I was feeling down. I was not yet an adult, so he kept a special eye out for me, even though he was miles and miles away in Queensland.

He's a great friend, and I love him. He's a great coach and I feel blessed to have crossed paths with him. On a recent TikTok video about me, someone wrote in the comments underneath words to the effect of *"Lee Addison did so much for Ronaldo in his junior years"*. That comment got over a thousand likes in no time at all. I couldn't believe it. It is a measure of the man and the impact he has had on me and so many others.

Ronaldo Mulitalo plays as a winger for the Cronulla Sharks and New Zealand. He needs thirteen tries in 2025 to become the third-highest try scorer in Cronulla Sharks history at only 25 years old.

2
Change Management

I was telling everybody I could. Whenever I could and wherever I could.

"It's going to be the best program in Australia very soon."

People were shocked when they heard those words regularly from me and often nodded uncomfortably in agreement, or faked an *"Of course, Lee!"* before scurrying off to no doubt discuss how crazy I was to think that. When I arrived in the City of Ipswich to coach at little-known Ipswich State High School, my sanity was often questioned. Historically, the school team had only achieved a few third-division titles.

Little over three years later it would be one of the best programs in Australia, and ten years later, THE BEST!

So, how did that change get started?

The vast majority of coaches, as I have personally experienced, are appointed to coach a team or club when things aren't going so well for that particular team or club! Rarely does a coach waltz into the perfect coaching environment and is only required to keep the engine running (a skill in itself)!

The reality is we are often a 'change manager' as coaches. If you're a coach of just a team and nothing else in an organisation, your change is directed towards the players and staff around that particular group in your care. If you are the Head Coach of a club or similar, you may need to take a holistic view to change – including developing your juniors and coaches. Over the following pages, you'll read examples of how to implement both these crucial elements.

FC Barcelona has spent a long time as one of the most valuable sports teams in the world. In terms of revenue, they are one of the richest football clubs in the world. They have won a record 77 trophies, 27 League titles, 50 domestic cups, 5 UEFA Champions Leagues, a further 12 European trophies and 3 World Club Cups. Their Academy produced arguably the world's best ever and most famous player. Lionel Messi. Enough said!

When describing the youth academy supplying FC Barcelona, Pep Guardiola, the former Head Coach and well-known trophy accumulator, was quoted in the book 'Another Way of Winning' as saying:

"All good academies should develop players and human beings and, instill in them, a strong sense of belonging, of identity. What is the key to this Barcelona? That the majority of us are from 'in this house.' This is our team, but not just the players, the coaches too, the doctors, the physios, the handymen."

With any team I coach, I often inherit groups that contain some players with different standards and expectations to the ones I have. In any of the lower-grade NRL or schoolboy teams I have coached, several individuals had NRL club contracts. This often proved difficult to manage at times as, invariably, these young players had experienced so many adults telling them how good they were all the time. When faced with this problem, you have to change their mindsets so that these players feel the hunger to improve again and to give them something to work for, to chase after and the desire to achieve.

At other organisations, I have inherited groups with low self-esteem Rugby League wise and this soon became apparent in their attitude to training. From the day I walked into Ipswich State High School, I said to anyone who would listen to me there, *"We are doing everything to a 'Best in Australia' standard from now."* I felt I had a fair grasp of that standard after some of my experiences. At the very least, I expected them to train as well as the Manly Sea Eagles, Penrith Panthers and St Gregory's boys used to under my watch. To give their all at all times. By now, James Tedesco had graduated to the NRL. I had won premierships coaching at that illustrious league school. The Ipswich players knew that I had something to back up my ambitions, even if they couldn't quite picture the pinnacle for themselves yet.

Next is a letter I wrote at the start of a 146-page development document I put together for all my support staff at Ipswich State High School. I wanted to **_set my standard from day one!_**

Here's a summary of the letter – originally written in 2012:

To the reader,

Make no mistake – by reading this document, you are in the process of joining or following a program which has one ultimate goal...

"To be the best schoolboy rugby league academy in Australia"

In my mind, us being aware and "living" the key performance indicators (KPI's) of what is required to be "the best schoolboy rugby league academy in Australia" is crucial. In the first instance, I would like to offer the following goals (in no particular order)...

Do you have any others that spring to mind? If so, these should be brought to light in rugby league staff meetings both formal and informal which will be a regular part of our practice from the start of 2013. These meetings will also help us revise our training environment, share best practices and develop a series of KPI's in the goal categories already outlined...

I am a big believer in KPI's. I would like them to form a huge part of our practice, our training, our games, our coaching and our program as a whole. For players to improve under us, they need to be accountable in every session for what they produce. They need to get better every session, every week, every game, every season. So do we as coaches.

This will see us going through the process of FORMING, STORMING and NORMING as a staff group, a playing group and a 'department'. A group development process identified by Tuckmann, a psychologist many years ago (1965 in fact.)

I foresee this process taking anything between 1 and 2 years as we align our thoughts and work out our strengths and weaknesses as a 'department' before we go into the PERFORMING stage, the fourth stage of Tuckman's model.

This is not to say that we will not 'perform' within the initial one/two-year window, indeed, I hope we win every game! That said, it would be almost impossible for us to get to our ultimate goal within the first year and I believe it is always possible to improve, regardless of the contents of the win-loss column.

Regardless of results, please never lose sight (and therefore allow the players to lose sight) of our ultimate goal and the incremental stages required to get there. To become the best program in Australia.

Some stages will be easier to conquer than others and, achievement of one stage may also mean achieving another simultaneously. You will also notice I have not added time limits here. I believe time limits would add unnecessary pressure or indeed, the opposite, make us relax when we shouldn't be.

To achieve these goals, It is important that as a staff, we plan and deliver a quality training and preparation environment for these boys in our care. It is also important that we identify talent in the most efficient way, both inside and outside our organisation.

When the program is at the level, we want it to be at, many of these boys will go on to Cyril Connell, Mal Meninga or Toyota Cup level. A select few may also go on to Q Cup and NRL level. The importance of giving them the best start possible to their rugby league career cannot be stressed enough. We have a very key role to play in the development of the young player in this district. I want our School to be seen as THE place to send kids for a future in the sport.

I believe that fundamental to the whole process at this age is that players should be learning lessons for the long term, the bigger picture as well as focusing on the here and now. Our success as a coaching and management group will be determined by how well we develop the players for the ultimate goal of winning the Australian title at senior level and we must not lose sight of this.

This pack has been designed to outline roles and responsibilities to help achieve this. I would like all coaches in this program to see themselves as Assistant First Grade coaches regardless of their current title.

I am a huge believer in a highly disciplined environment. I will put high standards and expectations on staff and players, with the aim that everyone reaches those standards and asks for bigger challenges.

I am also a huge believer in transparency and teamwork. I will be very hands-on at the start as I set out my own boundaries for the team. Gradually, I will be delegating more and more coaching and review tasks to other people, but please bear with me if I appear too 'hands-on' at the start. It will not last forever and I just ask you to be 'hands-on' and proactive in your support.

I have coached children from various backgrounds in England, NSW and Queensland and as a result of this, I believe that those at the start of this program will lack certain skills and training disciplines. The key for me is developing a system whereby we give them an appropriate amount relevant to their age group and ability, taking into account their backgrounds.

You will see within this document the '5 pillars of our program'. These are the 5 most important lines you will read in this document and they must underpin everything we do. Upon reading them, you will note that there are actually a few more coaching points than 5, but they are grouped into the 5 'pillars'. The reason for this is simple – the information is "chunked" because the disciplines in each pillar are all interrelated

This document aims to outline how we will go about our business in 2013 and beyond. When feedback has been received from all staff as we go through the Forming, Storming and Norming phase, it is hoped that this is the contract that binds us together, the text from which we work.

Indeed, this is a 'Handbook' as much as it is a curriculum document and a handbook should be there for all to benefit, for each staff member to have a reference point should they need help or assistance at any stage. The document is separated into clear sections and they should be your reference point. They will be available in those separate sections on the school network for easier consumption.

Most of all, this document in its various forms is designed to give us direction and resources and hopefully, we will all be pulling in the same direction over the next few years. If that is what we want our players to do then they need to see the staff doing just that as well. The whole document is written in the first person so any feedback or suggestions for improvement/correction should be targeted directly to me.

Enjoy the ride! (and the read)

Lee Addison (December 2012)

Changing the standards in a team

If you're a leader of any kind, you need to know where you are heading. How can you lead to somewhere you haven't identified? You then need to get that vision across to your team off the field, so that they can get it across to those on it.

If you are walking into a failing or underperforming team or organisation, you need to focus on changing mindsets from day one. If you are joining a winning team or club, or one operating on par, setting *your* standards is also super important, despite the fact you should also be taking the time to look at what is right and what is working well within that group.

A very common way of getting things started is to write a letter to all players, coaches and officials. Another useful method is to prepare an electronic presentation, such as a PowerPoint, to show to these people when they are assembled in a suitable room.

Every year, I try to do both! You've just read an example of one of my letters, and you probably gathered that I want nobody to be in any doubt about my standards, my ambitions and where I expect us to get to. I want the doubters to lift their belief levels from the off. I want to make them believe what they previously didn't believe was possible is possible. To those who are at the right levels already, I want them to know they can reach an even HIGHER level of achievement.

> ### Joel Gould, Queensland Times, December 22nd, 2013
>
> IPSWICH State High has taken schoolboy rugby league in the city to a new level.
>
> But this year's success is just the start. Deputy principal Mick Hornby and rugby league academy boss Lee Addison have much bigger fish to fry.
>
> "I want this school to be associated with national championships," said Addison

A men's representative team I took over responsibility for in 2014 was a seriously underperforming bunch.

The Ipswich Diggers is the representative side of the area of Ipswich in Queensland. The Diggers operate rep teams from juniors, with the senior team being the men's team. I was appointed Head Coach of the seniors in 2014 and stayed in the job for three campaigns. The team was made up of players selected from the local Ipswich 'A Grade' competition and the Ipswich Jets reserve grade side. All players were paid at their respective clubs, so in the UK, you'd say they were about Championship or Championship One standard and professional.

On 21st May 2013, the Queensland Times Newspaper (QT) ran the following headline in its sports pages...

'Bomber says Diggers lack pride and passion'.

The story underneath included the quotes of a player from an Ipswich Rugby League (IRL) club who had just represented the Diggers. Quotes such as *"not a memory he will savour"*, *"(a campaign to) rather forget"*, and talk of a return to *"the bad old days"* of *"several years of poor results"* after *"giving the comp a shake*

CHANGE MANAGEMENT

in the last two years" hardly painted a positive picture of the Diggers experience I was about to walk into. And these thoughts only came from the pen of the journalist! The player himself was quoted as saying the following:

"Being a rep side, you'd think you'd enjoy it, but I don't think there was as much pride in the jersey as there should be.

"When we went out there, it felt more like how good they looked rather than how well they represented Ipswich.

"When you're representing Ipswich, it should be about the team. But it seemed more about individuals and about getting the free gear.

"People weren't putting in."

There were also 'shots fired' at the selection committee.

"It seemed like they were trying to pick a name-based team rather than one based on form,"

OUCH!

The IRL Operations Manager of the day, Brendon Rose, was given a right to reply in the same publication. He stated that the preparation for the Ipswich Diggers would be *"reviewed by the Ipswich Rugby League"* but the following caveats were added:

"They've had the same preparation time previously and it has worked. In regard to the pride in the jersey, these things come out when you get well beaten."

I was appointed Ipswich Diggers coach in January 2014. In the first Chairman's Challenge of my tenure, in May of that year, the Diggers came the closest they ever had to winning the tournament. We beat the Gold Coast by two points in Game One but only managed a draw against Brisbane in Game Three of the round-robin tournament and lost the tournament on points differential. The same newspaper that carried so many negative comments about the Diggers experience a year earlier now had the back page headline 'Cruel Finish for Focused

Diggers'. The captain spoke of *"the pride and passion"* of the players' efforts and of a *"phenomenal performance"*.

That's change right there!

Fast forward two years, and the Chairman's Challenge trophy finally ended in Ipswich's hands. Ipswich Rugby League chairman Jack Rhea told the QT in May 2016, *"We've had nine years and the closest we came was a draw two years ago"*. He also spoke of the pride restored to the jersey after two huge wins over the Gold Coast and Brisbane opponents.

After three campaigns in charge of the Diggers, Ipswich was (arguably) the dominant side in the competition and on this evidence, was no longer the easy beats.

Now that IS what you call change!

But how did it all happen?

Meeting the Chairman and Former Coach

When it was first mentioned that the IRL chairman Jack Rhea was interested in me as a coach, I had to make it clear to him that I had to bring change and not just accept the 'status quo'. We had a meeting over coffee; we didn't keep the meeting to a time limit, and I asked Jack what his thoughts were on this approach.

To my enjoyment, what he said was music to *my* ears and I've since learned, so were my words to him – so it was a great meeting. Jack didn't want to keep things as they were, and he knew change needed to happen. He saw me as the change agent and was willing to back me to the hilt.

Change, in my eyes, meant being able to have complete control of the football side of the Diggers organisation, eradicating bad attitudes and only getting people involved who wanted to be part of it and who wanted to improve. That might mean saying goodbye to some.

I asked Jack to hand over the footy side to me and let me carry out whatever I needed to do in terms of selections of staff and players, how often we trained, where we trained and when we trained. He agreed. Not only that, but he also told me of a few 'unfortunate' incidents that had occurred during the last few Diggers campaigns and the players involved. He told me that he didn't want those people involved again, and I agreed to that, but it would be a fresh start for everyone else. We were up and running.

It didn't take a genius to work out that the Diggers 'brand' was in a bit of a confused state at this time. But it had nothing to do with me or the staff alongside me, so that we could look at it with fresh pairs of energetic and enthusiastic eyes. I didn't let the past impact my thoughts, and I encouraged those around me not to either. Our plan was to look forward with confidence.

Whenever I get a new coaching role, I grab a brand-new journal and write. I write down anything I hear about my new coaching environment. Not only that, I seek opinions. Opinions from previous staff and players associated with Ipswich Diggers. It was clear that there was a general 'malaise' around the concept and it was something that players and staff knew should be a proud moment for them, but for some reason, had turned into a chore.

The most important meeting I arranged was with my predecessor as coach. We shared coffee at a local McDonalds and chewed the fat for well over an hour. He told me of his experiences, why things were difficult, which players I should be looking at and which ones had let him down.

I'll admit, it was at this time that I started to have a tiny doubt creeping into my mind. The previous coach was a very experienced campaigner and was on the development staff of the NRL's Brisbane Broncos at the time. He was no slouch, he knew his football, and I had no doubt I was talking to someone who had given his heart and soul to this project in previous years. He is also a great bloke and cares about the City of Ipswich and the players he had in his care. I think it was at this point I realised what a sizeable rebuilding job I had on my hands.

I also noticed, from some of the people in 'club-land' in particular, that there was a sense that Diggers staffing and selections should be an 'equal split' between the clubs, so for example, a set number from each club or at least someone from each club involved. To put it mildly, I felt that this was not a particularly good recipe for success. In fact, I think that type of approach is a load of bollocks!

I had to make sure I had the right staff around me and in turn, we were going to pick the right players – but not only that, the right 'type' of player. By that, I mean, the right players to do the job but also people with the right attitudes towards the Diggers and preparation in general – namely, players who didn't miss training, players who were in good physical condition, reliable players and players who cared.

The coaching staff

Staff-wise, I went with the following people:

Assistant Coach – Josh Bretherton

Josh was my assistant in my day job as well and he is technically a very good coach. He is also very adept at editing and analysing game footage and moving forward this was to play a big part in our strategy. Josh and I both had sports analysis software on our laptops and Josh often edited and sourced clips which we reviewed together. It is such a big task that both of us needed to do it. Obviously, as head coach, my attention was frequently taken elsewhere, so Josh just ploughed on through the footage. We also had the added bonus of him knowing how I wanted my training and our team to look, so I didn't have to worry about 'training up' a new assistant coach.

I asked Josh to analyse the opposition weeks ahead of me, so that I could compare it with my own analysis. I did this nearer to the time of our game against a particular opponent. He provided me with great detail, and it was then up to me to decide how much of it I wanted the players to focus on. He was a key part of my off-field team.

Conditioning – Peter Poole

This wasn't as typical a 'conditioning' appointment as they usually tend to be. It was more about monitoring players' health and fitness, monitoring their fluid loss, their diet and any injuries. 'Pooley' gave the players weights and fitness programs to follow in their own time, on top of their current club commitments. Like Josh, Pooley was on my coaching staff in my day job too, so it made life a whole lot easier. He did this job for the 2014 and 2015 campaigns with a family bereavement sadly affecting his involvement in 2016. Pooley is an absolute guru when it comes to the health and wellbeing of us humans and he is the most organized man I have ever met in my life!

Various – Shane Harris

Shane was the youngest member of our staff and was a trainee with us during the daytime in 2014. He was destined for more in the future, both short-term and long-term, but back in 2014, all this experience was ahead of him. We brought him into the Diggers set-up as an extra selector and to observe the training and game day structure. By 2015, he was a full-fledged member of staff with the Diggers as a third assistant coach/manager/conditioner, as we felt we needed that extra pair of hands involved. By 2016 he stepped up to Assistant Coach due to Pooley no longer being involved.

It's fair to say that in 2014, Shane was still trying to work out what he wanted to be with regard to footy. He is one of those guys who is an excellent coach but also excellent in the 'trainer' role and he can actually referee quite well too! By 2015, he was clearly morphing into an Assistant coach as his knowledge of the technical nuances of the game was growing by the day. I also noticed he was studying coaching methods in his own time, so it was a pleasure to help him on this journey. He progressed to become the Assistant Coach and then Head Coach of the Ipswich Jets Mal Meninga representative side and assisted me with the Poland national side.

Admin Manager(s) – Byron Whitehead and Joe Colthorpe

Byron was the Treasurer of the IRL, and he was a great link between the IRL offices and the group. He also cooked up several great feeds for the players and looked after all off-field needs. The players loved him and referred to him as 'uncle'. Joe has been involved in some kind of capacity with the Diggers for many decades, so he was my link to the history of the concept, and it was for someone like Joe that I wanted to see us succeed. He'd never seen them win the competition and really wanted to. He also keeps statistics on everything. We had many moments looking for historical facts about the Diggers – anything to help prepare.

Round one of the IRL competition back then was always played at the Grand Final venue, the North Ipswich Reserve, meaning you can get to see every team in one sitting! (Manna from heaven for this coach!) Our coaching staff were given an executive box and supplied with food and drink to help get us through the day. In the box, we watched the games intently. The brief I gave all watchers was that if somebody showed anything, write them down as a 'possible' and we will study them in more depth. And when I say 'in-depth' – I mean it! I think this was the first, most important or game-changing thing we implemented.

Team selections

The video man Gordon was giving us a live feed of the game into our laptops, and Josh was 'tagging' the footage of the players we identified and starting to build files on them. So as soon as one game finished, Josh or I would get to work on editing it on our laptops. This always left two or three watchers free to keep watching live. We probably ended up with a shortlist of about fifty players at the end of Round One each year we did this job. This shortlist was narrowed down over the first five rounds of the IRL. We also watched the Ipswich Jets reserve grade side each year to identify their best players. The edited files allowed us to watch the players in isolation, which makes it a lot easier to build up a profile of that player. With the edited files, along with the coaches, I compiled a draft seventeen, a reserve seventeen and a third seventeen.

I can promise you, that each year we did this job, we never ended up with our preferred original seventeen! There are always injuries and players who aren't interested or available for very genuine and sometimes, not so genuine, reasons. In 2014, our squad ended up mostly from our reserve seventeen, 2015 it is fair to say we went into a fifth or sixth draft with close to thirty-two players unavailable, but 2016 was a smoother year and we ended up with the majority coming from our first choice seventeen.

Now for the second 'most important' or game-changing thing we implemented. Who we selected, how we selected them and why.

The competition the Diggers play in is a three-day round robin, with players having to perform twice in either a 24 or 48-hour period. I felt that, as a result, we needed mobile men. Men who were fit enough but also young enough to recover for that second game. With a thought that the Diggers needed a 'new broom' sweeping through it due to some attitudes, this meant that it was an opportunity to select an overall younger squad. I also felt a mobile brand of football would be easier to implement based on the players available and the tournament-style format of footy. I felt I wanted to let the opposition chase us around rather than picking big men to plough through their big men and get bruised up themselves in the process. You've read this from me before, as coaching a mobile style of play tends to be my default strategy if we have the players to do it.

'Non-negotiables'

I've always had a rule about training in all my coaching years, and it's one I will never change. If you don't or can't train, but don't have the courtesy to let the coaching staff know via a message of some sort, then straight away I'll just assume you don't care and give your spot to someone else. If there's a genuine issue, such as a work commitment, then if you let staff know they will work around it.

Also, when it came to training, the players were told they had to talk. They weren't asked. They were told! And I also gave them ideas of what to say to each other. I wasn't encouraging them to talk or asking them to talk; it was a coaching order, and something expected of a Digger as a bare minimum. If the talk was not sufficient, they would be told. In three years, I never had to remind the players to talk after that initial chat.

My third non-negotiable was that, as of our first training session, everyone was to treat each other as a brother. Again, there were no 'phasing in' or 'getting to know you' sessions. It was a coaching order, not a discussion point. Any club differences had to be put to one side immediately. These may sound like quite harsh approaches, but I found the players appreciated these things being addressed, being brought up straight away and being diluted as a potential issue without delay. After the difficulty of the previous years, I felt these actions were a necessary step.

Avoiding 'Over Coaching'

A golden rule I have always followed when coaching representative football is to put a huge amount of faith in the players at my disposal. They are rep players for a reason, and they have been selected because they have skills and abilities to bring to the table. Therefore, it's my job to bring those skills to the fore.

I have also worked out over the years that I can teach everything I want to teach the players about how I want them to play the game in three sessions of a maximum of ninety minutes length, each. So, 270 minutes in total.

One thing that you don't know before the first session, though, is how quickly the players will adapt to what is being asked of them.   In 2014 and 2015, we did six sessions to prepare over three weeks. Basically, this meant the workload for Diggers players doubled in length once I took over from three to six sessions. After completing the first cycle of sessions one to three, we could use sessions four through to six to zoom in on any areas we felt we were deficient in or, alternatively, just go over them again for repetition purposes. In 2016, I decided to condense the whole thing into a week of four sessions, but I planned for three of them to last 120 minutes rather than 90. But in 2016 the players picked things up especially quickly, which meant I actually cancelled a planned session and told the players to stay at home and rest instead. Bonus!

I told the coaching staff we had to be clear and concise in our coaching, do lots of coaching 'on the run', and to limit and 'chunk' the information so that we were focusing on doing only a few things but doing them exceptionally well. I also spoke with the coaches about what and how we corrected players who were doing things wrong. We discussed how we wouldn't be able to change the way a player would catch, hold or pass a football, but we might be able to influence the angle of run, or how he engaged a defender. We also encouraged the players to remember what they could, and to communicate it constantly because *"Not everybody will remember everything, but everyone will remember something - so tell everyone else what you have remembered"*.

Getting the boys together

It's one of the oldest tricks in the book but there is nothing like getting the players together for some time to relax, over a nice meal and a beverage of their choice and as many beverages as they want. The IRL supplied it all free of charge to the players, and in the three years, I found that if I treated the players like the adults they are, then they acted like adults. What they did in these bonding sessions helped relax them but also did absolutely nothing to impact negatively on their performances or the Diggers' reputation in the community. We structured the events so they were not at risk of being detrimental to performances.

Allowing Home Comforts

For tournaments that were held in Ipswich, I was offered accommodation in a hotel for our staff and players. I respectfully refused it. I wanted the players in their own beds and in their own homes with their own families to maximise the home advantage. We also structured video and recovery sessions in late afternoons to allow players to spend time with their families in the mornings and to carry out their daily chores if they needed to!

> **Joel Gould, Queensland Times, March 29, 2017**
> *Gold Coast and Brisbane representative sides play the Ipswich Diggers in a carnival for the Chairman's Challenge.*
>
> *Last year's big win by the Diggers under Addison, his third year at the helm, was the first time the side had won in umpteen years.*
>
> *"From where we were, to what we achieved last year was just a quantum leap. Last year we won the Chairman's Challenge easily".* Jack Rhea, Ipswich Rugby League Chairman

The lessons

Without the unwavering support of the IRL executive committee, headed by Chairman Jack Rhea, I wouldn't have been able to do my job, and neither would the staff around me. Any coach needs to know that they have the backing of the committee. Yes, we got so close to winning in 2014, but 2015 was a horrible year for us and it would have been easy for Jack and the committee to blame the coaches and look elsewhere.

In 2014, we implemented a plan as outlined above and with it, we came as close as ever to winning the trophy. It created a buzz again around the Diggers. On the back of that, Jack said I had the job as long as I wanted it, and I was happy to do it for the long term. Fast forward twelve months, and, what we considered to be a better and more refined version of our 2014 pre-tournament processes didn't work. Not only did it not work, but it also went horrendously wrong, with our Diggers suffering a disappointing loss on day one and an absolute hammering on day two.

Immediately after that terrible loss to the Gold Coast, I went up to the Chairman and Operations Manager of the IRL and immediately offered my resignation. I was told rather politely that it wouldn't be accepted and to file a report on what I thought went wrong so things could be fixed. The IRL committee at that moment showed their support to me and the staff and that is so important for any coach.

In my report, I identified some key areas of breakdown around the Diggers concept that I felt were outside of my control and, in an attempt to come up with remedies, used these key areas as the basis for my recommendations for the future. Obviously, that report is not for public consumption, but it is fair to say that no stone was left unturned in getting the Diggers to the top.

So, it wasn't easy. Anything worth achieving rarely is. That year was my last coaching the Diggers. There has not been a Chairman's Challenge win by Ipswich since.

Key Points from This Chapter

- We are often a 'change manager' when appointed to a coaching role

- Set your standard from day one!

- If you're a leader of any kind, you need to know where you are headed. You then need to get that vision across to your team off the field, so that they can get it across to those on it

- If you are walking into a failing or underperforming team or organisation, you need to focus on changing mindsets from the off

- If you are entering a winning team or organisation, or one operating on par, take the time to look at what is right and working well

- Write a letter to players, coaches, officials or indeed all of them

- Present to those people in a room, using some method of electronic presentation such as PowerPoint

The Work Before a Team is Named – By Brendon Rose

With all representative sides, a 'mission' or 'outcome' is the key. It's less about 'X's & O's' and more about culture, trust and single focus. With limited preparation time and players coming from different clubs (some with fierce rivalries), the ability of the coach to get the group of players to focus on the 'mission' and leave the baggage & personal glory at the door is imperative. That is why, if the player is not willing to get onboard, no matter how good or big a name they are, they aren't welcome.

In senior representative football, selectors are becoming obsolete. They are sounding boards for the coach because, at the end of the day, the buck stops with them. That is why total control has to be given to the coach (they will be held accountable for the result). Yes, there is communication from above on the overall mission, but the coach will be held accountable for how the team achieves that mission. The coach knows how they want to play, and how they want the culture in the team to be and as a result, they know what type of a player they want. Why confuse that with other people's clouded judgment? Give the coach the tools they believe can get the job done.

In dealing with Lee for several years, this is his biggest strength. His ability to communicate a mission and sell his message to players is exemplary. He could probably sell ice to an Eskimo! He doesn't play favourites. He knows how he wants to play and looks for the players that can do that job the best.

He has an uncanny ability to get a player to run through a wall, whether he spends five minutes or five seasons with them. He knows how to get in the head of players because he spends hours working to understand them and what makes them tick. He does this by studying tape, watching them play, and watching them train. Also, by observing how they interact in the dressing room, how they are as people & ultimately what drives them.

Lee has shown me that the majority of the work is done well before a team is named and the first session. It might only be a short preparation for the players, but a good representative coach has a long preparation cycle if done correctly.

Many of these traits can be implemented in season-long campaigns. The difference is that when selecting players, the margin of variation on either side of your ideal player can be increased as you can spend more time getting the player aligned with your mission. The creation of systems and culture to help the team develop can live long past the moment a coach moves on. Lee's creation of the Ipswich State High program is a testament to this. It has continued to develop and been successful based on the building blocks established under him both in the development of players and just as important, the coaches & trainers that he looked after. The program is continuing to thrive to this day, because of those key components.

Brendon Rose is a former Operations Manager of Rugby League in Ipswich. He is also a former Queensland Cup referee.

3
Footy and Coaching Talk

Football or bash ball? So many of our top-line players don't have the attacking vision that they should. I have been known to take a screenshot of a top-level game where there are glaring holes or spaces in defensive lines, yet the attack doesn't go there, often because they're not even looking.

A gentleman named Peter, a regular commenter on my Facebook posts, posted a reply that I read out in a slightly paraphrased fashion on The Rugby League Coach Podcast in December 2024. All I could say in response to it was... *"I agree"*.

Some of his concerns are listed here, separated into quotes exactly as he wrote them:

"The problem stems from robotic coaching methods at a junior level in development squads".

"Most coaches teach exactly the same X/Y ball philosophies, (and) they don't look or can't recognise individual skill sets and coach their squad about the players they have".

"At a junior level, I would realistically say on average a (bigger) kid would be 10/15 kg heavier and some a lot more so teaching all the kids the same way to play puts the (smaller) boys at a huge disadvantage to start with.

"Even when I was playing 30/40 years ago, we attempted to play a high upbeat running game keeping the ball in play as much as possible...when we played a team with a lot of (bigger) players,

and our superior cardiovascular genetics even out and more often than not beat their higher strength and power levels".

What Peter is also hinting at is that there is more than one way to win a game of football. We seem to have lost the ability to see that in so many aspects of our football at all levels. In Australia, some media types refer to it as the 'cookie cutter' approach to Rugby League. Such an approach is defined as 'denoting something mass-produced or lacking any distinguishing characteristics.'

I agree with those journalists but would add that there is a fair bit more to unpack. For example, if we are a 'cookie cutter' sport, how did we get to that point, and why do we remain there? Indeed, do we remain there?

I trace the start back to (and blame) the influence Gridiron (American Football in the NFL and College Football) has had on our sport - ironic considering that the roots of Gridiron can be traced back to it being influenced by Rugby!

Jack Gibson, officially the Australian Rugby League Coach of the 20th Century, was widely recognised as one of the first to embrace what they were doing in the United States. I will stop short of saying he was THE first because I want to focus on the tactical impacts rather than the historical back story. He is, however, definitely one of the first and one of the most successful at implementing his findings and adapting them to Rugby League.

Gibson would often travel over to America to watch Gridiron teams play and train. In particular, he was recognised as being a huge fan of coach Vince Lombardi. Lombardi is still seen today as one of the most successful coaches in the whole of American sports, not just the NFL. He also closely followed and got to know another coach, Dick Nolan and spent time with Nolan's San Francisco 49ers. So much so, that a lot of the innovations he brought into Rugby League were attributed to these trips.

When we look at the game in that era, namely the fact that six tackle sets were only introduced in 1971 in Australia, we can start to see why Gibson and others like him thought that Gridiron (with limited 'downs') was such a neat fit as a comparative sport. Prior to 1971, we had unlimited tackles in Rugby League, and then, in 1967, we introduced four years of only four tackles in a set. Jack Gibson's first official year of coaching was 1967.

The defensive line only retreated five yards or five meters back then, too. This didn't change until 1993, when Gibson hung up the clipboard. That year, we reverted to what we have now, ten metres between play the ball and where the defence retreats to. So, when Gibson was the top operator in the sport, players had half the space to play in than they do now.

To break down the defensive line, teams and, as a consequence, their half-backs, had to be more creative. As players got fitter and training methods advanced, defences came up at a rapid pace and had to cover less space than they do now. When the defence is on top of you in no time, you have to throw something different at them if you want to create space or gaps in that defensive line. Also, offloads in the tackle were hugely important to disrupt the rhythm of the defence. Gridiron teams have even less space to play in. That's why coaches in that sport have huge playbooks for their players to learn, and their quarterback is like an on-field version of that playbook and a purveyor of all its various permutations.

Those very same approaches also became common in Rugby League. Good coaches had detailed playbooks to give to their players, but even better coaches got their players extremely fit to carry out these plays constantly on the field, backing it up with energetic, rushing defence. In the early 1980s, there was one particular event that laid bare these changes to the game and on a world stage to boot.

The 1982 Australian Kangaroos squad toured Europe and swept all before them. The impact of their performances still resonates throughout the game today and influences so much of what still happens because it meant Australia were on the way to becoming the dominant force in the world for the next 43 years (and counting).

The 1982 Aussies were soon to be dubbed The Invincibles as they became the first Kangaroo touring side to ever go through a tour of Europe undefeated. They played twenty-two matches, scored 1,005 points and only conceded 120. That's an average of 45.6 scored compared to 5.4 conceded points per game, to be exact.

To put this into context, Australia had toured Europe every four years (unless there was a war), and Great Britain had won 9 of the 14 Ashes Series played in that country before 1982. Only Great Britain had managed a 3-0 Ashes score whitewash before and that was twice in 1933/34 and 1948.

There was a warning shot fired in 1979 when Australia beat Great Britain 3-0. But that was on Australian soil, and it was meant to be a different proposition in the Northern Hemisphere, with the softer fields, colder weather and noisy, parochial crowds.

As Australia landed in England on 10th October 1982, the Ashes series win tally was nineteen to Britain and eleven to Australia. The previous twenty years had seen the score at seven series wins to two to Australia, but this was not seen as uncommon, just part of the 'natural cycle' and the series were often close and finished 2-1 to someone.

1982 took it to another level and quite frankly, it was a blow that British Rugby League is yet to completely recover from while Australia set the standards that everyone else tries to emulate. There have been nine series played since and including 1982; Australia have won all of them, including four of them by a series score of 3-0. Indeed, Great Britain or England haven't beaten Australia in a match since 2006.

This 1982 tour impacted the whole world of Rugby League. The British deeply studied everything Australian and started their cookie-cutter approach throughout the sport in the mid to late 1980s and onwards. But by then, Australia was moving ahead constantly.

Listen to players from the earlier days of Winfield Cup first-grade football (Winfield sponsored what we now know as the NRL competition from 1982), and they will tell you how they *"Hardly did weights in those days"* and that most of the emphasis was on cardiovascular fitness and thus, lots of fitness training and ball work. By the late 1980's and early 1990's, players were doing some serious weight training in gyms, and only a few years later, the sport would go full-time professional on both sides of the globe, making this fitness, strength and power approach even more of a factor.

Throughout this period, England or Great Britain got closer to Australia in the Ashes Series and World Cups, but their inability to topple Australia in a series or win the world prize reaffirmed the thought that whatever was happening in Australia was market-leading stuff.

What also happened in the early 1990's was the game turned to the ten-metre rule in defence, which was essentially, double the distance between the teams that existed before. This is a change to the sport that I believe has never truly been fully understood by so many in the game due to its magnitude. Let me explain my thoughts.

This extra space combined with full-time professionalism meant it wasn't long until the symptoms from the collisions in the sport were compared to those that someone gets when they've suffered a car crash. That's only one collision on the field, by the way! To prepare for that, the physical composition of the player becomes of paramount importance, if nothing else, just from a safety point of view. And going back in defence ten metres also meant efforts had to be doubled in the fitness department to cut down attacking space if teams didn't want to be blown off the park.

One Australian-born UK Super League coach of the early 2000s made quite public his thought that the strength scores in the UK were matching, if not beating, those of their Australian counterparts in that era. Yet he failed to see that fitness scores plus football knowledge and know-how were often not even in the same ballpark.

On a podcast in 2024, commentator and widely respected football brain Phil Gould said something along the lines of *"We've only really learned how to be proper full-time professionals in the last ten years"*. If correct, that would mean that up until about 2014, we were in something of an experimentation phase that coaches were going through when it came to preparing for the physical aspects of the sport. That means that for two decades at least, we've been adapting and maybe even experimenting with training methods to get the absolute best out of each player.

Whatever happens in the top grades influences our youth and also the coaches of youth teams. As kids start in the game, they want to emulate their heroes and many have ambitions. Anybody who has played Rugby League as a junior since the mid to late 1990s knows that, once you get into your teens, a huge emphasis is placed on developing the body to meet the physical aspects of the sport and, so often, a lot less time is spent on core skill and decision making.

My own training regime after being selected for an 'academy' squad in the UK in 1995 meant two to three days a week of weight training plus two to three days on the field doing fitness or ball work. I was 16 years old at the time and I had been lifting light weights for almost two years already at home.

When this author turned into a coach a matter of years later, it didn't take me long to realise that I had been pigeonholed as a player. I was a prop or a back row forward, so I was expected to run directly and tackle. I had never truly been taught how to pass. Never taught how to play the ball and.... strategy? You're kidding, right? I was often told off by a coach at various stages for passing when I *"should have run"* and never did I see my role as part of a bigger strategic picture!

To this very day, there are junior programs in Australia that have been VERY successful over the years, yet many of their players come out of those particular systems with very poor skill levels. Instead, they are huge individuals who can bench press, squat and deadlift in a gym better than most adults can in society. There is a huge emphasis on creating big, strong, fast and powerful players. Some of our top NRL clubs even sign players solely based on their physical characteristics so this approach perpetuates.

Somewhere along the line, Rugby League started to become overly obsessed with physical prowess at the expense of skill and strategy. Stories abound of junior rep systems in Australia conducting three-hour training sessions that are predominantly strength and fitness-based and often include kids who have been doing exactly the same in a school footy program during the daytime, too.

The talk from media types and many coaches around the sport also laments the 'lack of halves' being developed in the sport, encouraging some NRL clubs to initiate 'halves academies' in a bid to reverse the processes that the community game has gone through to produce them. The big problem is we are asking our halves to do the wrong thing a lot of the time and expecting the wrong outcomes. Let me explain!

One common thing that frustrates me is the thought that *"Halves need to run the footy"* or *"They're not playing well - they're not running the footy"*. I hate that. I coach that the halves should always go at the line with themselves as an **option** to run. They might bring forward attacking shapes in the form of teammates with them to their right and left whilst keeping their hips square or at a 45-degree angle when carrying the ball. Doing this means that, if space opens up, the half can go themselves towards the gap - but only if it opens up, and players should be coached in how to recognise it.

Instead, what we have is a game full of halves who sometimes feel the premeditated need to run the ball to keep their coaches and media happy that they're running! Good halves can make other players look good, and don't always feel the need to get on the highlight reel themselves. Coaching like this also takes the pressure off young halves everywhere.

Kids are now bigger than ever before they even reach a gym in many cases. Many junior coaches can assemble a big squad and win their competition easily by steamrolling everyone else. Sometimes the half just needs to share the ball around the big people to ease the workload and to kick if the opposition manages to hold them out for a set. Smaller teams have to be a bit more creative – but the problem is, tactics have been left behind in the quest to build big powerful players and many halves are often given bucket loads of instructions via a playbook, just like the halves of the 1970's and 80's or NFL quarterbacks. Either of the two approaches above results in one thing – players being taught robotically. They are instructed to *"Do this set"* or *"Do this play"* over and over again.

These kids that came through this system have become teenagers and adults and lack the vision to play football in many cases, or, if they have that vision, they have a coach who doesn't trust that they have it and puts crazy, intricate playing structures in place. But as I outlined earlier, there's a ten-metre gap now between the play the ball and the defensive line, and this is why I don't believe the game truly understands it or has truly embraced it.

A good half doesn't have to pull as many rabbits out of the hat as one of twenty, thirty or forty years ago or more. I cannot understand the strategic rationale of so many coaches in the world who are obsessed with robotic plays at the expense of encouraging their players to play what is 'in front' of them.

I casually refer to Rugby League as a sport of 'motion and emotion'. The motion element refers to how attacking teams attempt to generate momentum with fast play the balls, whereas the emotion aspect concerns how we deal with that momentum. More of how to generate this momentum attacking-wise or prevent it in defence will be discussed over the following pages. The same with the emotional aspect on both sides of the ball.

What I will say at this juncture is that anything remotely robotic should be parked by the coach until the team has mastered the art of how to generate momentum in attack without obsessive structure. It starts with keeping things simple...

Keeping things simple

There's an old saying about Rugby League that I have heard plenty of times:

"It's a very simple game overcomplicated by idiots."

I like to think I explain it in a bit less of an insulting manner:

"Einstein would have trouble doing his scientific equations if he had 13 people in a different colour jersey trying to bash the shit out of him".

To me, there is a simple reason for that, and it's something that applies to many sports too.

White noise & fight or flight mode.

I firmly believe much of Rugby League is played with white noise and even in fight or flight mode sometimes because a player is playing against thirteen people who, quite frankly, want to bash the ball carrier.

Coaches need to coach so simply that it cuts through the white noise of any game. So, instead of telling your players how smart you are at everything or coaching to the gallery that is watching around you, be really succinct with what you say. Be really clear and repeat it often. Your messages will then cut through because you want your players to know what to do in the heat of the battle when there's all that white noise and they're in fight or flight mode.

Get your team to do ***simple things***, do them **excellently** and do them ***ruthlessly, repeatedly*** and better than any other team in the competition or even the world (why not?) My teams always have a maximum of five key things to underpin everything they do throughout training and then the idea is this becomes second nature when it matters - in games.

Below is an example of four I have used most regularly with teams:

- Discipline and patience

- Core offensive skills

- Core defensive skills

- Defending as a unit

We will now look into each in more detail:

Discipline and patience

Players need to be taught about why they are being asked to do certain things. Even though they must 'focus on the moment' during every play in the game, they must be made aware and therefore, become aware of the bigger picture of the game situation. This involves teaching them about the sport they play beyond one phase of play or their involvement. For example, giving away fouls or penalties through a lack of game sense can have a huge detrimental impact on the team. Yet that particular player did it for a reason, be it tiredness, laziness, ignorance, not knowing what to do or a lack of focus on the bigger picture.

Another important skill is that of staying patient in a game rather than trying to force things to happen (Game Sense). The tendency for many players is to try and do something risky on many sets of six tackles, yet if that team plays simply for two to three sets, that is enough, at many levels of the sport, to force the opposition into errors and for it to lead to points scored. Most sports fixtures are <u>lost</u> by someone making a mistake and an opponent capitalizing on it, rather than <u>won</u> by someone doing something amazing to break open the opposition. If the latter does happen, the chances are other scores in the game were a result of mistakes from the opposition.

Most dropped balls at many levels of Rugby League come from a lack of concentration, collisions and players forcing their hands when they get excited about a potential line break or opening. It's important to address this in training and preparation as close games tend to be lost by one team rather than won by the other.

Core skills in attack

I always believe in coaching and empowering the player to make good decisions within a basic team framework rather than structuring the player so much that they are like a robot! To coach like this requires a heavy focus on core skills, decision-making skills and lines of run and it requires patience from the coach.

In Rugby League, this means ensuring the players catch, hold and pass the ball excellently, have the ability to apply vision to each situation and are aware of how the defence would react to any line of run they employed. In some cases, kicking skills are also added, but there are always some players who can't be let loose with that in many contexts!

Now, this may all sound very simple and obvious, but in this sport, the focus on strength & conditioning has often led to skills work being sidelined either significantly or entirely. I continually get frustrated with how many players at the mid to lower end of the two full-time professional competitions in the world, namely the NRL in Australia and Super League in Europ, lack some basic core offensive skills.

'Winning the collision' is a huge Key Performance Indicator in Rugby League and this can be achieved either in offence or defence. In offence, this is namely an attacker landing 'on their front' when tackled and getting a quick play the ball. You will read more about winning the defensive collision very soon.

For now, let's focus on winning the offensive or attacking collision and something that can help when it comes to the handling of the football. I always approach the coaching of this as Soccer coaches would approach their players with the round ball at their feet. If you imagine the best Soccer teams in the world and how the ball seems as if it is attached physically to the feet and body of the best players, then I like to think of Rugby League Football in a very similar manner.

In League's ecosystem, I only rarely see this in action. Yet it is an approach I have honed over the years. For example, going into the collision, the attacker should not 'present' the ball to the tackler. As I write this sentence, I am watching a UK Super League game live, and a player has literally just done what I am saying he shouldn't do. He ran with the ball tucked under his right arm and led into the tackler's shoulder with that side of the body and ball-carrying arm. He then laboured to his feet and played the ball with his right foot after placing it down with his right hand, and it all happened 'in front' of the defender. It wasn't a particularly quick play the ball.

Imagine, instead, the player had a two-handed carry and, on approach to the defender, he switched the ball to his left and fended or bumped the defender with his right arm. He would likely go to ground with the ball in a better place to play it with a left hand and foot. He would also be more likely to have an advantage over the defender, who would still be prone on the ground while the ball is being played. The play the ball would be a second or two faster, and under current rules, the referee might urge the defender to move away.

This may also sound like a subtle difference in advantage in that particular collision, but if this is happening in most, if not all, collisions, then the incremental wins add up for the attacking team and would be telling throughout an attacking set, a half of football and a full game.

In addition to the handling of the football, we need to know what to do with it when carrying it in offence. Do we just run? Run and pass? Or just pass? We could even kick it, couldn't we?

Picture that you, the reader, are the attacker I am talking about. That decision, in any given attacking moment, is dependent on what impact your movement has on the defence. Surely, you're not going to pass if there is no one in a better position than you to advance? Surely, you're not going to kick if the game situation doesn't lend itself to that action, and of course, the simplest option is to just tuck it under your arm and charge into the defence!

You, the reader, are hopefully imagining yourself now in that scenario.

In Rugby League coaching culture, most players don't get taught what to look for in that scenario, never mind, make the right decision! Forwards (the big players) tend to get taught to go one way – forward. They get pigeonholed and restricted. How dare they think of passing! And if they do get taught to pass, it's premeditated and robotic!

As you keep reading this book, you'll see methods promoted on how to develop vision and skill amongst players. Yet, despite a coaching culture that primarily encourages forwards to 'just run' there is also a distinct dearth of teachings about 'how and where' said players should run and the impact that will have on the defence and the game in general.

If the player runs straight (no deviation) with a ball 'tucked under' their arm, a defender or group of defenders only has one decision to make – how they're going to get this marauding person down to the ground. They will likely advance forwards at speed towards the attacker and use the full force of their shoulders and body in order to carry out this task. It could be painful for the attacker!

Imagine instead, this attacker (Player 1) carries the ball in two hands after receiving it from their right. The attacker also has two teammates in support. We will call them 'Player 2' on the left and 'Player 3' on the right.

Player 1, when advancing, steps subtly off their right foot to their left and then quickly off the left foot to their right. As they step to their left or right, they throw a subtle dummy pass to Player 2 on their left about two metres from the oncoming defender. They can do this because they are carrying the ball in two hands in front of their body. This subtle stepping and dummy, plus the support of Player 2 makes the defender 'check' their movement and, instead of advancing at full speed, they are slightly hesitant and may even turn their body two different ways as a result of the steps and dummy (which they thought in that split second was a pass). The defender then has to re-adjust to the first step and then again, to the second step as the attacker (Player 1) changes direction with a subtle step at almost the same moment as throwing the dummy.

Imagine now you're the defender, you've hesitated after the first step from the attacker, then you've lurched to your right as you take the dummy, but now you have to go back to the left. Instead of tackling with your shoulder, you might be able to tackle with your arm, somewhere near the attacker's chest or waist

If you're an attacker, would you rather run the ball at someone's shoulder or their arm? It's a lot easier to burst through one or two stray arms (as long as they're not around the head!) than it is to run into one or two shoulders, which allow a defender to get all their weight behind the tackle. Again, we are looking at an incremental attacking 'win'. A win that, if repeated more often than not, will result in even more positive outcomes later in the game.

This attacker (Player 1) rather than just charging into a defensive line, is playing some football – thinking of their movement and the impact on the game. Because they have stepped subtly back into the place where the ball came from, they have also kept the defence tied up thus keeping the space available for wider players to attempt to exploit.

When Player 1 is further developed, they may even learn when to recognise when to actually pass rather than run! After three or four carries, the defenders will start to think that all Player 1 will do is dummy, so they can stop 'taking the dummy' and instead, put all energy into tackling Player 1 instead.

However...

Player 1 has been taught how to recognise this and notices that the defenders all 'turn in' to the tackle. This means that, on the outside of each defender is now space for Player 2 or Player 3 (in support) to potentially exploit. If a successful pass is at some point delivered, then the defence really is on the back foot and the game will be significantly easier for the attackers moving forward, as defenders are constantly hesitant. To help you understand what you've just read, feel free to head to YouTube and search for *'Rugby League Advancing at the Ruck'* on the Rugby League Coach YouTube channel.

Note: *As I wrote this section, the UK Super League game I referred to has continued and the number of errors and poor discipline from full-time professional players is alarming. Also, so far (6 minutes remaining) not one goal kick has been successful. Full-time professionals should not lose the ball as often as I have just seen. Kickers also need to practice their goal kicking more. These are basics that are seemingly still not getting honed as much as they should be deep into this century. I am not expecting it to be perfect at all times, don't get me wrong. But if full-time rugby players and teams can't hold a footy consistently or kick goals more often than not then they have an awful lot of work to do in their day job. And what chance do we have of getting kids to focus on it if their heroes aren't?*

It's like a soccer team having no control over their feet or missing all shots at goal with no defenders in the way. In Soccer, they'd be playing in a local Sunday league, rather than the elite level of the game.

Phases of the game

Teams in Rugby League tend to attack with sets and I basically only have three basic set structures that I use with my teams. They've always worked well for my teams too!

One very common set is a very simple 'exit set' to start every game. We will take either a run directly from dummy half or one pass from the ruck to a runner on, let's say, the right, who takes it directly into the defensive line. We will then take the next one to the left for the next play the ball. Then right, left, right we go and then we kick to a pocket of the field. This kind of set is known often as a set that works a 'channel' as these sets work over one area or channel of the field. Imagine the field divided vertically into three such channels as we are looking at the opposition try line. A left channel, a middle channel or a right channel. My teams might be under instruction to target one channel constantly or to work the channel from where they have received the ball. This means that if the opposition kicks it to our left, we use our possession to attack the left channel.

The key after doing a couple of these types of sets to settle into the game is, the next time we get the ball, do we do that set again? Do we do it down a different channel? Do we carry out the set in the same way but wrap it across all three channels? Or do we do a different kind of set entirely?

This is what I refer to as the phases of play. If we change set types or change the direction of our set, we are going into a different phase of our attacking play. I have seen NRL teams seemingly play in phases of about four minutes. Their first couple of sets will be wrapping across the field for example and then they will switch to other sets that are more direct (or vice versa).

What influences phases of the game? Early in a game, you want to keep things as simple as possible, keeping play nice and direct which is what the 'channel' set will help with. But then once settled into the contest, it might be a combination of channel sets and other set types.

If you ever coach against me, this is what I tend to do with my teams.

If I start with a channel set, I'll do it twice to settle into the game (as a minimum) before either changing sets or keeping going with the channel sets until that doesn't work anymore, or I find something else in the opposition to exploit. My exit sets are a combination of the channel sets or 'plus ones' that wrap across the field. A plus one is a pass from dummy half to one of the halves, who then passes to an oncoming runner, meaning the ball is a lot wider from the play the ball when it is being carried into the defensive line. Halves can also use plays or different shapes of attacking formation here if they like or if guided towards that by coaches. Some teams at all levels of the game often wrap across with these sets or use them to get to the middle, before going back to where they came from, hoping to exploit a tired defender.

There can be different phases when we get down to the other end of the field too. My team might quickly set up near one of the 'scrum lines' (20 metres in from each touchline) when attacking the opposition try line, then we might do three long passes to the opposite side of the field, or two long passes, followed by a short pass. We can keep rotating around the different permutations here, including just one pass, or one long pass for one short pass to surprise the opposition.

Explaining these sets further, let's consider what each individual might do within that lateral passing framework, particularly the halves. With a typical 'front and back person' shape, they might play to the 'front person' for a few repetitions before hitting the back person or vice versa. Halves also have the freedom to put on any plays or formation shapes in this framework. If three long passes are delivered with each passer of the football (hooker and two halves) performing a shape or play as a way of getting the ball to the next in the line, then we have a very convoluted attacking play that the defence has to read very carefully.

When we think about phases of the game and coaching, its important attack doesn't become readable. Players do subconsciously react to patterns and trends on the field and coaches should aim to be ahead of the game in that regard. If your team is regularly taking the ball in for three tackles before your half touches it, then a smart coach in the opposition dugout and smart defensive teams will pick up quickly what's going on. I always advise coaches not to waste those three tackles and instead, try and use them to become a bit more unpredictable. Never let the opponent relax!

The next time you watch a match, have a look at the phases of the game. Do the team stick to one set for a while? Are they working over a certain defender? Are they working with the opposition laterally as a team? What are they trying to achieve?

Another consideration in regard to phases of the game is the 'temperature' of the game. If a team has been under pressure for say, eighteen tackles in defence, are they going to be taking risks in the next set or should they just carry the ball out relatively slowly to regroup? You may have heard this referred to as 'game management' in recent years in the media.

In the past, I've instructed players to get up slower to play the ball after a set like that and to kick the ball downfield to walk to the scrum to get their breath back as a group. Good halves and good coaches recognise the temperature of the game. Does the team need to keep forcing play if they're ahead twelve on the scoreboard or do they just relax (relatively) in possession and frustrate the opponent? It's very hard to maintain a high-tempo type of football for a full game and it may be that the team needs to take its moments to rejuvenate mid-game by keeping things basic and not taking any undue risks.

Let's imagine a team is 8-0 up with five minutes to go, and all that team does is carry the ball up from each play the ball in a form of channel set that is lower risk before kicking the ball so that the restart is from a scrum at the opposite end of the field. The team has sensibly eaten up some of the clock and there could be only three minutes left by the time the opposition gets possession again. One solid defensive set from the team who kicked the ball, and the game is more or less won.

This is a far better way for the team to close the game out than them forcing their hand trying to make it 14-0. If, by taking more risks they make a mistake on the halfway line to give the opposition possession there, then it means the opponent has a chance to get four or six points with four or three and a half minutes to go. This would allow the opposition to sight victory in the closing minutes. Managing the phases of the game means balancing fearless expression with cautious consolidation when needed.

> *"He's a very astute judge of the game and knows a shed load about league".*
>
> ## Steve Renouf, Brisbane Broncos, Queensland and Kangaroos legend

Attacking Strategy

To get onto the same wavelength as me as a coach, you need to watch a game and look at it from this standpoint:

Our game is 13 v 13

In attack, 13 players are allowed to attack
In defence, there are often two players at marker and one full back.
That leaves ten players in the defensive line.

Using this way of looking at the game, it means that, on every play the ball, the game (if you do things right) is essentially '13 v 10'. Throw in the principles of passing the ball to 'someone in a better position than you', props and back rows running in order to get 'little wins' and creating space for the next play and everyone aiming for quick play the balls, the 13 should 'win' the play the majority of the time, getting at least a passive tackle or at best a partial or full line break.

This is exactly how I coach Rugby League Football and have done for nearly two decades with plenty of success at various levels. Of course, there is a lot more to it than that, but essentially, these statements form my footballing philosophy.

Watch a high-level Rugby League game through this prism of thought, and we can hopefully get on a similar train of thought for our football discussions!

Team 'playbook' and calls

I am a firm believer that, if coaches produce a playbook several pages long, they are potentially giving players too much, at many levels at least. My 'playbooks' always fit on one piece of A4 paper. Here is an example:

Sets
Zero, Bridge, G3, G2, G1

Plays
Boss, Yellow, Snap, Bash, Flash, Dash, Big Bash

Kicks
Fly or Drive – Lane, Channel, Road

Defence
Set - Green, Hold and Fold, Effort 1, Effort 2, Edge 4

General
Next Action

Now here are the explanations for each:

Zero, Bridge, G3, G2, G1 – these are the sets! Zero is the 'channel set', Bridge is the 'Plus one – wrapping' set, and anything with a 'G' denotes 'Good Ball' which is the opposition half and the number after it is the amount of long passes we will play from a play the ball on or near a scrum line. These sets tend to be called by the halves.

Boss, Snap, Yellow – 'Boss' means 'give me the ball on the long side of the field', 'Snap' means 'give me the ball on the short side of the field' and 'Yellow' means I am pretending I want the ball to fool the opposition (subterfuge). Any player can use these calls, but it tends to be the 'runners' more than the halves who do.

Bash, Flash, Dash, Big Bash – these are the names of plays that are very common in Rugby League. I would like to refer you to a YouTube video as this will be easier, although I apologise the videos are not in the same order as listed here. Type in *"Rugby League Plays Coach and Player"* on YouTube and you should see a video of yours truly with players running around in red. 'Bash' is the code name for the 'Block Play' you see in this video, 'Flash' is the 'Face Ball', 'Dash' is what a 'Drop Off' would be from the video and 'Big Bash' is known as the 'Block Plus' in the video.

Fly or Drive – Lane, Channel, Road – 'Fly' means a high kick, and 'Drive' means a low kick (grubber). 'Lane, Channel, Road' refer to the code for left, centre and right.

Set - Green, Hold and Fold, Effort 1, Effort 2, Edge four – 'Set' and 'Green' refer to calls when organising the defence line. We 'set' the line and 'green' means go! 'Hold and fold' is the marker system at the play the ball. One marker stays in place (holds) while the other takes one step in the direction of the ball (folds). 'Effort 1' is the initial tackle, and 'Effort 2' are subsequent attempts at slowing down the attacking play the ball. 'Edge 4 means the last two defenders on the 'long side' of the defence have to spread a little further apart from each other.
We go into depth about defence in the next section.

'Next Action' is a call that refers to focusing on what happens next, not dwelling or 'dining out' on what has occurred before.

> *"Lee is a very good coach, knows a lot about the game and is great to play under!"*
>
> **Phil Sami, Gold Coast Titans**

Defence

So far, we have focused on the attacker and how they can manipulate the defence to achieve their desired outcomes, but now, it's all about the case for the defence! The reality is that in most sports, we have to attack and defend, so it makes sense to spend as much an amount of time as possible, if not, an equal time or more time on defence in the training sessions delivered.

It amazes me how many coaches ignore this very, very simple doctrine. At some of the highest levels I have coached at, I have gone against many coaches who don't put enough detail into their defence. Firstly, we need to backtrack to our attack a bit to explain an approach that can go a huge way to resulting in victory.

There are three outcomes available to any Rugby League contest anybody takes part in:

1. Win

2. Draw

3. Lose

Some of the more exciting professional sports teams we have seen have tried to take number 2 out of the equation in a method colloquially known as 'shit or bust'! But even the 'Bazballing' England cricketers of late or Kevin Keegan's Newcastle United in the 1990s soon learned that pragmatism needs to be considered quite a lot too.   Many people, including Sun Tzu, the revered Chinese military general, will tell us that *"You win by first preventing your defeat"* and that when you do that, you can essentially only draw or win.

In Rugby League terms, this would mean your attack turning possession over at the end of their set, deep in opposition territory and regularly. The term 'completion rates' is heavily used in rugby league coaching and analysis. This means, an attacking team holding the ball for either all six tackles they are allowed to take or holding it for five before kicking to gain field position.

The other reality that is regularly overlooked is that, if your team has the ball, the opposition can't score. So, the absolute BEST way to defend is to have hold of the ball, preferably at the opposition's end of the field.

Virtually everyone in Rugby League would agree completion rates are important. Former Ipswich Jets coaches Ben and Shane Walker were successful in using another approach that focused on 'time with the ball'. It saw their players running sideways a lot and backwards sometimes. It was great to watch! The 'standard' way of playing the game means many sets of six tackles take about one minute to complete. With the Jets, that time was sometimes doubled! Ultimately – completion rates and time on the ball are much of a muchness in the sense that, the opposition doesn't have the ball.

One of my Ipswich High teams were low points scorers, so we just focused on high completion of channel sets and forcing repeat sets, backed up by a tough uncompromising defence. We lost two games all season and they were close affairs too. Following a more direct method of completion means a team can enjoy 'time on the ball' by forcing the opposition to defend those repeat sets. You win by first preventing your defeat, after all.

Now, let me give you something of an 'in-play' kicking tip. When kicking to the opposition and expecting them to return with their set of six plays, I have found that the overwhelming number of teams struggle to make as many metres when exiting from their left to right rather than right to left. Why? I hear you ask. Well, approximately only 3.5% to 13% of the world is predominantly left-handed and ambidexterity accounts for a further 1%. At best, 87% of players who play Rugby League are right-side dominant. So, if the ball is returned from right to left, they can use their right hand to keep defenders at bay and will likely prefer leaning into the tackle with a right shoulder to bump off the defender.

Coming from the other side, they have to try and fend with that weaker left hand or shoulder! If they have a strong right footstep, this difficulty can be reduced somewhat but that would bring them directly into contact with the defence. I have found over years of study before big games, kicking to our right shaved anything between twenty and forty metres off opposition sets!

I am hoping I am painting a picture of a team that holds lots of ball and, if they do change possession to the other team, they ask the opposition to return the ball under some very tough circumstances.

But now to that defence...

In 2004, I was on an English RFL National Camp, watching former Newcastle Knights, St George Illawarra and at the time, Great Britain coach David Waite address a group of the nations' best under 13's, 14's and 15's. He was showing them the importance of strong tackle technique towards achieving desired match outcomes. And what I witnessed will stay with me for the rest of my coaching life!

Waite was showing the kids a video of the English under-18s against the all-conquering Australian schoolboys. He showed how, early in the game, the English were tackling high up the body, with an open chest and with arms wide open. This meant the Aussie attackers could 'find the floor' easily to get quick play the balls and thus, attacking momentum. He then went on to explain that the instruction or reminder was given to the English to tackle with 'Shoulder, Shape and Studs' during that game.

'Shoulder' meant top-of-the-shoulder contact from the defender. 'Shape' meant the defenders had to crouch, meaning their body looked like it was forming an 'S Shape' and 'Studs' meant the defenders had to keep their boot studs in the ground while tackling and throughout the resulting 'wrestle' to get more purchase in the ground.

The impact of this change was amazing. Australia, seemingly marauding in previous attacking sets were now being comfortably controlled by the English. The elite kids in the audience were sold on this concept almost immediately.

As I continued my coaching journey in the ensuing years, I embraced Shoulder, Shape and Studs, and indeed developed the acronym 'SSS' for players to remember it more easily. In 2008 and 2009, during my time at Manly Sea Eagles, I started strongly using video analysis and editing software to help my coaching.

In '09, I sourced the original of the video Waite used to display to the kids. Upon deep study, I found something else that hadn't been mentioned that day. The Australians were making far less in terms of metres in their sets as a result of 'SSS'. In one case, they only achieved 50 of the available 100 metres after a kick at the end of their set. Without 'SSS' They were getting 80 to 90 metres.

A little later, I also found a book in a second-hand bookstore about Olympic wrestling, namely freestyle or Greco-Roman wrestling. I was now intrigued about what could be achieved with this tackle technique and I wanted to be sure the defenders' shoulders were targeting the right area of the attackers' body. Olympic wrestlers don't have ten metres in which to sprint up to their opponent and that opponent isn't sprinting at them, so to do a take-down requires specific targeting of the body, preferably with the shoulder!

I read in this book that a common tactic was to target between 'elbow and hip'. If you imagine a wrestler, with hands in the air just below the face then this gives a clear route to 'between elbow and hip' for the 'advancer' in the wrestling contest. This jumped out at me because, when a Rugby player carries the ball, they often carry it under their arm and against their chest when getting close to collision, which also gives a clear space between the ball-carrying elbow and their hip for defenders to target.

I then turned my attention to what happens after the collision. I started asking my players to dominate the 'contact line' (the point where the defender connects with the attacker) and if successful in doing this, drive the opponent backwards.

The impact on my teams and coaching in general was unbelievable – it was like I had cracked a code. It is a code that will work for you, even in today's increasingly litigious society, where tackling is under scrutiny more than ever, as the idea is to go nowhere near the head with the tackles.

I find that successful statistical returns in contact lines and then defensive rucks 'won' have a huge impact on my team's winning games, more than I ever thought possible back in those days when I started to wake up to this method. The tackle alone doesn't help you win the ruck though; you need something after it and, what we are going to talk about now is taboo in many areas. It's called 'wrestling' in some places, 'grappling', 'dancing' and just plain old 'ruck control' in others.

Either way, like it or not, the game has created this issue and teams everywhere, desperate to give their defensive sides something of a chance to get back ten metres and up again in time, are doing everything they can to 'win the ruck'. So, here is my shortcut of how to do it!

It is an easy way to teach ruck control in a few easy steps. If you listen to commentators on the NRL or Super League, you'll start to think it's quite complicated, but I found I've been able to get it down to quite a few easy steps.

As mentioned already, the first thing we're going to look at is the hit. Player 1 will carry the ball into two defenders who both tackle with 'shoulder, shape, studs'. Imagine now that there's an imaginary line underneath this tackle. I always tell players to imagine it's the try line itself.

The ideal state that we want the attacking player to get to as defensive coaches is for the attacker (Player 1) to end up on their back, facing away from our try line. This makes the players' journey to play the ball significantly stretched out. This is the furthest or the longest journey for them to play the ball and it would take a full re-adjustment of the body to get to a play-the-ball situation. If Player 1 was to end up on their front after carrying the footy, then all they have to do is get up and play it.

Most collisions are not extreme like the one just described and there is a myriad of possibilities as to what can happen from the contact line until the ball is played. Rarely does an attacker find their front immediately or get knocked on their back immediately. Most are a 50/50 grappling contest between an attacker with the ball in hand and defenders. I call this phase, 'Effort 2' for the defenders. Remember that we are trying to stop Player 1 from scoring a try on our imaginary try line which is underneath us. Player 1 is battling, trying to get down on the grass to play the ball whilst defenders are trying to keep Player 1 up so that the ball can't be played quickly. I have found that the most efficient way of doing this is to wrestle Player 1 'away' from the direction of our imaginary try line and our actual try line on the field. The call used by the defenders to carry this out is *"Away, away, away"*.

The second coaching point is to get Player 1 as far as you can from this imaginary line. Sometimes, though, defenders end up 'behind' the attacker as the ensuing struggle unfolds. The key here is to ensure that all defensive forces are moving in the same direction and not pushing 'against' each other (very common). Summarised very simply, defenders should imagine that they will lose points if that attacker gets to the ground quickly and do all they can to move that attacker away from that imaginary try line.

I know this sounds unbelievably simple. That's because it is (in an ideal world)! Tackle properly and defenders can have full control of the attackers' body weight. Once in control, they need to work in tandem with forces going in the same direction.

It is not an ideal world, however, and attackers put up one heck of a fight against those defensive ambitions, yet to outline absolutely every scenario here would be a book on its own! Therefore, I encourage you to go to the Rugby League Coach YouTube channel and look up the 'Coach Playlist' and you will see some scenarios outlined with visuals there, including one named *"A simple way to coach ruck control"*.

Defending as a unit

There are several defensive systems and ideas out there. You can group them into two main ones – 'up and out' and 'up and in'. 'Up and out' encourages players to stand tighter in the defensive line and slide across the field in tandem, moving up initially and then out towards the sidelines as the name suggests. 'Up and in' is essentially the opposite as defensive players stand wider apart, move up first and then in towards the play. Both systems (should) focus on maintaining defensive line integrity for as long as possible.

One of the ways I describe defence to my players is to change their attitudes to it straight away (if it needs changing that is). Mainly, I focus on the pack mentality aspect of defence. Defence in Rugby League is the one thing most of the team can do together and each team member has a very, very similar job description. Most of them tend to move in a similar direction, together and they (mostly) need to focus on fixing any problems posed by the attack, together. Offence, on the other hand, is often thirteen people moving in different directions – namely lines of run or angles, yet also, preferably synchronised, in tandem.

Players love to attack. Any sportsperson dreams of hitting a shot, scoring a goal, a try or a slam dunk. Defence, on the other hand, can be seen as a chore by some! Players love to attack, but they HAVE to defend.

Be really clear in your coaching messages and repeat them often.

Key Points from This Chapter

- Get your team to do simple things, do them excellently and do them ruthlessly, repeatedly and better than any other team in the competition, or even the world (why not?)

- Have a maximum of five key things that underpin everything in your preparation and game strategy

- Coach all players to play 'football' rather than to follow a robotic game plan – but be patient with this way of coaching

- Use set types or change the direction of sets to go into a different phase of attacking play and also consider the 'temperature' of the game

- Keep the playbook simple

- The best way to defend is to hold the ball

- Sound tackle technique and defence line integrity are essential to successful ruck control and defensive structure

- Defence is an attitude

A Coach and a Leader in the Rugby League World – By Matthew Elliott

In 2009, I had the privilege of meeting Lee Addison during a pivotal moment of his coaching journey. Lee was interviewing for a position at Penrith Panthers where I was Head Coach. While impressed by his enthusiasm, vision, and understanding of the game, some external factors prevented him from landing the role. However, fate had its own plan, as Lee found his way to the Western Sydney Academy, largely by chance after bumping into key figures at a development carnival while still with Manly.

What truly stands out about Lee's early approach is his hunger to learn and immerse himself in the world of coaching. He spent a summer with us, working alongside my assistant coaches and myself. During this time, he absorbed everything he could, hanging around and offering to help, even jumping on the field to participate in games.........he thought he was best on field most days, a dream we let him run with! Most importantly his commitment to the craft and willingness to pitch in wherever needed showed early on that he had the qualities of a dedicated coach.

That summer was particularly significant for us, as we were studying Parramatta's run to the Grand Final with the help of influential figures like Brandy and Freddie. Lee wasn't just watching from the sidelines; he was actively involved in the analysis, soaking up lessons from the best. Lee's ability to connect with players to relate directly, certainly motivated players on a personal level.

Our connection grew stronger over time, and by the end of 2010, Lee had secured a job at Penrith for the 2011 season. However, the real turning point came mid-year when I reached out to him with an opportunity to assist with the USA Tomahawks during their 2011 qualifiers. Lee eagerly took up the challenge, and together we navigated the highs and lows of that campaign. Qualifying for the 2013 World Cup for the first time in USA rugby league history was a massive achievement for the team, and it was a rewarding experience for both of us.

In 2011, as I transitioned to the Warriors, Lee continued with the USA program and was instrumental in their build-up to and during the World Cup. It's been incredible to watch Lee develop into the coach he is today. His journey has been one of continual growth, marked by his relentless pursuit of knowledge, adaptability, and passion for the game.

Now, as Lee writes his coaching book, he's drawing on these very experiences and stories, that reflect the lessons he's learned and the value of mentoring in coaching. His journey from our first meeting to where he is today is a testament to the power of dedication and hard work. It's been a privilege to be part of that process and to see Lee's evolution as both a coach and a leader in the rugby league world.

Matthew Elliott was Head Coach of Canberra Raiders, Penrith Panthers and New Zealand Warriors in the NRL, as well as Bradford Bulls in the English Super League and the USA national team. He has also been a commentator on the game for ABC Radio Grandstand.

4
What to Coach

What do you want your team to learn? Can you define it?

Often daunted by the thought of planning a whole year out, it benefits coaches if they can break the planning process down into manageable parts and there are several ways in which we can do that.

When working with coaches during the off-season, and as we sit down to plan the season out, I first ask them... *"What do you want to coach?"* This is the first essential step when it comes to planning and, providing a tangible record of it can also ensure nothing is missed when the team finally runs out for that first match. I find most coaches don't think of taking this simple step before starting their planning, whereas I am of the belief it is essential.

The obvious distinctive columns when listing points to coach are 'Offence' and 'Defence'. I ask the coaches to develop these thoughts by taking them through a process. I ask them to list Offence and Defence so they can be organised laterally on a page, while also adding three vertical columns labelled 'Core', 'Unit' and 'Team'.

Core, Unit and Team are defined as follows:

Core

Any activity that can be practised alone or an individual is responsible for. Examples include grip, pass, catch, carry and tackle technique.

Unit

Any activity that involves more than one person but less than the team. I often define this as between two and five players. Unit skills could refer to skills such as a two or three-person tackle, set plays, decision-making skills and the right or left edge, or left side and right side of the team in offence or defence mode.

Team

Any activity involving the full 13 players of a team. Often, coaches list the offensive sets they want to coach and the patterns of defence they will require the team to follow in different parts of the field.

Main core and unit coaching points

Next is a list of the core skills and unit skills coaching points I want my teams to focus on:

Core skills

In Offence, all individuals should/be/show/have the ability to:

- Look up to determine where and how to attack. Look 'out to in' (left and right)
- Organised support left and right

- Ability to avoid markers (positional specific instructions)
- Good two-handed pre-line carry
- Hitting the advantage line
- Awareness of defensive movement for pre-line decision-making (give or go)
- Hips square, 'unders lines' or straight run to the line
- Footwork at the defensive line
- Bring the ball to the body just prior to collision
- Find arms, not shoulders, 'spaces not faces'
- Have a 'run to bust' mentality
- Have a strong compact body position in the collision
- Leg drive after the collision
- Post-collision decision-making skills (eg: offload or not?)
- Find 'elbows and knees' after the collision
- Quick play the ball
- Reload after an action (ready for next)
- Push through (in support or anticipation of the ball) on each play shouting designated calls

In Defence, all individuals need to:

- Be LOUD
- Compress the line

- Call 'Set' looking left and right to ensure their teammates are with them
- Call 'Green' before using explosive speed to move off the defensive line
- Emphasise getting up at the 'A' defender position
- Nominate and communicate the opponent they are marking
- Move 'up and out' after the ball has passed, when they are at a distance from the ball (more than 1.25 metres)
- Move 'up and in' to the ball when the ball carrier is within approximately 1.25 metres
- Tackle with 'Shoulder, Shape, Studs' (Effort 1)
- Seek to dominate the contact line
- Initiate a second effort or surge after the initial collision to dominate the contact line and win the floor (Effort 2)
- Initiate one of the three 'floor work plans' when the collision reaches the floor (Dominant, 50/50 or elbows-knees)
- Markers must split in a 'hold and fold' style and be tactile with each other. There will be no set direction for this so the defenders must communicate to each other during each ruck. The first marker can chase in the opposition 20-metre area
- Retreat without backpedalling. Must check over their shoulder a maximum of three times in the direction of the ball and the last three steps are crucial

Middle Players

In addition to the individual skills listed previously, middle players (lock, props) need to:

- Stay in their channel/general area (lock may be the exception based on their specific characteristics)

- Get to six to eight metres width from the play the ball before taking a hit-up

- Run at 'C' defender, back into 'B', or B back into 'A'

- Put extra emphasis on getting quick play the balls whilst maintaining composure with the ball in hand (no forced passes unless the game plan dictates otherwise)

- Hit available holes on sets where the halves receive the ball at 'first receiver'

- Hit available holes/run decoys on sets where the ball is moving laterally between halves

- Be aware of kick calls in case middle players are kick chase priority team (rare in my teams but sometimes it happens)

- Have an extra emphasis on getting up at 'A' in defence

Edge Players

In addition to the individual skills named above, edge players such as wings, centres, second rowers and sometimes the full-back need to:

- Keep shape at all times when attacking

- Cover shape for someone else (such as the centre covering the winger shape if they come infield for whatever reason)

- Runs from dummy half must follow a 'C' line and must be done in tandem with other members of the back line

- Follow the same width from the ruck rules as middle players on normal hit-ups

- Run at a defender on their outside shoulder to inside shoulder (and vice versa)
- Hit into holes and disguise the intended line of run for as long as possible
- Always look up and communicate numbers
- Push through on every single play, shouting designated calls
- Keep hips square when attacking and run 'unders' lines
- Make good decisions - getting the ball to space is a priority
- Place particular emphasis on the vagaries of the defensive pattern ('up and out' v 'up and in' relationship)
- Place particular emphasis on maintaining line discipline and working as a unit with those alongside
- Winger has the option of becoming 'elastic' on a wide-open side in defence
- 'Long side' edge has the option of 'edge four' defence structure
- Be aware of kick calls in case edge players are the kick chase priority team (common)

Key Points from This Chapter

- It is important to list all the coaching points you want to deliver to your team before planning sessions

- Refer back to previous pages to for specific coaching points you can use

"Lee Taught Me Some Invaluable Lessons" – By Brock Shepperd

I first met Lee in 2008, when we were both completing a master's degree part time at Sydney University. Lee is never short of a word or an opinion and never held back on a criticism or a point of view. That would be understandably shocking for those who know him.

I was a second-year coach, 22 years old trying to find my way, and realistically I was far too wet behind the ears to be passing opinions and giving anyone advice. My only goal was to listen, learn and build relationships with experienced coaches such as Lee.

Ironically, twelve months later Lee presented me with my first opportunity to coach on a Junior Representative staff with the Penrith Panthers in 2010. At that stage I had coached within development programs at the club for three years after finishing up as a player. To be involved on a junior rep staff was a huge deal for me. I remember after four rounds we had lost three and drawn one. Lee never wavered in his philosophy or approach. Sitting near bottom of the ladder we managed to win five on the bounce to make the Finals.

When Lee was coaching at St Gregory's in Campbelltown, as a St Dominics Penrith old boy it was hard to cheer for the "Pom" during his time there. But he built a strong program which managed to rival and compete within both the MCS and Schoolboy Cup competitions. He continued this strong schoolboy resume at Ipswich again building a program which competed strongly at a national level.

We only spent a short time working together, but Lee taught me some invaluable lessons which have become staples in my own approach. His organisation and attention to detail was second to none. Lee wanted to develop players - winning was always important but not most important.

He has a wicked sense of humour and an interesting way of building relationships with players, giving them nicknames, singing songs about some and taking the mickey out of others. He is the ultimate competitor but never forgets to have a joke or to allow the players to have a laugh and enjoy each other's company. With no wins through four rounds in 2010 his approach did not change, a great lesson for me as an aspiring leader.

These lessons played a role in forming the foundation for me as a coach and leader which sets the tone for how I approach every day in my current role. Lee kicked me off on this coaching journey, and I owe him a debt of gratitude for how he mentored me during these early years as an aspiring coach.

Lee is always looking for new ways to develop Rugby League players and coaches. He has a level of passion for the game few possess, and the game is all the better for having Lee involved.

Brock Shepperd is an NRL assistant coach with the Canberra Raiders. He has also coached at Penrith Panthers, Wests Tigers, Mounties, and Manly Sea Eagles.

5

How to Coach It

When introducing a skill, it's always best to do it when the players are relatively mentally and physically fresh. You need the players to think and concentrate on the skill.

Structuring training

I strongly recommend taking them through the stages of 'Isolation, Opposition and Game'.

'Isolation' allows you to teach it, 'Opposition' to test it and 'Game' to see the skills and talented players in action!

I pride myself on making my teams very fit and very skilled, so every training session I ever lead contains games, either for skill or fitness development and sometimes both. It pays to take the players through stages before introducing them to a game scenario. It was a process I used for the very first time in 2009 at the Manly Sea Eagles. I have refined it since then and trust me, it tends to work a treat!

Before we see the details behind each stage of the method, let me share with you some of the things I have unearthed using it.

Many coaches are often worried about doing games in training because of the lack of control they feel over events. Back in 2009, I started a process of doing pre-season training that was 10% 'drill' and 90% 'game'. There was a kid called Luke Vescio who came to me as a wing but also as a 'year young', meaning he had another year up at this age level. He was fast and elusive but small. In one preseason small-sided training game, he routinely got himself in at dummy half to run and he was electric! I got to him after training and asked him to show me his dummy half-pass. It was average. I said if he wanted a crack at the hooking role, he needed to pass at least five hundred times a day, left to right, and then the same from the other side. He did just that and started the season at hooker for us. He also played National Youth League a few years later for Parramatta Eels and represented New South Wales and Australian Schoolboys!

The majority of the 2010 games I did at St Gregory's were '13 v 13' and they allowed me to help develop and see repeatedly the wonderful, natural skills of a certain seventeen-year-old called James Tedesco, who went on to captain Sydney Roosters, New South Wales and Australia with distinction.

Another success I remember from the small-sided games approach, this time at Ipswich, was when I was struggling to find a replacement five-eighth (stand-off) for my team when our first and second choice was injured for the season. Watching small-sided games allowed me to notice a player called Corey Kurnoth get in to move the ball around because his group had no one else to do it. Corey was a backrower who I'd only ever seen run and tackle. But he had a very stable passing game, could pass equally well on both sides and had an above-average kicking game. Out of necessity he then became my first-choice number six, and we had another great season, only losing two games all year by the finest of margins. He also went on to play at Wests Tigers.

All of the small-sided games I use are intended to develop core and unit skills, but also fitness. The 2010 and 2011 teams I had were exceptionally fit then and went on to win games against all odds. During my subsequent years at Ipswich State High School, I was essentially a full-time coach as we trained in the daytime during timetabled lessons. I also had access to GPS data which allowed me to track how many kilometres the players were covering and the intensity of their work. They were doing a lot more work than any fitness trainer could put them through that's for sure!

As a result, all my drills, game fields and player numbers, plus work-to-rest ratios are all measured and considered strongly before each session I do. I have all the 'physical demands' information and years of experience doing it to benefit me in my decision-making processes. Most importantly, the players love this kind of training!

Next is a model outlining the essentials of 'Isolation, Opposition and Game':

From Isolation...

Coach teaches a skill with no opposition or pressure so that players get accustomed to the movement patterns and techniques. This is the 'How' of the skill. An example is a *'Grip, pass, catch, carry' drill in a grid.*

To Opposition...

Coach places opposition in front of those executing the skills. Often when the basics of the technique are mastered. Players can also be asked to react in a certain way to create a certain response for those executing the skill, an example being 3 v 2 drills with the presence of one or more defenders moving up and in.

To Game

A game, structured to regularly highlight and isolate the skills practised previously, can be devised. The game introduces the 'where and when' of the skill and encourages the players to recognise opportunities to use certain skills. Games are structured and have pressures of their own. An example is an 8 v 8 touch game with turnover for poor carry, the ball hits the chest or spin pass

Once players are familiar with skills, the isolation stage can be taken out or just done in the warm-up. The ability of the players and their place on the skills continuum would dictate the length of time spent on each stage. Coaches may have to revisit the isolation or opposition stages for correction at times.

Nature of Sessions

It is my belief that training should be a major 'event' in itself, not something players just have to 'get through' ahead of the next fixture. Often, a positive training week leads to a positive performance on game day.

I developed this thought process when I was under Des Hasler at Manly Sea Eagles. Des's sessions were great events, taken seriously in the lead up with serious preparation done by support staff to prepare for the session and Des and his coaches ensuring the highest standards were met at all times.

Bilateral learning practises are also essential. Using passing as an example, the players should be asked to pass to the left and pass to the right in ***exactly*** the same amount. Use a stopwatch to time it on each side of the body or count the number of passes completed in the phase of activity. You should even monitor who is on the left of the grid, the right of the grid and in the middle and it can be programmed so that players move around to get repetitions of everything required in equal measure.

With tackle shields, ask the players to do three tackles on their right shoulder and three on their left. Make sure, whatever number of repetitions are used, the players work on both shoulders in equal amounts. I often use six for the simple reason there are six tackles per set in our game. Even if you are asking your team to do unopposed sets in a light, non-intense manner, make sure they target the left, middle and right of the field in equal measure with their sets or that they start them from the left, middle and right in an equal amount.

Everything about training should also be as specific to the game of Rugby League as possible. I firmly believe that most coaching environments have time for little else to happen, particularly coaching activities that are not specific to the game. For example, if you set up a drill, are the defenders ten metres away like they would be in a game? Is the distance you want the attacking players to run and pass all a replica of what happens in a game, too?

If players shake hands with each other before a match, then they should shake hands before training and enter the training field focused and ready to give their best effort. Likewise, they should celebrate the completion of a positive training session as an achievement and something that will benefit them just as they would celebrate a win on game day.

There are some other key considerations when attempting to make training an 'event'. The main ones for me are a constant focus on correction where needed from coaches and the importance of high communication levels amongst the whole group.

Correction

There must always be energy from coaches with ongoing correction of activities at all times, creating a vocal and encouraging atmosphere.

Too many coaches I have witnessed first-hand watch their drill or game unfold and don't correct things that are going wrong. I find this happens an awful lot with training games. Many coaches get lost in the game and watch it as a referee or a spectator! Either they don't know how to correct what's unfolding or cannot recognise it amid the activity with bodies and ball(s) moving everywhere.

One little diagnostic activity I do with coaches I mentor is to watch five minutes of a match with them, and I don't say a word. I ask the coach I am working with to outline what they see as it is unfolding. I also ask for what their interventions would be.

Good coaches recognise what's unfolding in front of them in a drill, training game or on match day and can, if needed, act on it appropriately.

There are, of course, types of and times for, correction. For example, if the players are warming up for a session or carrying out an activity that is designed to improve their fitness, even if you have made the activity game-specific, you should correct 'on the run' while the players are carrying out the task, rather than trying to constantly stop and correct them. Likewise, if they are warming up for training your key job is to warm them up, not coach them in the finer points.

On the contrary, many skill development sessions lend themselves to deeper and more detailed correctional practices. I often help coaches step back from drills or games and observe and watch, to look for the things that aren't being carried out perfectly, then to assess if it is something other players are also doing. My golden rule is if I see three or more players that have the same issue, I have permission to stop the session briefly to tell the whole group about a problem I have seen that needs fixing before we start again.

Communication in training

People are creatures of instinct and many also suffer from reservations such as shyness, anxiety or fear of 'messing up' in group settings when they are at a training session. That's why one of the most common questions I get from coaches is *'How can I get my players to talk?'*

Here is what I respond with:

1) Make it a non-negotiable of your coaching environment that players have to talk during training and games
2) Teach them what to say!

When you do the above with your players, you should be amazed by how many of them start talking, particularly after applying the message from the second statement. That simple step of actually giving them something to say goes a long way. What do you want them to say?

Once some of the players are talking, others will respond. It's then that you can start to drop less information into the group, and they will 'coach' each other. Keywords that you use in a drill could soon be all that's needed to spur your players into communicative action. I refer you back to the 'Clap, Grip, Tip, Flick' method of coaching outlined earlier in the '13 Things that Coaches do Wrong' section, when it comes to considering keywords and how they can be shared in training.

In a training game, it is a good idea at times to just tell them the rules once and then use your whistle to award turnovers of possession or penalties. They will soon communicate to each other what they think you are looking for as a coach!

Other ways of ensuring your training is like an 'event' include:

- Players and coaches should be working as a team in all aspects of training.

- They must emphasize communication, encouragement and praise.

- When one person talks, the rest listen.

- Coaches should not talk to the group until they have complete silence.

- There must be a huge amount of respect all around, with the promotion of mateship, teamwork and communication.

- Coaches should work to ensure the highest quality in everything done in training. When they are happy with technical input, coaches should set goals in training such as, for example, ten successes in succession, or one minute without errors. When success is achieved, they can move on to the next task.

- Coaches should encourage player feedback, empowering them to make some decisions, and making them feel that they themselves have come up with the answers and it is 'their' structure.

- Coaches should always work ahead of the group by always having the next activity ready. Players should never have to wait.

Creating Competition in Training

If your players are competing as often as possible in training, it prepares them for the real competition when it comes around. By putting players into small team environments, they can get to know a number of players quickly, on a deeper level and it also provides talking points and some light-hearted 'banter' with the other teams.

Creating competition in training also lifts standards! There are many out there that will tell you participation is what truly counts, and I guess they are right, to a point. Yet a bit of training competition will teach young players, in particular, how to deal with the 'twin imposters' of winning and losing in an environment that is hugely safe and supportive, whilst older players will thrive on it too.

In addition to the fun and enjoyment surrounding any training competition, there should be a huge focus on skill development that the players can enjoy and learn from under more intense training conditions.

Training drills can also be competitive because competing against each other in drills stops players 'going through the motions.' Also, as mentioned earlier, many games can be played to help the skill and athletic development of the players.

The game's approach allows players to problem solve, learning when and where to execute certain skills. Players learn to recognise game situations by duplicating them in the training environment and it also adds a little bit more (manageable but noticeable) pressure to every task. At the very least, it will add a lot of fun to training and allow for quick team building.

Skill-based conditioning games can be used to develop the skill and fitness of players, with mean heart rate and blood lactate responses during these activities almost identical to those obtained during competition.

So basically, tell players there is a prize for everything and they try a lot harder! Next, I will suggest a format and games you can use in your own training.

The Rugby League Coach Cup

Divide your squad into small teams, give the teams funny team names or let them make their own up and get ready for the fun in training to begin! These teams could be named after members of the coaching staff or important people or places associated with the team. Squad size will determine how many small groups you can split them into. If you have more than one staff member, each one can then be in charge of general motivation for their team throughout the preparation.

The teams then compete throughout the season program at varying stages for the imaginary cup, imaginatively titled here as 'The Rugby League Coach Cup!' Winning a drill that is designed to be competitive in training could earn a team, let's say, one point, whilst winning a game will earn them three points, for example.

Prior to each training session, the coaches will decide on when Rugby League Coach Cup (or RLCC) points are up for grabs and also what game will take place. If there is a plan sent out before sessions, ensure 'RLCC' features on the plan if decided in advance.

A sample session for a seventy-minute training session might be focused on a theme of ruck advance, numbers around the ruck and decision-making. The warm-up is a grip, catch, pass, carry drill and is followed by dynamic stretches taking up a period of ten minutes. After drinks, we then conduct a drill focused on technical coaching of the push-through at the play the ball, angles of run and so on. It progresses with the introduction of opposition in the form of one, two then three defenders. This is all practiced for a total of twenty minutes before players are given a second drink break.

The players then play a game for RLCC points. The game is in 3 x 8-minute segments with a drink in each break followed by coach feedback. The game is a form of 'channel footy. Teams get a maximum of two passes per play, and they have six plays in controlled, semi-collision conditions. There are no kicks allowed and poor carry, tackle technique or no push through in support is punished by turnover.

Games Options

Ruck advance/ruck defence game

- 8 minutes with 2 minutes rest and feedback from a coach, who monitors each game from the best vantage point.

- Each team has 4 'tackles' with the ball. On the first two tackles, the team will be allowed one pass only. On tackles 3 and 4, two passes are allowed before a turnover. There is no kicking.

- To teach defence, use full collision when safe, legally cleared and appropriate consent is collected. If not, a two-handed grab alone can be enough, or it could be followed by a re-creation of a dominant defensive floor position. In this instance, a one-handed touch will be followed by the re-creation of a negative defensive position where defenders are not allowed to slow the play the ball (PTB) down. The referee awards a 3-second PTB for a passive tackle or one-handed grab and a 6-second PTB for full shoulder contact or two-handed grab.

- The game will create a situation where players will strive to get a quick play the ball and will quickly learn what they can do to avoid a two-handed grab. They will also work hard to create go-forward situations on tackles 1 and 2 as well as 2 v 1 and 3 v 2 situations on tackles 3 and 4. In defence, players will realise that getting good feet position will help get them a slow ruck and therefore, more control in defence.

- Coaches should look for poor carry, poor footwork and poor decision-making in attack and will 'punish' players with turnovers accordingly.

- In defence, we can also 'punish' backpedalling in the defensive line with a repeat set.

Variations

- Each team has 6 'tackles. On the first two tackles, the team will be allowed one pass only. On tackles 3 and 4, two passes are allowed whilst on tackles 5 and 6, players are allowed three passes before a turnover. There is no kicking.

- Dropped ball – if a player loses the ball in possession via a forward pass or knock-on, the opposition will get nine tackles, with the same rules applying for the first four plays and three passes allowed for the rest of the tackle count. This rule is so that players learn to respect possession.

- Piggyback penalties or being split through the middle in defence will result in the opposition restarting their tackle count with three passes allowed on all plays.

Ruck Channel Game

- Ensure the game is small-sided, no more than 8-a-side.

- Create a (relatively) thin channel in which to play, no wider than near post to corner flag and no longer than the length of the field.

- Using the same sensible approach to contact rules as mentioned earlier, allow six 'tackles' where there is no more than one pass allowed at the ruck, nor offloads. You can include offloads as a variation.

Games for promoting width and vision

Double Double *(This game is also known as 'four hand touch' or 'AB touch')*

Teams get two 'tackles' only. A tackle is two, 'two-handed' touches by two different players.

- If an attacker is touched by one player, they can continue the game by passing the ball and the tackle is not completed.

- The best teams split from the ball, stay alive and keep the ball moving.

- Variation-wise, you can change the direction of the game from a 'north-south' direction to 'east-west' at short notice, using a whistle.

'Look up and play' ruck recognition game

- The idea of this game is to isolate each player's ability to 'look up and play'. Also, it is designed to teach players how to recognise when go-forward momentum is needed prior to lateral shifts as well as the need to keep 'attacking shape' in order to maximise attacking opportunities.

- Depending on your coaching goals, possession can be shared as per a normal game, or one team can hold the ball for a full period of play or half a game before switching. Each failure to score or poor technique can see the attacking team return to the starting point in this instance.

The rules of attacking:
- The players have a set (6 plays) with the ball. However, they are limited to only one shift/line shot per set. A line shot is defined in this instance as a play that includes more than two passes. A try will not be awarded from anything that is not a line shot.

- The players are required to look up, communicate space and get the ball to where the defence is short or penetrable. So, for example, in an 8 v 8 game, with two markers and the ball in the centre of the field. The defence will either put three on each side of the ball and therefore be numbered up correctly. If they have a four and two defensive formation, there would be a weak area where the two defenders are.

- The attack can advance towards any point they choose and don't necessarily need to identify poor defensive numbering up. They must, however, employ the appropriate attacking strategy and will soon learn the value of a speedy PTB and good ruck recognition.

- The ball will be turned over, or the team will be brought back to the start for core skill indiscretions or a 'poor decision' as judged by the coach, who will monitor from behind the attacking line.

- Instead of returning to the halfway line for the restart, a sprint return to the start line (try line) to restart the set is good for fitness levels and energy in training.

- The defensive players will have ample opportunity to practice defending the shift and therefore, putting into practice those teachings.

Find space game

- The idea of this game is to isolate the ability of players to 'look up and play', to teach them how to look up in search of space and to communicate what they find.

- The same 'end of set rules' as the previous game apply here, as do 'collision level' rules of previous games.

Rules of attacking:
- The players have three 'tackles' with the ball. However, they are limited to one shift/line shot per set. A line shot is defined in this instance as a play that includes more than two passes. A try will not be awarded from anything that is not a line shot.

- The players need to look up, communicate space and get the ball to where the defence is short or penetrable. If the attacking team finds space, they are rewarded with another three tackles to complete the six.

- Variations include marking wide areas on the try lines from the corner flag to the scrum line and awarding extra points for tries in that zone. Defenders could also have one or two fewer players than attackers.

13 v 13 game ideas

- Normal scrimmage – 3 seconds PTB for passive tackles, 6 seconds PTB for front-on tackles

- 'Find Space' game (as above)

- 'Exit' set/ 'get to kick' game – teams don't shift; they just exit to get to a kick during their attacking set.

- Put limits on when teams can shift the ball, including from a designated launch pad on the field, or when the team crosses the 60-metre line (examples).

- The 'Aim Up in Defence' game - the defence team kick-off or do a '5th tackle' kick and have to keep the opposition in their own 40-metre area for 5 'tackles' or to stop them getting to another designated point on the field.

- 'Goal Line Defence' game – the defence does a dropout and defends as many tackles as possible (no limit) until a try is scored. The winning team is the one that accumulates the most tackles in each attempt at defence.

Coaching principles to work to

If the session coaching is done in a certain way, then every isolated drill or game will be seen as 'game preparation' and, therefore, specific game preparation sessions will fit in seamlessly with all drills that are delivered.

When planning or carrying out anything in practice, it pays to ensure you can make the following statements with confidence...

"This game/drill/practice has very specific relevance to a movement pattern in the game and duplicates almost entirely what the players will face in a game"

"This game/drill/practice has clear aims and objectives that fit in with the overall direction of the group."

"The importance, relevance, aims and objectives have been communicated to the players. They know why they are doing this."

Encourage players to do skill-based extras

If you arrive at training and some players are already there and have access to footballs, there's a very good chance they'll have either arranged a game of some kind or be kicking and catching a ball to each other!

When players are in groups conversing before training, rather than leaving them just 'kicking' the ball, encourage them (but working under their own initiative) to set up small skills and practices without the formality of structured coaching.

What follows are some pre-and post-training tasks that players can carry out on their own or in small groups during these situations and also after formal training. I am a firm believer that, when arriving at training, players should definitely be socialising! I would, however, rather them do it whilst they are practising! It's a good idea to encourage/demand that the players do not stand around doing nothing and get them doing the tasks that follow over the following pages.

During this time, players should be encouraged to get the 'feel' for a movement rather than being overloaded with any technical coaching points.

The 'ball familiarity' program

As a potential top-line player, individuals should aim for the shape, patterns and trends of movement of the football to be second nature to them. They should also practice reflexes and catching difficult balls on a regular basis.

Here are some things they can do:

Individually

- Two-handed and one-handed finger flicks of the ball
- Carry one hand and switch
- Bounce the ball in front and catch
- Throw the ball up above the head (forward) and catch after the bounce
- Throw the ball at the wall and catch it before or after the bounce

In pairs or small groups

- Normal passing*

- Players bounce the ball to each other

- Roll or grubber to each other

- High pass/low pass *

- Fancy passes *

Important all passes are backwards as per a game

Positional specific extras

Ideally, these tasks need to be practised for about thirty minutes at a time with a high number of repetitions. Intensity is not important, but quality practice is. In each session before or after training, tasks such as these or the ball familiarity program should be done before the main team warm-up.

Full backs/wings
High ball retrieval (catch), scoot ('C' line dummy half run)

Centres
Catch and pass (hands up, quick transfer), decision making, scoot (C – line), line-running

Halves/ball playing lock
Kicks (all types), catch and pass (hands up, quick transfer), decision making

Hookers
Ball straight from the floor, variety and disguise of next play intention, roll out

Front Row

Body position in a collision, footwork at the line, finding the floor, quick play the ball, lines of run, timing

Second row/edge
Body position in a collision, footwork at the line, finding the floor, quick play the ball, lines of run, timing

Key Points from This Chapter

- Introduce skills to players when they are relatively fresh and take them through 'Isolation, Opposition and Game' stages

- Bilateral learning practises are essential

- Everything about training should also be as specific to the game of rugby league as possible.

- Good coaches recognise what's unfolding in front of them in a drill, training game or on match day and can, if needed, act on it, appropriately

- Creating competition in training lifts standards

- Encourage players to do skill-based extras

- There are many benefits to using games to coach your players

"His knowledge of the game is second to none" – By Noel Cleal

I have known Lee for almost 20 years from when he started work with us at Manly Sea Eagles and he has worked before and since then in all aspects of Rugby League from NRL to grassroots. He comes out to country areas regularly to give coaches some guidance and I have worked with Lee since our Manly days, as have other members of my family, including my brother Les Cleal.

His knowledge of the game is second to none and his ability to educate all things Rugby League is exemplary. More importantly, he is a thorough gentleman and has a real presence about him. I feel honoured to call him a mate.

Away from footy, Lee is a joy to be around. He does, however, think he's a connoisseur of beer. How can he be? He's a Pom! Despite all his denials, it seems the beer here is a bit cold for his liking! The day after I announced my retirement, he showed up on my doorstep for 'a beer' and he didn't leave for what seemed like an eternity. My beer stocks had run dry by the time he left!

His general sports knowledge, especially around the English Premier League used to come in handy on Sunday mornings whilst I was attempting to get the sports crossword done in the paper.

For years I invited Lee to come out wild pig chasing with my friends and family out bush, and he used to look at me strangely. I met him when he had just come over from England so chasing pigs was about as foreign to him as a cold drink and a good wash.

Despite all these faults, he goes ok for a Pom!

Noel 'Crusher' Cleal played 245 First Grade games for Eastern Suburbs (now Sydney Roosters), Manly Sea Eagles, Widnes and Hull FC. Played 10 times for Australia and 13 times for New South Wales. Recruitment Manager of Parramatta Eels, Manly Sea Eagles and Canterbury Bulldogs since retirement from playing.

6
How to Plan It

Quite simply, all coaches worth their salt need to get into the habit of planning their training, carrying it out and then reviewing it. How good are you at planning your training? Good or not as good as you should be? How can you be a leader of others if you don't know where you are going yourself?

If you are serious about your coaching (which you probably are because you're reading this book), you should be planning your coaching, at a minimum, one week ahead. That's a minimum standard, by the way.

If you're not a serious planner but want to be, I believe your time to sit down and plan for weeks ahead is before and during your pre-season. That's because those 'would be' planners who try to start mid-season often end up falling back to a short-term focus, namely focusing on what happens during a weekend game and trying to work out how to fix that. Therefore, if it's mid-season as you read this, go week to week for now. Don't put too much pressure on yourself to plan weeks and weeks of work.

The other thing with planning and reviewing is we tend to stay in our own minds a little bit and sometimes we'll just plan what's comfortable for us. Try and review with others in and around the team to see if what you're doing is the best thing that you can do in that circumstance. Also, consult any mentors you may have.

It's a conscious decision you have to make to be a better planner. This is because coaches get washed up in the whirlpool of the season and washed up in the whirlpool of life and family once the week-to-week grind of football starts. It's like they're on a treadmill that can't be turned off. Then, at the end of the season, they get off that treadmill for a while and possibly start reflecting on their coaching practice to try and become a better coach the year after.

Does this all sound familiar to you?

If you can, try and intercept this treadmill journey each week. Get off that treadmill for an hour or two a week and just 'think'. Rather than 'just doing' a session, ask:

- *"Why am I doing this session?"*

- *"What am I doing this session for?"*

- *"What am I doing this training week for?"*

- *"How can I make it better?"*

Two decades ago, when I started to form this habit, it initially gave me some mental torment because I was never happy with myself. I soon realised that it's a really good habit to get into because it is an essential process to go through. That's one of the big ways you can improve as a coach.

One of the biggest indicators of a good training session is if your players enjoyed it and if they had fun. A team that's having fun is happy. Fun is a cause of happiness, so if you can factor that into your coaching, you're on to a huge winner. *(See Chapter 7 for my 'Ten indicators of a good training session).*

Listing the content you want to coach

As mentioned in Chapter 4, before putting anything into a plan, the first stage of the planning process is to start looking at the skill and technical coaching aspects that are needed during your preseason or, indeed, any period of coaching throughout the year.

Start this process by forming a **content table**. I help coaches do this by breaking the game down into a few distinct sections. First of all, look at the wide array of skills involved in our game and then look at what skills the players are actually able to execute in the game commensurate with their age and ability.

Sorry to say the obvious, but the game is separated into offence and defence. They're signified by two horizontal columns on our table. You may remember from 'What to Coach' in Chapter 5 the concept of 'Core', 'Unit' and 'Team' skills. (If not, there is a reminder of them below the table).

We can add these elements in vertical columns as follows:

	Core	Unit	Team
Offence			
Defence			

It is worth a reminder here of what our definitions of 'Core', 'Unit' and 'Team' are:

Core
Any activity that can be practised alone or that an individual is responsible for

Unit
Any activity that involves more than one person but less than the team. Normally involves no more than five people.

Team
Any activity involving the full thirteen players of a team.

We can now start to think of some of the content that can go into the content table. To help you understand the concept of the table, we will drop one coaching point into each stage. For example, 'grip, pass, catch, carry' is an individual skill in offence, so that would go in 'Offence – Core'

In defence, tackle technique would be an obvious one. So, our planning table now looks like this:

	Core	Unit	Team
Offence	*Grip, Pass, Catch, Carry*		
Defence	*Tackle Technique*		

When it comes to the unit skills required, many coaches look at areas of the field such as the left side, right side and the middle of their offence and defence set-up. In attack, this could mean set plays that you want the team to learn (we will list three generic ones), whilst in defence it could refer to the marker and 'ABC' defence system on either side of the ruck. Here they are in the table:

	Core	Unit	Team
Offence	Grip, Pass, Catch, Carry	Face Ball Block Play Drop Off	
Defence	Tackle Technique	Marker System ABC defence	

Team skills are quite often the easiest to put into this table because a coach normally has a good idea of how they want their team to play. Every coach has got different types of sets that they'd like to teach the team. I tend to split mine into 'Exit' sets and 'Good Ball' sets but other coaches may divide the field up even further. In the next version of the table, we see the sets listed: (I have used labels for the sets identical to the ones referenced in Chapter 4).

	Core	Unit	Team
Offence	Grip, Pass, Catch, Carry	Face Ball Block Play Drop Off	Zero Set Bridge Set G3, G1 Hamilton
Defence	Tackle Technique	Marker System ABC defence	Red Zone D Green Zone D

You may notice there are two defensive terms in there. Many coaches apply slightly different defensive systems in different parts of the field. The 'Red Zone' in this instance refers to when defending in our half of the field, whilst the 'Green Zone' refers to the opposition's half. Many coaches will apply slightly different defensive systems in different parts of the field, often altering defensive formation or movement patterns depending on what they expect from the opposition.

The list of things added to this table is not exhaustive at all. You should now think about all the different technical aspects you want to coach your team in any given season and drop them into the appropriate sections. This can be done on a device or written by hand in a notebook or journal. The advantages of doing this using technology such as a computer, tablet or phone are that you can easily edit this and share with other people should you need to. It also makes things easier when we move to the next stage of planning. I carry out this process with pen and paper first before committing my work to a Word document on my coaching laptop.

What else do we need to coach?

It is not enough to simply coach your player's skills, plays and tactics; you will also need to consider several other things. These include elements such as fitness, speed and agility, mental aspects of performance and general philosophies.

As a general rule, I tend to leave until last, the adding of the fitness-related components I want to include in my coaching. I do this because I base all fitness work around the technical work that is being undertaken, as discussed in Chapter 5.

I strongly encourage coaches to think about how they will go about this. It is crucial to take some specialist advice before putting any focused fitness work into a plan. When it comes to the stage of putting it in the planning table, simply do the following (three exemplars included):

	Core	Unit	Team
Offence	Grip, Pass, Catch, Carry	Face Ball Block Play Drop Off	Zero Set Hamilton Bridge Set G3, G1
Defence	Tackle Technique	Marker System ABC defence	Red Zone D Green Zone D
Fitness	Conditioning games MAS Runs* Speed & Agility*	N/A	N/A

*= As an example, only. Must be planned separately and specifically upon taking specialist advice. MAS stands for Maximal Aerobic Speed.

The mental aspects of performance and over-arching philosophies of preparation and play can include general concepts such as team disciplines, 'team first' ideals and elements such as positive communication and having a culture of using 'no negatives' when speaking to teammates. In our content table, we will simply include some of the principles that were mentioned earlier in Chapter 3. These would feature in an additional section of the table which you can place either above or below all other components.

Mental Aspects & General Philosophies	*Doing SIMPLE THINGS, doing them EXCELLENTLY and doing them RUTHLESSLY and REPEATEDLY* *Ball Control* *Discipline (reduce penalties)*	*N/A*	*N/A*

Using the content table to plan pre-season and in-season training

When the content table is fully completed, we are left with a thorough and detailed list of 'what to coach'. The next stage is to consider when each item gets coached, how it gets coached, how much time we spend on coaching it in a session and how often we revisit it. If your content table is in a computerised document this is very easy as you can 'copy and paste' items from the table into a plan. If it's in another format, just use the table as a checklist and mark off what you have added to your plan.

At this juncture, I encourage coaches to plan a four-week cycle of all technical and tactical work to ensure that all latecomers to pre-season or in-season training are catered for. When the coach sits to plan the pre-season and in-season work, instead of looking at the year as a whole, (let's say 40 weeks), it can instead be planned as 10 x 4-week blocks. The idea of this is that the coach just repeats that original four-week block of work (with a twist). The twist is that coaches need to cover the same elements of the game but consider delivering it differently on each occasion that each facet of the game is visited.

Using decision-making with the football as an example. On the first four-week cycle, this could be delivered in a three-attackers versus two defenders (3v2) drill format. On the second cycle, this could be delivered in a '4v3' drill, and on the third cycle, a 5 or 6v4 can be considered, and so on.

To make sure the team is as good a defensive side as an offensive side, it is important to plan an equal mixture of offence and defence for every session, every week or every two-week cycle. A strong suggestion is to start with a '50-50' split of offence and defence in every session and, therefore, each week. This gives players the message that defence is as important as offence. It is better to teach defence very early in preparation and get that right than to try and 'catch up' on defence later in preparation. How much defence is being coached also depends on the complexity of the defence systems being employed. It is always easier to put slightly less defence into the training at a later date rather than to try and cram in even more.

Much of the coaching work planned will need to be revisited in every session or several times, whilst other elements may need to be touched on only once or twice. For example, the football's grip, pass, catch and carry is a skill that always needs practice to keep players 'sharp'. Think of coaching tasks like this as just like brushing your teeth! (We have to do it regularly or else standards drop alarmingly and quickly!). The mental aspects and general philosophies you want your team to be strong in will likely need referencing in every session whilst other elements of the game, such as teaching the team how to exit their danger zone simply, may need only one short introduction and some gradual reparations along the way.

Sticking rigidly to a plan at the absolute expense of what you, as the coach, see unfolding in front of you is dangerous, particularly if correction of what is seen in training or on game day becomes more urgent. If, for example, many players are starting to look overly fatigued because pre-season is hard on their bodies, not pivoting to provide a more palatable training offering for a session or two could prove detrimental to the overall morale of players in a squad.

When in-season, if dealing with younger players, it is important to always maintain an element of training that focuses on the long-term development of every player, rather than the short-term need to get a better result at the weekend.

Key Points from This Chapter

- It is not enough to coach your player's skills, plays and tactics; you will also need to consider several other elements such as fitness, speed and agility, mental aspects of performance and general philosophies.

- You should be planning your coaching, at a minimum, one week ahead.

- Sticking rigidly to a plan at the absolute expense of what you see unfolding in front of you in training or in games is dangerous

- Some coaching work planned will need to be revisited a number of times whilst other elements may need touching on only once or twice

- When in-season, if dealing with younger players, it is important to maintain an element of training that focuses on the long-term development of every player, rather than the short-term need to get a better result at the weekend

"His work ethic and attention to detail is up there with the best" - Dr. Vinny Webb

Many things connect the best mates in life, but for me and Lee Addison - Salford, Man City and the cricket are NOT in the running. That's no disrespect for any of the mentioned, but they are not on a list of things that float my boat. Even more so, Lee once went to work at the world-renowned rugby league club, Wigan Warriors and I am a Warrington Wolves man. To be correct, I was until the last few years when my daughter started working at Wigan, and to be honest it's the best culture in a club that I have witnessed. We used to coach Matty Peet, Wigan's Head Coach! So maybe Lee and I have something more in common now.

Rugby League appeared to be the initial 'glue' that connected us, but as a lifelong friendship evolved, the connection is now bound by love and care.

Specifically, the friendship. Well, it was not that at first, but I saw something in Lee that intrigued me. This intrigue started in the British Student Rugby League back in 1998, where I was Performance Director and Head Coach, and Lee was the only first-year student selected by his university team to attend the open selection event for the newly formed GB Student Rugby League squad. My first thoughts were that he could either play a bit or his forthright manner had got him selected. The trials would tell and if all else failed, he was from a rugby league background with some pedigree.

The trials were part of initial preparations for a trip to play France in a 'test' match and a tour to Australia the following year. I'd coached several successful teams before this 'gig' which were made up of players from what is widely known as the UK's Rugby League M62 corridor. The students turned out to be a very different challenge, and Lee provided proof of that in good and bad ways.

Back then, Lee was, and still is, a gregarious character. I identified he could play a bit (in fairness, probably more than quite a few of the players) and he would also certainly ask a lot of questions of me as his coach. This was challenging in many ways. Some were good challenges, but others were less so. I'm very serious about Rugby League, and back then, Lee, on the surface, was less so and he was even more gregarious with a huge sense of fun. I have what I call my 'too hard bin' and Lee was in danger of going into it as he was 'zapping' all my focus.

I'll be honest at first, he used to frustrate me no end. The coaching team and I tried different ways to understand Lee and to integrate him into the team, but the reality was I found it hard to see how we could pick him for an international side with serious ambitions and a dedication to preparation. He would be talkative and sometimes disruptive when in drills, the loudest in the team meeting, on the bus or before and after training and it is probably fair to say he struggled with some of the more technical tasks required of a back-row or front-row forward. However, as a coach, your job is to try and develop players who want to progress and if I'm honest I'm not sure Lee did want to progress. He was happy being there mixing with some new buddies and having a 'giggle' and hopeful of getting a bit of 'swag'(kit).

But they do say you should never judge a book by its cover and to be balanced in my comment, a challenge as a coach is also helpful in your development, and I was challenged many times which I now know has contributed to my personal development as a coach and coach developer.

I have since learned that Lee has never been one to completely 'buy in' to several 'peripheral' conventions that bind so many in the sports or commercial performance space. Many coaches and corporates are cagey with each other when they interact, never truly being authentic, keen not to show weakness or to give their contemporaries any clues or secrets as to the direction they're planning to take. They have their guard up because they believe in the 'secret sauce' that wins you games or cups. Let's be clear - that's a sporting myth. So-called marginal gains are the top point 1% of preparation, good old hard work and contextual practice are the sauce; the coach is the chef who mixes multiple ingredients to help players perform at their best. It's their best and they must own it.

In my mind Lee is authentic, individual and has been for all my time knowing him. He still bucks the trend in many people's minds as a (sometimes) non-conformist which ruffles some proverbial feathers in the institutions of Rugby League and beyond.

To be fair, the squad support team and I didn't realise until sometime later that Lee was being Lee. There is nothing wrong because he was being his authentic self and not conforming to convention. You just need to take time to get to know him. Maybe more people being authentic would help the world of sport and maybe we would have fewer people behaving like robots!

What Lee tends to be very good at hiding (and I know this isn't intentional it's just who he is) is his steely determination and drive to succeed. He is arguably the living embodiment of 'work hard- play hard' as his work ethic and attention to detail is up there with the best I have witnessed. His preparation of his players and development of young people is first class and stands above many I've seen and witnessed first-hand over some of my 30 years of experience as a coach and coach developer, not just in Rugby League but across multiple sports that I have worked with.

So, these opposites do eventually attract, namely Lee the 'entertainer' and 'sensible' Vinny.

Back to the GB Students.

In 1998, we fully expected him not to make our GB squad, but his performance in the trial could not be ignored. After starting as a standby member of the squad to tour France, he made the final trip.

We didn't, however, pick him for a game on the tour - but that wasn't the end of Lee Addison.

Just before his second year at Uni, he got selected for England Students ahead of several of the players who had been chosen ahead of him in France. The coach at the time, John Kain, seemed to have the same issues I had with Lee in training and kept him on the bench for the trial match. Seemingly non-plussed as he sat on the bench, laughing and joking while waiting for his opportunity, Lee eventually had to be chosen as one of the first-picked for the England side after taking to the field and playing a blinder!

I have since learned that Lee felt burned by his non-selection in France, so he dedicated the following months to ensuring it didn't happen again, preparing meticulously, training hard and steeling himself for the challenges ahead. He spent the rest of that year as a student international.

I would next cross paths with Lee three years later, but this time he had a clipboard in his hand and was an ex-student. He told me he'd ended up in Rugby League administration whilst in his final year in Uni and had ended up coaching 'by accident'. The student representative side he was in charge of was prepared meticulously and played an enterprising brand of football. There were some players that I'd hardly ever noticed before doing things I'd never seen them do before!

A few weeks later, I saw Lee coaching England Students against the New Zealand Army side that had swept all before them in the four games they'd played against the Armed Forces sides before meeting this group of small, yet focused and determined students. The England Students beat the NZ Army, and it was a very memorable win.

We were determined to bring two of the coaches of the 'Home Nations' with us as Assistant Coaches on the tour to Australia with the GB Students. Lee was one of the two we selected. It wasn't just me as the Head Coach who picked him, it was a panel, and we also interviewed players who'd played under him. I also didn't want assistants who were just going to carry out my suggestions without questions. I wanted people who could challenge me! So, from being that player who I couldn't truly work out, Lee was now one of my Assistant Coaches and we would be spending an awful lot of time together either in person or via communication devices over the following eight months!

The Lee I got to know has what philosophers call a sophisticated epistemology (e.g., source of knowledge, methods, truth, validity, beliefs and opinions). That's one thing (sophisticated) I would not have previously said about Lee, but getting to know him over the years it does explain his approach and, indeed his personality. In other words, he's not a cut-and-paste coach. He questions and wants to know how it works, why it works, how it is perceived and why it is perceived so. He doesn't always accept knowledge as it is presented, so he was never going to just coach like he'd been coached or everyone else coached if he could find what he felt was a better way of doing it.

Lee challenged the strategic way we played, and he was also adept at being intense and demanding with the players on the training field, yet would approach those same players away from the 'work 'and enjoy periods of downtime with them and our staff. It's important to remember, contextually, that this was the early 2000's. This was still an era where the coach was 'boss' and players were to do what the coach said. I was too intense back then. I was focused too much on football and not necessarily building strong relationships with the players. I kept my distance somewhat.

I'd won the Emerging Nations World Cup, with the British Amateur side only a couple of years earlier in the year 2000. When I asked these experienced and seasoned amateurs for their opinions on how we prepared our players, it was not what they wanted. They wanted a boss – they wanted to be told what to do. It was the other way around with Lee and the Students in general. It was a stark contrast between the Students and the Amateurs who were representing their country.

My coaching approach and philosophy changed significantly during this time, and 2002/03 when Lee and I were working together, was smack bang in the middle of that evolution of my coaching. I was a fan of structures and set plays. Lee brought what appeared on the outside to be a more cavalier approach, but the reality is very different to that. Lee helped me believe that we were constraining players with too much structure and it's an approach I still agree wholeheartedly with today.

Years earlier, we both thought we were opposites, but the reality is that this period proved we were exactly the same in our approach to what we both did. Coaching. We wanted the same outcomes, as did all the staff group - it was a collective of like-minded people. We kept to a framework originally set by me, but we improved it. The questioning approach is exactly what I was looking for at that stage of my working life, as was a better balance between work and 'play/downtime'.

In the years before leaving to live-in Australia full time, Lee was with us in the Rugby Football League's (RFL)Performance Department, working as a coach in a wide range of our programs on the player and coach pathway, working with the best young players and coaches in the country. At the time, I was a Coaching Project Manager for the RFL before I became the Head of Coach Development for the game in England, so I bumped into him a fair bit. In 2005, Lee was invited to attend the Coach Education Department's National Coaches Development Camp as one of only twelve coaches in the country and then the English Schools Rugby League Association also identified him as a future coach.

It was an exciting time for the game in the country after David Waite arrived and the huge investment in our sport that we received was starting to pay huge dividends with results that we'd never seen before. But despite all this and having a very promising coaching future in England, true to form, Lee decided to test himself in Australia, where the game is at its toughest and competition for everything is more intense. Lee, was once again asking the question *"Is there a better way of doing this?"*

He's had some amazing experiences since he went to Oz and in many of the Facetime conversations we have or when he visits us in England, it's great to hear the latest on this most unique of journeys and our friendship has grown from strength to strength. Our most recent Facetime chat a few days before this book was printed was a two-hour affair, where the first hour saw us debate the state of the country I live in and the political landscape here and in the USA. The second half was all about coaching, philosophies and a better way of doing things. Which is probably not a shock to you now!

Dr Vinny Webb is a former Head of Coach Development for the Rugby Football League and Head of Education for the hugely successful British Cycling, the national governing body. Now a Head of Workforce Governance and Sporting Bodies and a consultant for a variety of sporting bodies, Vinny has also coached at Warrington Wolves, the multiple premierships winning Woolston Rovers and was Head Coach of Great Britain Students, the British Amateur Rugby League Association (BARLA) Great Britain side, Georgia and Russia.

7
How to Manage It

It's the most annoying, horrible and frustrating job any coach has to carry out – navigating lower-than-expected training turnout. Is there anything more annoying for a coach than planning for a session containing twenty players to see only ten turn up?

What do you do with players who miss training? How does that impact your training? How different do those sessions look? How can you coach a team when half the players don't turn up a lot of the time?

Coaches need to make sure training is important, implementable to games and enjoyable or else players will sometimes choose not to do it. They'll just turn up at the weekend and expect to play - and that's it.

If you've got players who work their socks off all year long but don't always make your run-on side because some others, who swan in after doing no training at all, get picked ahead of them, don't be surprised if the committed ones start complaining, or worse, start looking for elsewhere to play. There's nothing worse for team progress and morale than late-comers to training who throw the ball around in a way that looks nothing like the team structure you've worked on, even if they score a try or two in training and are capable of doing it in games too. Despite the obvious benefits that person scoring tries brings, bringing these players straight into the team at the expense of other, more committed ones can render all previous coaching work completely null and void. It's a fine balancing act for a coach.

Develop non-negotiable coach rules

When coaching in a high-performance environment, I have several rules and regulations that are **non-negotiable** as far as I am concerned when it comes to creating a fantastic culture amongst the team. When it comes to deciding how 'firm' to be with your players, a lot will depend on where the team sits on the recreation to performance curriculum. (Which you will see in Chapter 8)

I am always happy to discuss the contents of my non-negotiables and how best to convey these protocols with the staff I work with and the senior and responsible players in my care, yet I am steadfast in my belief that strong, basic rules are the core behind a strong team ethos and would take some persuading to change them.

My rules in a high-performance coaching environment tend to look something like this:

Attendance

- Players must attend every training session ***without exception.*** Players in the team will be subject to a one-strike rule. If they miss training once with an 'unauthorised' absence, they will be cut from the squad or at the very least, demoted from the starting lineup to the bench for that week's fixture ***without exception***. There is always a consequence for non-attendance at training.

- Absent players must make themselves an authorised absence by discussing this with the team manager no less than 24 hours before any training session or 48 hours before a game. Players injured or sick must attend training if they are physically or safely able to and will be advised on the next required action at the discretion of the coach and any available medical staff. The inability to train due to illness must be supported by a medical note or onsite team medical staff.

Punctuality

- Players must arrive at training ***on time.*** Appropriate actions to take against lateness are dependent on the group's circumstances. Any lateness must be recorded for team records.

Uniform / Kit

- Players must wear training kit provided to them during training and games. Appropriate actions to take against any indiscretions are dependent on the group's circumstances. Any infringements must be recorded for team records.

Ten indicators of a good training session

The 'ten indicators of a good training session' is a framework I developed for my team during my first season at Manly Sea Eagles in 2008 and, having reviewed it every year since, I still believe it is fit for purpose. Basically, the first point about dropped balls can be hard to achieve, but really, the other nine are non-negotiable!

If you have low standards as a coach:

- Your players have not got a very high bar to attain and therefore, success is highly unlikely

- Training will be based more on 'going through the motions' rather than being something to look forward to with an improvement focus.

- Your players will soon be uninterested in your sessions.

In the words of the rapper Pitbull, we should *"Reach for the stars, and if you don't grab them at least you'll fall on top of the world"*!

I call my roadshow of clinics the Aim Higher Program because I want every player who comes on it to get out of their comfort zone. The program and its name are designed to attract the players and coaches who want to get more out of this game. I think that as a coach you need to do the same. Set your bar high!

The ten indicators are:

1. Less than six balls dropped in any one training session

2. All players are present or accounted for

3. All players arrive on time

4. All players arrive in full uniform

5. All players are doing 'extras' as directed

6. No player is seen to take a short cut such as starting to slow down after nine metres on a ten-metre sprint

7. No player is to be seen as 'giving up', taking an easy option or breaching any training disciplines as set down by coaches (such as walking when they should be jogging.)

8. General communication amongst the group is 'excellent'

9. Success is high. Group improves at a good rate, understanding and learning are high and the general 'feel' for the session is good.

10. No negative vibes were noticed around the group

Aiming higher

As the sport of Rugby League has evolved from part-time to a full-time professional pastime in some parts of the world, so too have the opportunities available to youngsters who play the game. These players originally join a club for fun and as a 'consumer' who pays a fee to play. There are, quite frankly, far more opportunities to make a full-time living out of the sport in 2025 than there were in 1995.

Players who sign for clubs as juniors are essentially the 'customers' of the sport. They pay their registration fees to join a club that has a duty to cater for those who want to enjoy the sport for recreation purposes only. Not everyone has high hopes in the sport. The emergence of more opportunities for paid employment in the sport, however, means many don't just turn up to play for fun; they also have (at least at the back of their minds) desires and ambitions to 'go further' in the game. There is nothing wrong or evil about this, but it creates a difficulty for club providers, and it is becoming harder and harder for some clubs to cater for everyone.

The Recreation v Performance Continuum

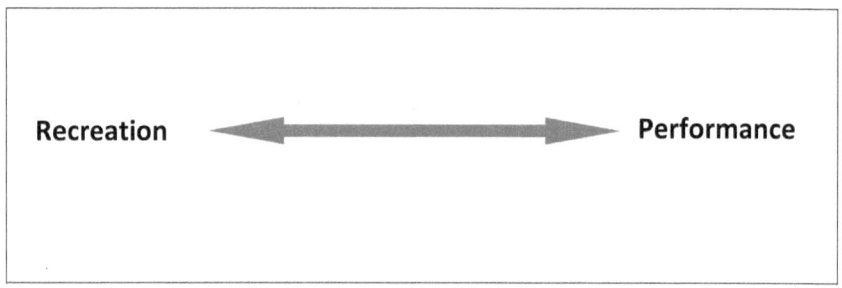

Looking at the model above, if we imagine a recreational approach to sport at one end of the continuum and elite performance at the other as per the model above, we can also begin to understand some of the challenges that can make life difficult for rugby league providers such as clubs, schools and their coaches.

Let's start with some definitions for each type of participation. Active recreation is defined by the Western Australian government as:

"...activities engaged in for the purpose of relaxation, health and wellbeing or enjoyment with the primary activity requiring physical exertion, and the primary focus on human activity".

Sport is defined by the same organisation as:

"A human activity involving physical exertion and skill as the primary focus of the activity, with elements of competition where rules and patterns of behaviour

governing the activity exist formally through organisations and is generally recognised as a sport".

Sports clubs, such as those that cater for rugby league can fall into both the recreation and sport categories described above. Many participants will endeavour to play according to the rules that govern the code, yet will have less care for the result or indeed, as is happening more and more in many jurisdictions, play in competitions where the points aren't officially accrued. In essence, they play a sport, recreationally!

The same government website also states that their *"High-Performance Department"* is:

"...committed to creating a sports system that allows our athletes to achieve their ultimate potential in both national and international sport".

It could be argued that many of our rugby league clubs are (often in an unspoken way) expected to provide such an environment too.

Most coaches that work in the game and the clubs that host them, therefore, tend to have to strike this balance between providing a 'sport' to be played 'recreationally' and a provision of activities that can allow those players who want to reach their ultimate potential to believe they are in the right place to achieve those goals.

How coaches can deal with this problem

Teachers in education know this problem as 'differentiation' or, in other words, approaching each student differently. The New South Wales government refer to differentiation as *"The responses that teachers make to learners' needs".* We can easily apply this to sports coaching too.

As a kid growing up in the delightful North of England, I wasn't a naturally talented player. It wasn't until the age of 15 and 16 that I started to get some accolades from the game. The fact remains that if I hadn't been so keen on rugby league, I may have drifted away from the game, and it wouldn't have played such a big part in my life. I was probably written off by many coaches and not invested in a great deal beyond some basic instruction. I was told by some coaches not to risk passing the ball because I was a *"forward and forwards shouldn't pass the ball"*. I was told by others I couldn't tackle very well and I remember one rep coach telling me that he felt I needed to *"get bigger"*. That was the only bit of advice he could give me when I didn't make the side that day and I am not sure how I could do that before the following week's fixture!

Needless to say, I am not a fan of that kind of coaching! I have always tried to do things differently by giving everyone a chance, as much as I could. A big problem is that not everyone responds to the kind of coaching geared towards the standards required for elite-level football.

It is also essential to consider current knowledge regarding learning disabilities. The chances of your team containing at least one player with some form of difficulty when it comes to learning are extremely high. Statistics suggest at least 15% of the world has some form of disability.

If a coach is dealing with a team and trying to differentiate, here are some approaches that tend to work:

- If they are capable, ask the more experienced players in your squad to mentor the less talented throughout your training

- 'Less is More' – for every three bits of feedback you give to a talented or more experienced player, use only one for the less talented, those less experienced or struggling to understand.

- Build rapport with every player, regardless of ability – most people just want to be acknowledged.

- Give more positive feedback than any feedback that can be construed as negative. Find and acknowledge what the players can do, rather than what they can't do.

- Many players will know if they are unlikely to be in your run-on side so it's a chance to help them create a new positive mindset around some new, more realistic goals. Tell them the reasons they aren't in the side, give them ways they can correct that and set them a target to make that team in the future.

- Remember players just want to have fun. Make training fun.

- Many children who are not confident in rugby league are often 'gun shy' when it comes to collisions. Approach this issue with understanding and care and also liaise with parents.

- Follow a '*Whole – Part–Whole*' or '*Whole–Progressive Part–Whole*' model of coaching where you can.

A '*Whole–Progressive Part–Whole*' coaching approach to a typical Rugby League scenario might start with a coach asking their team to carry out an attacking set structure in full, whilst accepting that the lines of run, handling and timing will not be up to standard immediately. By doing this, the coach has allowed the team to see what the ultimate goal is. They will also be able to picture how the team will be playing in the future.

The coach can then move the team to the '*Progressive Part*' phase by separating the set into each of the five distinct plays that traditionally lead up to the 6th tackle kick. The coach may focus on the quality of catch and pass each time it is done, and/or the angles that are required to be run. The team may practice this in distinctive left-side, middle group and right-side groupings, practicing their role on their own away from the other groups.

'*Progressive Part*' involves putting the parts together in a sequential way, in the order as they would happen in the 'whole'. As per our example, let's say that one of the plays in the imaginary set involves the team shifting the ball from left to right as they attack. The coach adds the 'middle group' of players to the 'left side' group once the left side has done their element of the work satisfactorily. The same approach is taken to the addition of the 'right-side' group when the left side and the middle group execute their parts well.

When this is all done to a satisfactory standard, the hope is that the coach can return the team to the '*Whole*', expecting the set to be carried out with better understanding and hopefully also, successful execution of the many parts that constitute the full set.

How clubs and schools can deal with this problem

There are some subtle and not-so-subtle changes and interventions that can be considered by a club, school or any organisation that provides Rugby League as a pastime to players with a varying range of ambitions and goals. For simplicity, we will just use the term 'clubs' from now to indicate all places where the sport is offered.

The traditional thing that clubs have done for many years is select 'A, B and C' teams in each age group based on ability. Other clubs, and even some competitions, require teams not to be 'tiered' in terms of ability. As a result, equal-ability teams at the same club are often named or labelled with a colour or a team moniker.

There are now many competitions that limit competitive elements until later ages, and it is something I have debated and discussed on social media and podcasts before ad nauseam. I am not going to delve deeply into the arguments in this book because I want us to focus on what we ***can do*** rather than what we cannot do. There are some excellent arguments on both sides of the debate and I encourage you to listen to both sides. Current Queensland Rugby League Chief Executive Officer Ben Ikin has been an excellent proponent of the reasons why 'non-competitive' games have been introduced in junior grades in Queensland. He compellingly argues the case.

Yet what I will say at this juncture is that I am definitely of the belief that it isn't the kids in the competition that are the problem, it's the adults watching or volunteering that can't control their own emotions. I also believe competition through sport teaches us some amazing values and, if they are managed correctly, they stand us in good stead for later in life.

But that's enough of that.

The fact remains that, regardless of the competitive or non-competitive framework, many families still crave what they perceive to be the best for their kids, which is often defined as a career in Rugby League. Clubs that don't provide for that or don't know how should really promote heavily and clearly the fact that their club is there solely for fun and recreation.

Instead, I have found that most clubs haven't yet gone through the process of recognising the distinction or alternatively, they face confused approaches by their masses towards recreation and performance sport unfolding in their orbit. At the same time, other clubs, fully cognisant of the different motivations of those in their care are trying to balance a fine line between both with a mixed bag of results.

Schools (in Australia at least) are, on the other hand, very good at clearly defining the goals of their rugby league programs. High-performance rugby league academies at schools on the Eastern seaboard of Australia have become very commonplace in society and their popularity amongst families as the vehicle of choice for the Rugby League development of their children is arguably at its highest ever. This doesn't mean kids at those academies don't want to play club football (in most cases). Most still have the desire to play the game as much as possible and also enjoy the time with their friends. But for those not able to or choosing not to attend a school academy, they only have club football as their pathway to the elite. This is the conundrum for the club coach and the organisation in general.

Teams can be full of players with mixed abilities. Those who want to progress in the sport can sometimes get upset about a lack of standards around them or a perceived lack of quality coaching or opportunity. This can see players (and sometimes their parents) vocalising their concerns in the training environment or on game day. This can also see players leaving to go to what they consider to be greener pastures for the following season.

It is a good idea for your club to set up a program for players who are either aiming for further honours or are ahead of their peers to accelerate their development. One such program is the Aim Higher program that we at Rugby League Coach have run at many clubs around the world since 2021, but other clubs also administer and carry out their own.

The key characteristics of these programs are:

- They bring more intense training and higher demands than normal club training as the 'best' or 'more committed' players are pitched together in a new, specialist environment. This also includes standards of punctuality, behaviour and where applicable, uniform.

- There is a huge focus on Core and Unit skills that the players can take to any team with them which holds them in good stead for their footballing future. They can help mentor other kids who play in their club side, thus peer coaching is promoted and it aids the later developers in the team.

- Players are given correct and contemporary dietary and training advice.

- Coaches who have a desire to improve can come to the program to coach and be mentored by senior coaches or an external provider. They can also benefit from peer coaching and interaction.

I have run over sixty of these Aim Higher Programs since the start of 2021 all over Australia plus parts of New Zealand and the UK. I often bring coaches with me who are specialists in coaching groups of players with mixed abilities. During these clinics, I have watched coaches emerge as much as players. Tamati 'Tambo' Elers is a former primary school teacher who went on to become a junior high school teacher and rugby league coach at Mabel Park during my time as head coach before helping the girl's Academy become the first school to win the new Australian Schoolgirls title in 2023. Tambo has been a dedicated coach on the Aim Higher Program since its inception, specialising in coaching the youngest who attend. Brisbane-based community coaches Tim Cheeseman, Nathan Drage, Chris Neale and Damien Kiely plus Rob Vai in Sydney, are other coaches that have grown exponentially during their time on these clinics, with all gaining the necessary experience and confidence to pursue coaching accolades at a higher level than before they joined.

Key Points from This Chapter

- Coaches need to make sure training is important, implementable to games and enjoyable or else players will sometimes choose to not do it.

- Develop non-negotiable coach rules

- Focus on 'differentiation' in your coaching. It is also essential to consider current knowledge regarding learning disabilities.

- If they are capable, ask the more experienced players in your squad to mentor the less talented throughout your training

- It is a good idea for your club to set up a program for players that are either aiming for further honours or are ahead of their peers to accelerate their development and lift the standards of other players around them.

"A Leader Who Extends People" – By Mick Hornby

Lee Addison is a powerhouse in the schoolboy Rugby League world but is much more than just a coach.

I first met Lee when I was trying to establish a Rugby League Program at *The* Ipswich State High School. I had communicated wide and far that I wanted to establish a Rugby League Program in search of everything from sponsors to support, anything and everything as we were starting from scratch. The Big Pommy flew into town after hearing whispers through the community. He was teaching and coaching at St Gregory's Campbelltown and looking for a change. We were in desperate need of teachers and coaches, so it was a perfect match.

After only three months teaching at the school and living in the community the change was palpable – students were arriving at our school in their droves, teachers wanted to get involved in the program in all capacities and the students were starting to train in a program with a high standard expected. Within this three-month period I had organised a one-off Rugby League match against the most dominant schoolboy program in Ipswich at the time. They had been in operation for around five years and had, by far, the best schoolboy program in the city of Ipswich, a huge area for rugby league and an historical nursery for talent.

I played to the egos of the Principals of both schools and bought a great big trophy and named it after them both. I even got us on the front page of the local newspaper!

Lee was in his element. I had given him an enormous challenge to start a Rugby League Program from virtual scratch and put the senior team against the best team/school in Ipswich – he not only thrived on the challenge but loved the pressure.

After you get to know Lee, you know that he not only loves a challenge but also a beer. So, what better way TO motivate and encourage the Big Pommy than with a drink or two? I stated I would shout him one schooner if he got beat by less than 30, two schooners if we got beat by less than

20 and three schooners if we got within 10 points. He came back at me without hesitation and said *"What if we win?"* I scoffed and stupidly said *"Six schooners if you win"* – no way did I think he could even get close, our opponents had been in the best schoolboy competition in Brisbane (the Broncos Cup), were well established and even affiliated with the GREAT Canberra Raiders.

The day came and we turned it into an event – Marching Band, Cheerleaders and an estimated 10,000 people – it was the biggest Rugby League match anyone had seen in the town for a very long time. In pouring rain, we beat them 36-6 and some referred to it as a 'flogging'. At the end of the game our Principal accepted the trophy and a new era was born – Ipswich State High School were about to become a Rugby League force within Australian Schoolboy Rugby League. More than that, Lee Addison announced himself on the Queensland Rugby League coaching stage. He left the schools footy scene a decade later, having brought Ipswich State High and then Mabel Park State High (where we joined up together again) to the top of the School Rugby League tree.

In closing, Lee Addison is more than a Rugby League coach. He is a mentor for players and coaches, a person with passion and integrity, and a leader who extends people beyond what they think they are capable of. He has proven himself on the international stage and has produced some of our most exceptional Rugby League players in the league nurseries he has helped to build, develop and nurture. He has developed more than just Rugby League, or the skills associated with the game, he has produced exceptional human beings.

Mick Hornby was Executive Principal at Mabel Park State High School and Deputy Principal at Ipswich State High School.

8

Long-term Player Development

"The best among us are no more gifted than the rest. They just take little steps each day as they march towards their biggest goal in life. And the days slip into weeks, the weeks into months and, before they know it, they arrive at a place called EXTRAORDINARY."

That is a quote from 'The Greatness Guide' by Robin Sharma. I am not sure how much this celebrated leadership expert and author knows about the greatest game, but his quote certainly hits home to this League coach!

Whether a coach of a Rugby League team, a club executive or if you were (or are) a player at any age, you likely have experience of a youth development system. Any developmental outcome could have been a result of a well-designed, planned and well-thought-out program, or it can be the result of a series of events that were not coordinated in any way, shape or form, and as a result, they have mixed results.

Youth Development Programs

Most successful sports programs around the world have a structured youth development framework in place to provide a pathway to senior team representation within their organisation. In Rugby League, the most famous youth development pathway of recent years at the time of writing has been that of Penrith Panthers in the NRL. Wigan Warriors in the UK Super League also have a storied and proud history in this regard and are once again, standard bearers in that part of the world.

To understand player development models, it is important to understand some precedents and the importance of context. The processes and mechanics of a successful development program from a club, state or country don't always work when duplicated, yet the main principles of each development system often do. Let me share with you my experiences of working in some successful systems from around the world of Rugby League before I add how I put these learnings into practice when setting up two of my own programs that were very successful.

Development stories

Without doubt, the best youth development program I have ever witnessed and been a part of is that overseen by former Newcastle Knights, St George Illawarra and Great Britain coach David Waite when he was the Rugby Football League's Technical Director between 2000 and 2004. His work was assisted and then very ably continued by another excellent operator, Chris Chapman. To understand the magnitude of the work undertaken by Waite, Chapman and so many other excellent people during that era, it is important to understand the context in which this work was conducted and the void that exists still to this day.

Many junior Rugby League coaching programs before and since are characterised by 'short term' thought and highly structured gameplay with little flexibility given to the individual player in a game situation. Short term in this instance, is defined as one year, a season, or a six-to-ten months cycle. My experience suggests that this happens at most of the junior representative levels as well as junior club (or local amateur) levels on both sides of the world.

For an elite junior player progressing through the age groups, his or her sporting education is traditionally delivered via a combination of representative and junior club pathways. This combined pathway can contain duplication, a lack of long-term planning, high playing structure and a lack of quality measurement as well as a lack of player-centred approaches, long-term measurement of learning, skill development and game sense.

There is a distinct lack of research on long-term talent development in Rugby League players, particularly from the 'skill development' and 'decision maker' perspectives. Seemingly indicative of the apparent lack of literature, a 2015 book containing academic writings published by my mate Craig Twist and Paul Worsfold titled *"The Science of Rugby"* stated that it is:

"The only book to examine the scientific principles underpinning the preparation of rugby players for high performance."

The chapters within the book cover a wide range of issues in both league and union, including physical preparation, match day strategies, travel and jet lag plus performance analysis.

Long-term skill development, developing decision makers and reference to specific skills within the game are issues that aren't considered within the book. This is not a criticism of the aforementioned book or its authors, but it could be argued that this lean towards 'physical preparation' is indicative of the approach of many coaches in the sport worldwide.

Waite, an Australian, arrived in England with significant knowledge of this void, and his experiences as a schoolteacher, as well as his time as an NRL Head Coach, helped him to form a significant curriculum designed to increase the performance of English national sides. Waite arrived in England at the perfect time to conduct such an activity. Under the Labour government of the UK, which was elected in 1997, huge efforts were made to prepare British sports teams for the 2012 Olympics, which were to be held in London. Many sports, not just Olympic ones, were significantly funded to develop juniors to elite level and Rugby League was one of them.

The benefits of this funding and Waite's work paid dividends almost immediately. The development models Waite oversaw from the year 2000 resulted in England overcoming their Australian counterparts for most of the next decade at Under 18's level. Before this, England, nor any other national side from around the rugby league world had ever beaten the Australian Schoolboys in decades of trying.

Australian Schoolboys Rugby League has been the national representative side for schoolboy-aged male rugby league players since 1972. Before the bi-annual series in 2002, the score in matches between the two countries was England 0 – Australia 20 (a 0% win ratio to England). Between 2002 and 2010, the balance shifted significantly, with England winning five of the nine games played (a 55%-win ratio). They also won four of the six games played in England (67%) and were unbeaten in all games played in 2002 and 2004.

If I have not convinced you of the strength of this development program yet, it will likely be because the peak performance of each national team group in England came not at the senior level, but at the under-18 level and not much higher. If you're thinking that England or Great Britain's senior male sides have not beaten Australia or won a World Cup in over half a century of trying then you are absolutely right!

Before I left for Australia, I sat for dinner with some past leaders of this pathway in what was essentially a farewell and reflective chat before I headed to Australia to take up the challenge of coaching here. They discussed the frustration they had with the 'bottleneck' being created as talent that was being produced was often ignored or overlooked by impatient professional clubs that invested in senior experienced players instead. When we consider some of the vagaries of the English professional system, it becomes clear why this bottleneck could exist.

Firstly, there are three professional leagues in England. Sometimes there are two. A huge part of the British sporting psyche is promotion and relegation between the leagues. This has been part of Rugby League for most of its history in the country apart from occasional times of league restructuring or when Super League places are given out based on 'franchising'. The Super League is a competition that contains players who are full-time professionals. The second and third tier (if there is one) contains the odd player that is full time but they tend to contain a vast majority of part-time players who hold full-time jobs and train in the evenings.

Often, talented players who are still waiting to break into the 'big time' can earn more money as a part-time player whilst holding down a well-paid, full-time job in a different sphere. Not that the big time is always the answer. Wages in the Super League are not as significant as in the Australian National Rugby League

(NRL). Firstly, the salary cap clubs need to adhere to is higher in Australia and secondly, it's a far bigger commercial enterprise.

As an example of this, in an October 2020 article, headlined:

'Not so Super League! British fans stunned by star's salary reveal'

George Clarke of Fox Sports in Australia wrote that a Hull Kingston Rovers Super League player, who was also a Scotland international, had told an English reporter that he was:

"...only earning £14,000 (AUD 25,000) per year while at Super League club Hull Kingston Rovers".

At the same time, the minimum wage for a squad player in the NRL was listed as $110,000. Matthew Shaw, the journalist who originally interviewed the player, wrote on the social media platform 'X' (then Twitter) via account @M_Shaw1 on 3rd October 2020 that:

"(it) probably gives a bit of insight into why players can't always agree terms with clubs"

Adding that it was a:

"...harsh reality of what some players are having to do to get an opportunity at the top".

Shaw's original article on totalrl.com stated that the player, Ryan Brierley, had:

"...been left out of pocket during the season, earning just £14,000 a year while renting accommodation near the city to aid his preparation for training".

Born in 1992, Ryan Brierley started his professional journey in the Academy of Super League club Castleford Tigers in 2009, so he was certainly a product of the development systems of the RFL we've outlined. Unable to crack the first team at Tigers he headed to second-tier club Leigh Centurions in 2012, where he soon moved into the top five try scorers in the club's history. For context, the Leigh club was founded in 1878 and, by 2012, had won two top-tier titles and two Challenge Cups. They are a famous old club.

Brierley switched to Super League club Huddersfield Giants in 2016, scoring over a try every two matches, before heading back down the divisions to the ill-fated Canadian outfit Toronto Wolfpack. 2019 saw him return to Leigh on loan, where his second tier try-scoring exploits continued. This brings us to 2020 and his ten games at Hull Kingston Rovers on the aforementioned wages. By 2021, Leigh returned to Super League and got Brierley back for a third stint before he moved to fellow Super League outfit Salford where he continues to be a fan favourite.

Ryan Brierley's story is both very inspirational and extremely sad. Inspirational because of the drive, ambition and tenacity he has quite obviously shown to carve out such a career. A career that seems to be ending in a great place, playing in the division of football his talents suggest he should have probably been playing in all along. I am sure, just like me, you hope he is earning well and enjoying a comfortable existence as this is the absolute minimum he deserves for his efforts.

His story is extremely sad, however, because it clearly shows the difficulties caused by the bottlenecks caused. Many of the clubs Brierley has played for were either in the bottom half of the Super League or near the top places in the division below and attempting to get into the Super League. Both circumstances create a perfect storm for short-term thought to thrive at clubs and it is very hard to blame them when you consider the economic impacts of relegation from the top tier or the commercial impact of promotion to it.

Both relegation avoidance and promotion-chasing teams are not ideal places to blood a talented youngster who may be a year or two off being the 'finished article'. Survival in Super League is a very powerful motivation in particular, and clubs faced with it often plump for older, more seasoned professionals (often from overseas) to ensure it. This would have likely been the conundrum facing Castleford Tigers as Brierley was coming through the ranks as a junior. At the time, the Tigers spent more time near the bottom of the Super League than the top.

Leigh on the other hand, would have seen him as more of a 'blue chip' player - a Super League calibre player facing many part-time opponents. Yet, as he got older, his inner drive to play at the highest level brought him back to the lower echelons of Super League. Indeed, Matthew Shaw's article quoted him as saying back in October 2020 that:

"I just wanted the opportunity to be honest and to prove I can play Super League".

In the latter part of his career, it is very hard to escape the thought (which is highly ironic) that Brierley is now that 'seasoned professional' who may be keeping some other youngsters from a first-team place in a Super League squad!

It is also not a far stretch that suggest that if Ryan Brierley grew up somewhere on the Eastern Seaboard of Australia, he would have spent the vast majority of his career in the NRL. With sixteen and then seventeen teams in the NRL top tier as opposed to the twelve or fourteen teams in the English top tier, there is a very good chance that the sheer numbers of first-grade calibre talents required would have seen him employed regularly. Secondly, he would have been training full-time throughout his career, alongside top-tier players and playing against top-tier players week in and week out, which would have no doubt seen him improve. Thirdly, financially, he would likely have been better off.

So now you can hopefully see why much of the work of Messrs Waite and Chapman et al has failed to translate into England or Great Britain senior teams winning Rugby League World Cups, or even beating Australia in a single match since 2006. The development system was absolutely brilliant, and so much of it could be duplicated anywhere, but, even in the country of its inception, the roadblocks to fulfilling its early promise were there.

When I travelled to Australia, I arrived very swiftly at the Manly Sea Eagles. Famed recruitment manager and former Sea Eagles, NSW Blues and Australia back-rower Noel 'Crusher' Cleal took me under his wing. A few years later, I was at Penrith Panthers, and at both clubs, I saw first-hand the development pathways and challenges that existed.

The area of Manly Warringah where the Sea Eagles call home, is often referred to as one of the 'weaker' junior areas (in terms of numbers) in Sydney. The term 'weaker' sounds harsh but you can understand it when you consider that in their Annual Report of 2021, the Manly Warringah District Junior Rugby Football League Incorporated claimed to have 2,453 players registered and a higher figure in later years could not be found. Albeit a few years later in 2024, Parramatta

Junior League claimed 5072 junior participants, whilst Cronulla-Sutherland claimed 4937 and Penrith, 8342.

What the 'weaker junior league' phrase completely ignores, however, is the amazing first-grade numbers that have been accrued by some local juniors who started in Manly Junior Representative teams in 2007, which also happens to be the year I started at the club. My first representative sides at Manly Sea Eagles included three well-known surnames that anyone involved in the game knows plenty about, almost two decades later.

When I first arrived on the peninsula, the footy community were talking extensively about a kid called William who was only 14 years old but 'carving up', as the Aussies like to say. Carving up means 'playing extremely well' in Australian rugby league vernacular. I saw this dissection of opposition defences for myself when this kid, playing against boys all older than him, was scoring tries at will (no pun intended). Warwick Bulmer, a Life Member of the professional club and the Junior League in Manly, once told me that he was *"The best I've seen since Fittler"*. Brad Fittler, who was known as one of the finest footballers of the 20th century, was the most capped New South Wales player ever and was also the youngest to ever play for the state, so it was a huge compliment.

I was to be coaching *"The best since Fittler"* a year later when he would actually be playing representative football at his own age group rather than in the one above and he certainly didn't disappoint. At the current time of writing, William, Albert and Lehi Hopoate, all sons of former Sea Eagles and 209 first-grade game veteran John Hopoate had followed in their fathers' footsteps to pull on the Manly first-grade jumper a combined total of 41 times between them. William Hopoate played a further 174 elsewhere and also became the second youngest player to play State of Origin for New South Wales, making Warwick Bulmer's statement valid. Albert is currently at Canberra Raiders and has (at the end of 2024) played a further 36 games for them, whilst Lehi, aged only 19, will certainly add significantly to his 14 appearances thus far. Jamil, the second oldest son, played 12 first-grade games for the Brisbane Broncos. Another brother, Sione, was reported in early 2025 to be having a *"very positive"* pre-season while on a train and trial contract at the Broncos. When the Hopoate family sat down for Christmas dinner at the end of 2024 there were 491 games of first-grade experience sat in just five places at the table, with no doubt more to come.

Whilst we are talking of talented families that reside in that district, we have to also talk of the 'Turbo's'. I coached the first Trbojevic brother to play first grade for the Sea Eagles Jake Trbojevic. Others were always quick to tell us about his talented younger brothers, Tom and Ben who were quickly coming through the ranks. Those three brothers currently have 423 first-grade appearances between them at the end of 2024, not to mention Jake has been Manly and New South Wales captain, playing for his state 19 times and Australia 13 times. Brother Tom has played 10 times for New South Wales and 7 times for Australia.

As recently as 2022 when William retired, the Manly Sea Eagles' first-grade side could have had four Hopoate siblings and three Trbojevics and 'King Gutho' in their thirteen-man run on side if all the stars in the sky had aligned. Clinton Gutherson was also a talented local junior during my time there and he ends 2024 with 211 first grade appearances under his belt, plus 4 for New South Wales. In the 2024 season, the three Trbojevic boys and Lehi Hopoate all played regularly for Manly Sea Eagles on their march to the NRL finals, Albert Hopoate was a regular in the Canberra Raiders side whilst Gutherson played his ninth season at Parramatta Eels, his fifth as captain, before signing a new deal with St George Illawarra Dragons for 2025.

It would be hard to predict what would have happened to the Trbojevics', Hopoates' and Clint Gutherson if they grew up playing in the Penrith district - the area I started to work in when I switched to Penrith Panthers after several great seasons with Manly. It's all too easy to say they would have had the same or even better careers because there are almost four times as many juniors in the Penrith leagues and it requires far deeper analysis.

The competition for places may have meant others getting picked over them in representative sides at key stages of their career. The inevitable 'politics' that occurs within some clubs and selection panels may have done for them at various stages too. Also, what of the increased standard of competition that nearly four times as many players undoubtedly provide? Who's to say the younger version of any of these players would have handled that well as children?

What certainly wouldn't have helped them get to the top in Penrith at the time I started there was the fact many juniors and their families had started to look further afield. Murmurs were everywhere around the game in that area and many talented juniors had gone to other areas of Sydney to play in their junior representative teams rather than risk missing out on making the cut at Penrith.

Penrith and Parramatta also are, and were, such strong junior leagues that they agreed to collaborate to field a 'third' representative team of their combined talents in the junior representative competitions. The two districts started supplying their 'next best' from their playing squads to the Western Sydney Academy of Sport who fielded teams that were 50% 'Parra' and 50% 'Penrith'.

Phil Gould arrived as General Manager in 2011 and almost immediately set about stopping the talent from leaving in droves. He is certainly the chief architect of the development program that exists today for over a decade at the foot of the Blue Mountains.

It's not just systems that make development programs good, great or indifferent. The people within these systems – namely players, coaches and other stakeholders - are key to their success or failure.

I am going to tell you two stories of very talented players who should have achieved a lot more in the game than they have. They are still playing NRL but have reached nowhere near the heights that their junior talent suggested they would. One was touted as a future Origin half and the other, a future Origin forward,

'Player A' was a halfback who qualified to be in the regional representative team that I was coach of. But he didn't train, nor did he or his parents get in contact with our staff or provide any medical certification or explanation as to why he didn't. So, I didn't pick him. Simple.

All his supposed mentors (teachers in this instance and also the recruitment manager at the NRL club he eventually debuted for) cried foul that he should have been picked, for no other reason, it seems, than because he was 'Player A'. In response, they organised for him to play for another team in the carnival, just so he could be fast-tracked all the way to New South Wales and Australian selection.

I hope you agree with me that the only lesson that a 17-year-old 'Player A' was learning at the time was that he didn't have to follow all the rules that the nineteen other players had to follow. May I add that the other players in that squad included a half-back who has gone on to play Origin and for Australia. He also trained in every session I held, carried himself very professionally and was a credit to his family, club and school. There were also several other future NRL stars on that same side. They all trained without fuss and fanfare. We also won the competition we were preparing for very convincingly.

'Player A' then played against a team I coached a few weeks later in the domestic competition. He scored a try and decided at that moment to run over to me on the sideline and tell me exactly what he thought of me. His coach (a teacher still very heavily involved in Rugby League to this day) laughed at seeing this and didn't admonish the kid at all.

The half who did train in all my sessions, doing the right things at all times whilst acting like a young professional, went on to great heights. 'Player A', who acted like a spoilt and petulant child (all behaviours reinforced by adults), has been one of the more maligned players in the NRL in the last decade.

'Player B' was with me at a big club. He was, to put it mildly, a handful. Any rules I had in place, he liked to break. I am also aware he was a handful at school too. I went to the head of youth at the club and suggested we drop the kid from the team for one week to bring him into line. Instead, I was told that I *"wasn't managing the situation properly"* and *"that I need to learn man-management skills"*. I was also told that this player would not be dropped under any circumstances. 'Player B' had been recruited to the club by this particular head of youth.

The same head of youth who gave me those pearls of leadership wisdom also questioned me about why I wanted to drop a centre who had missed eight tackles the weekend before and had trained poorly for weeks. The centre was, funnily enough, another player he had recruited. I showed Mr. Head of Youth the incriminating clips on my laptop, but he told me I was seeing things and that this centre had not missed tackles. Honestly, I could not believe what I was hearing, especially when I played the two clips where the player lay prone on the floor while an opponent ran right over him each time.

Other hard-working players were missing out because these two players – Player B and 'the centre' were protected species. Dropping a sixteen-year-old for a week for failing to meet standards whilst explaining why and giving them clear criteria to get back into the team seemed a good way to teach them about life requirements if nothing else. Allowing them both to get away with things just reinforces that they are invincible and untouchable. And some kids keep testing those boundaries.

Indeed 'Player B' has been a club hopper and also ended up incarcerated for a short time in what he described as one of the scariest moments of his life. I will say to the day I die that, if I had been allowed to take a jersey off him that week, the impact on him would have been so profound that there's a chance he might not have got into any of that trouble later in life as he would have understood boundaries and values in this world. Neither he nor 'Player A' had ever been dropped from a team before in their lives.

Much has been made of NRL player behaviour in recent years. Maybe without even realising it, in Australia, the game has put many of our rugby league players in a bubble since childhood. 'Player A' and 'Player B' were certainly in a bubble at 16 and 17 years old and no doubt they were before and after that. There's a whole generation or two of players who know no differently.

Full-time professionalism has only been an advent in Rugby League for about three decades. Up until not so long ago, we had an Under 20's National Youth Competition that brought the profile of talented 18, 19 and 20-year-old footy players through the roof. They were TV stars before they'd become full-time professionals. Some, before they'd even turned into mature adults.

It's something I've seen countless times. A young player gets given a contract at 16, 17, or 18 and, more often than not; he thinks he's 'cracked it' until a good coach, teacher or mentor keeps his feet on the ground.

The problem is finding those good coaches, teachers or mentors because so many adults contribute to the thoughts of the talented kid that they are 'untouchable'. They fail to hold the talented kid to account the same way that other players are held to account. It's human nature for many kids and their families to sign with the club and side with the people that tell them what they want to hear and makes their life easier.

Quite often the ultra-talented kid, when at junior clubs or rep teams, might be able to sit out training or even games so they can avoid injury. The professional club may hear of a discipline issue at school regarding one of their talented juniors and whilst some clubs are excellently supportive of teachers, others are all talk and zero support. There is also a strong correlation between the clubs that act in the latter manner and poor performance on the field for all their grades, including the adults.

If in a junior rep system, a player's whole life outside of school is dedicated to training, sometimes up to five times a week with their club, there's not much time left to be a normal kid. That's why I don't blame 'Player A' and Player B' at all and it's the so-called adults I have a problem with.

I don't know 'Player A' personally but I know plenty of people who do and am led to believe he is a really nice person. 'Player B' I do know well and have seen him a lot ever since I coached him and got on with him very well. He now understands what I was trying to do back when he was a junior and he appreciates it.

The talented kid, when leaving school, might get a job for a while whilst playing junior reps or Colts, but if their boss is a supportive league fan, they will get time off work to train and travel with their team. They may be removed from heavy duties and will not do overtime, missing out once again on what are the realities of life for many.

Without even blinking, a kid has gone through their teenage years without experiencing the 'arresting' moments other 'normal' teenagers might encounter. On top of that, all the training they do in the evenings and the games they play at weekends stop them from doing what many consider to be normal teenage things. They spend most of their adolescence and teenage years as a commodity rather than a child, teenager or young adult.

Coaches, teachers and well-meaning adults often talk to kids about the pitfalls of what will happen if a player doesn't 'make it' and how they need a back-up plan in terms of trade or education so they can earn elsewhere when their sporting dreams don't come true. I truly believe, however, that there are many things for our game to learn in terms of mentoring the player whose dreams DO come true. Whose adolescence and young adult life is something akin to a fairy tale. The player who has schoolmates and crowds chanting or cheering their name gets asked for autographs and gets all the trappings of being a young professional. The player who has had many things go his or her way or has been helped on his or her way all because he or she can play footy.

Is it not human nature to think, if most people are pumping your tyres up all the time, that you are invincible? That you can get away with things? That everyone who comes into your life is a true friend and doesn't just want to know you for what you can bring to their life?

Many of the players who have been in alleged incidents in the last decade or so probably fall in most, if not all, of the above categories. They were probably on TV regularly while their childhood mates were looking online for a job. They stood out from their peer group. It seems we have produced a generation of elite footballers who have 'gaps' in their life lessons. Their knowledge of what is right and wrong, sensible or silly still needs attention because they've only been in the rugby league bubble. A bubble where the training demands are higher than ever.

Coaches at all levels, teachers, recruitment managers, scouts, agents and indeed any rugby league officials need to ensure that they don't overly 'pump a player's tyres up', keeping the feet of the players in their care firmly on the ground. Any development system needs to be just as good at managing these things as they do the systematic elements of their program.

Putting these experiences into practice

By the time I left Sydney for Queensland and had the chance to launch a youth development program for myself at a place that wanted to become a big player in the school's Rugby League world, I felt I had an abundance of experience and learnings behind me, and I was certainly passionate about that area of coaching and planning.

As I have mentioned already in this book, from day one in Queensland I would tell everyone who cared to listen that Ipswich State High School would one day be the best Rugby League school in Australia, and I remember people thinking I was crazy at the time. I also gave the players and the coaching staff this message constantly and that's how we judged everything we did. We asked the question constantly from the start – *"Is this happening to a 'best in Australia' standard?"* It was a standard we aimed for in each activity we carried out from the start of my tenure. As you already know, Ipswich indeed attained that goal a decade later and both the school programs that I led from 2013 onwards achieved great things and continue to.

What follows is an outline of many of the approaches towards youth development taken by me from the moment I could run my own programs in Queensland and how I would run anything similar to this day.

The 'High Performance Pathway'

In the manuals I supply to coaches on the program, I write the following:

"There will be no such thing as the 'finished article' when it comes to footballers. We will always give them areas to improve".

This is my way of saying that we are never going to switch off and always look for ways to improve. This applies to all staff and players.   The Japanese call it 'Kaizen' which means 'continuous improvement'. It was also a way of keeping the 'feet on the ground' of young players in particular. (See the end of this chapter for a deeper analysis of the Kaizen concept).

I also now share what I found when studying successful sports youth academies around the world. Namely, three main principles that shine through above any others:

- *Every youth team must be trained based on the same concepts and in the same manner as the first team.*

- *The top kids need to be pushed out of their comfort zone and played at an age group ahead, sometimes even two.*

- *The 'jewels' of the system need to be accelerated to first-grade football.*

The winning/losing dynamic and the lessons from each

I feel that all coaches must teach players the important lessons from both winning and losing. Particularly when coaching young kids who are still trying to put winning and losing games into the context of life. It means that:

If we win....

 It doesn't mean we are unbeatable – we have only won that game.

We must ask...

What did we do well?

What can we improve?
What are the dangers/threats moving forward?
Is complacency/ego creeping in?

If we lose....

What are the lessons we learned?
It's not the end of the world – it's a lesson learned. Deal with it accordingly.
Sometimes, to appreciate winning, you have to understand and suffer losing.

Next is a model outlining the characteristics of the ideal player arriving in first grade:

Is a "good person"

Understands and "lives" the importance of possession.

Has good Grip, Pass, Catch, Carry Recognises and plays to space

Has efficient Play the Ball

Knows the sets

Runs good lines (under)

Tackles with Shoulder, Shape, Studs (Effort 1) and a knowledge of Effort 2

Is fit, healthy, lives a good lifestyle ·

Has strong core strength

Has good functional strength

Has solid training habits (warming up / cooling down / stretching etc)

Hydrates permanently
Eats well

In terms of player development, I tell all junior coaches that it is important that they are seen by themselves and others as 'first-grade assistant coaches,' regardless of their coaching title or what age group or role the particular coach is assigned to.

As we work down the age continuum to the younger age groups, less of the focus of coaches should be on winning 'the next game'. Instead, much of the focus should be on the long-term development of players. When it comes to any decisions made by coaches regarding how to approach any decision with regard to players, **all roads lead to first grade.**

"What I want to produce for the city of Ipswich is a player that can do all the fundamentals in the game... so he's fit and strong, his core strength is good, his diet is good, and he can grip, catch, carry and pass it left and right. We hammer tackle technique as well. We have five fundamental things that we do and the whole program is measured on that.

"Last year we relaunched the program and a lot of boys from the Ipswich area decided they want to join it. The numbers have gone through the roof.

"We don't want bad eggs. But in my years as a teacher and coach I've learned you have to look at a kid's heart. When deep down there is a good person in there, you can coax that out of them."

My words in a Queensland Times article, December 22nd, 2013. Written by Joel Gould

---

There are many models and theories of Long-term athlete development (LTAD) out there in 2025. Back in 2013, we operated by basing our work on the models of renowned expert Istvan Balyi whose work in the area was all the rage in that era, particularly in the United Kingdom and Australia. It was also heavily studied and implemented by the Rugby Football League, responsible for the program I describe as the best I have ever witnessed or been a part of.

By this time, Balyi's version of LTAD was a seven-stage 'Late Specialisation' model that represented an athlete's life from childhood to retirement. With a focus on athletic development and all that entails, the seven stages were/are:

1. Active Start

2. FUNdamentals

3. Learn to Train

4. Train to Train

5. Train to Compete

6. Train to Win

7. Active for Life

Forgive me but I am not going to go into detail about the Balyi LTAD model here. I will, however, tell you how we applied its principles, or at least interpreted them, at the school when setting up the youth development structure.

11 to 14 years

We essentially started at a combination of Balyi's *"Stage 3 – Learn to Train"* and *"Stage 4 – Train to Train"* stage based on the players in the program that entered directly from primary schools or at the different stages we had students join the school and its program. I wasn't completely happy to start with a combination of the stages there because I was hoping that some basic training principles had been given to most kids we inherited. The reality, however, was that some kids were only new entrants to the sport, others had played at clubs where finding appropriately qualified coaches was tough plus there were adjustments to year level requirements in Queensland at various stages.

When we inherited players at eleven or twelve years of age, our adherence to Balyi's work suggested that it was essential that coaches were made aware that these are the crucial stages of athletic development. Deeper analysis also suggested 'games' as a way of developing fitness and body weight and medicine ball-type approaches to strength development - definitely no heavy weights! It is suggested that, if players miss this stage, they don't excel. If we were to fully take on board what Balyi suggests then we could not miss this stage.

The *'Train to Train'* stage asks us to consider differing maturation levels when dealing with junior athletes, so in the gym, we referred to those approaching thirteen and fourteen years old as in the 'boys to men' phase. Our strength trainer would determine when they were ready to start lifting weights rather than their body weight, for example. Other considerations, including positive and educational approaches to wins and losses, were crucial, as were the advanced approaches to training and disciplines associated with it.

During this phase, the players were given simple introductions to training methods such as:

- Guidance and coaching in HOW to train
- Nutrition
- Hydration
- Core skills in Rugby League.
- Emphasis was on as much fun-based learning as possible.

Players were coached to master the basics such as:

- Grip, pass, catch and carry (GPCC)
- Decision-making (via games and 3v2 practice in particular)
- Shoulder shape and studs tackle technique
- Effort 2 (ruck control) introduction
- Play the ball efficiency
- Defending as a unit

The main emphasis in this age group was talent identification and long-term planning. Players were taught that dedication to improvement is the key and received an introduction to basic skills and training patterns. Any player who came into the program at this stage had access to top-level coaching with an emphasis on basic skills and training patterns, starting in January and February and continuing into March and April. In school terms in Australia, this period is Term 1.

During Terms 2 and 3, coaching was tailored to meet some of the needs identified after each game, but a curriculum of work was still adhered to with a view to the long term. There were (and are) generic areas of improvement required amongst most members of a team when they're in juniors. As the players got older and closer to thirteen and fourteen years old, this was where they started to shape themselves into 'serious' footballers, and some started to see a future in the game. Therefore, training was also tailored to reflect that.

Once on to this stage, players received personal feedback on a very regular basis. They also started to do weekly skills and fitness sessions with higher standards required. They were prepared as a 'High Performance' squad, and the head coaches in those age groups coordinated all of their work.

We put a very heavy focus on:

- How to train

- Nutrition

- Hydration

- Core skills

Also, a very heavy focus on:

- Grip, pass, catch and carry (GPCC)

- Decision-making (via games and 3v2 practice)

- Focus on self-improvement as an individual

- Unit offence/defence

- Basic team patterns

- Focus on self, team principles

- How to win games in pressure situations

- The very basics of opponents

15 to 18 years

This age group was adapted by us to combine our interpretation of *'Stage 4 - Training to Compete'* stage and the *'Training to Win'* stage that comes after it in Balyi's model. It is important to note here that Balyi's work suggests that males should only reach this stage at eighteen years. We had 'opens' teams at schools that were 'under 18's' and the stakes were high, with games televised, live-streamed, covered in print media, online media and with trophies with prize money attached, on offer.

The younger players in this group were exposed to a higher level of technical and tactical training and higher standards were expected. More high-intensity training was provided as well as recovery programs and psychological preparation that was tailored to their needs. Players also started to receive more comprehensive feedback one-on-one, using video analysis software.

This was the age group where it started to become apparent who the representative quality players were, and, dependent on their physical maturity (and date of birth as per competition rules), some were considered for first-grade duties. Only the 'blue chip' players reached first-grade status very early in all my years in schoolboy football. Ronaldo Mulitalo, now of the Cronulla Sharks, was one. Alex Leapai Jnr, who had a contract at Gold Coast Titans but decided to pursue a career in Boxing, was another.

The majority of talented players in this age group were good candidates as our future first graders. It was crucial at this stage that we 'kept the net wide' and that no major decisions were made in terms of omitting players from the whole representative and future first graders program to allow for those who were likely to mature later.

The grades at this age were close to a mirror image of the work that the opens (seventeens and eighteens) team did. They followed a very similar program up until competition time, where team specifics started to dictate to an extent. For the opens team, or first grade as we liked to call them, it was all about maximising performance. The players were trained to peak at the right times. It was of a higher intensity but periodised, with rest periods factored in.

Technical training was all game and tactically specific and very high standards were set across the board. Video analysis was deep and players received appropriate amounts in team, unit and one-on-one situations.

Some other characteristics included:

- Tactical and strategy teaching that also had some focus on opposition strengths and weaknesses where appropriate.
- Specific game plan teaching, such as spotting defenders, kicking constantly to certain opponents or sides, targeting certain areas of the field etc.

Upon leaving this section players were expected to be able to:

- Use footwork
- Pass both ways
- Have consistent carry and the ability to switch to fend
- Recognise space
- Tackle on both shoulders
- Have a battery of knowledge on how to win the floor.
- Have an inherent knowledge of their strengths and weaknesses

- Be able to direct their learning to an extent

Kaizen - Don't compromise your standards

The Japanese term 'Kaizen' means a never-ending process of making incremental improvements. Some of the key points include:

- Never tell players what to do without explaining why.

- Talented teachers make difficult material easy to learn by explaining simple concepts clearly before building to more complex ideas. Systems like the New England Patriots system under Bill Belichick and Tom Brady were about as basic as they get. It is thought that the biggest difference between the Patriots back then and the others was relentless training. Patriots coaches were obsessed with player development, focusing each player on one or two training objectives at a time.

- Understanding a play or skill intellectually is not the same as being able to execute it. You have to repeatedly practice every play or skill to ensure each player FEELS it.

- Encourage players to strive for excellence and take pride in DAILY improvement. There should be performance goals for each training session and each game.

- Encourage each player to improve at least one aspect of their game each week and hold them accountable for it, regardless of the team result.

Quite often, when I am coaching, the feedback I get from the coaches in attendance tends to be that my sessions are 'intense' and that I place a huge emphasis on things being done right. I'd like to think I'm almost obsessive about things being right and like to insist on the work we do being of the highest quality, with the highest energy and focus.

In a youth development program, a good rule of thumb is that the youngest kids get the most leeway, and with the older players, you can demand a bit more. You don't have to scream and shout to ensure standards are met. You just need to have standards and stick to them. What you let go is what you allow!

Also:

- There is no substitute for repetition

- No coach or player should ever stand still to admire their work.

- Encourage the reserves/seconds to put performance pressure on to help improve the firsts, allowing the coaching environment to focus on them as much as the firsts. This can also apply to the top 13 v the rest if there are not enough players for the reserves.

Key Points from This Chapter

- Most successful sports programs around the world have a structured youth development framework in place to provide a pathway to senior team representation

- Raise expectations immediately upon your arrival in a coaching job

- There is no such thing as the 'finished article' when it comes to footballers. There are always areas to improve.

- Teach players the important lessons from both winning and losing. Particularly when coaching juniors

- Never tell players what to do without explaining why

A Storm-like Coach – By Billy Kitt

I attended St Gregory's College in Campbelltown, Sydney whilst under contract at the Wests Tigers and was coached by Lee Addison for my two years there. My two years were both premiership-winning years and I had the pleasure of being half-back of the team that won the 2011 title.

Mine and Lee's relationship was very similar to that a father and son might have. It was a relationship full of mutual respect, but we did butt heads a lot too!

Lee helped me to see the game differently from how the coaches of the Wests Tigers did and although that style wasn't enjoyed at the Tigers, I then moved to the Melbourne Storm where it was fully appreciated. Lee's program at St Gregory's was super close to the program I experienced at the Melbourne Storm in terms of training intensity and focus on skills and far apart from what I experienced at the Tigers.

Without the guidance of Lee at St Gregory's who coached so similarly to those at the Storm, I know I would not have had any success in Melbourne. The good coaches at that club are good coaches for a reason and they are in a stable organisation. That is why Craig Bellamy and so many of his staff have been at the one club for twenty-plus years.

Whilst I didn't always enjoy the lessons as a 16-year-old, I came to appreciate them all in later years.

The moral of the story is, to listen to those who know Rugby League. It will set you up for greatness in great clubs.

Billy Kitt has played at the Wests Tigers and Melbourne Storm. He is now the coach of Bathurst Panthers in the PMP Premiership in Country New South Wales

9

A Strength and Conditioning Overview

If we want to keep involved in the game when playing days are over, two of the most common pathways available are to become a technical/tactical coach or a strength and conditioning coach, more commonly known as an 'S&C' coach. S&C coaches tend to get characterised as not having sufficient football knowledge to influence that side of things, so they are often encouraged to 'stay in their lane', whilst us technical or tactical coaches tend to get pigeonholed as just that, and as people who need to leave the fitness and gym training to the experts.

It probably won't surprise you at this stage to know I have resisted as much as I can the need to pigeonhole people in my coaching staff or to separate completely the fitness and skill work that the players under my care will take part in. Neither do I like to be pigeonholed myself!

I took the decision almost instantly upon deciding I wanted to coach, that even though I never wanted to be an expert at strength & conditioning, I would always strive to know enough to have my 'finger on the pulse' and to be able to ask the right questions of any S&C coaches I worked with. As a result, I believe I have developed some excellent working formulae, and they have returned some excellent results.

I have for many years, taken the approach that the 'whole session is conditioning'. As soon as the players start warming up, their heart rates will start increasing and the process of conditioning begins. I have worked extensively with S&C coaches over the years to formulate sessions that do the trick.

Some of my earliest coaching experiences saw me work closely with one of the UK's most respected experts in strength and conditioning-related disciplines. He also coached me as a player when I played for an international universities side, and I remember clearly the moment he introduced these 'new' stretches to us that involved doing a series of dynamic, whole-body movements. He was asking us to do these as far back as 1998.

For asking us to carry out these movements (which none of us had ever seen or experienced before), 'Twisty' copped some playful yet cutting barbs from the squad who were confused as to what the benefits of our new movements were. (I think at one stage I asked if we were doing Michael Flatley's 'The Riverdance').

The movements Craig Twist was showing us are now commonplace in the sporting world and known as dynamic stretches. This method of stretching was shown as an alternative to the static stretch routines we had been so used to and brought up on. Confused as to how we could be ready to train after doing the Riverdance for ten minutes, many of us used our drinks break as an excuse to crack out some of the more familiar shapes that we were experienced in. Imagine twenty large, hairy blokes cracking out some amateur yoga movements, questioning Twisty's sanity, confused about our masculinity all of a sudden as we were complaining about the 'fairy stuff' we'd just been asked to do, and you'll get the picture. Enjoy that picture in your mind with my compliments!

The Craig Twist who put us through that ordeal in 1998 is now Professor Craig Twist, Subject Head and Professor of Sport and Exercise Science in the School of Sport and Exercise Sciences at Liverpool John Moores University, which in 2018 was ranked as the 60th best University out of 1907 across 108 countries and regions in the world. He was also one of the authors of the book I mentioned a few chapters ago titled *'The Science of Rugby'*. I was lucky to play under Craig and then, as a coach, cut many of my coaching teeth working closely with him.

By 2002, when I was on the coaching staff with him, he was furnishing us with graphs outlining the physical responses of our players during games, broken down by position on the field. The players had taken to the field in heart rate monitors, which at the time, were at the cutting edge. Even the new breed of player was complaining about the inconvenient contraption they had to wear! They were complaining even more when they were also required to don them in training, but this constant stream of accumulated data was then used to help us plan training at either 'below match intensity', 'match intensity' or 'above match intensity'.

The weight training sessions we asked the players to do lasted half the time they (and we) were used to. They consisted of five or six exercises, most of them functional 'whole body' movements and all very specific to the game of rugby league. By the time the players had finished their core and abdominal exercises, many were feeling that they were somehow cheating and that they needed to train for lots longer because they weren't ready to collapse. A few months later, some of our players (all students at Universities or Colleges and therefore part-time, amateur players) went up against some full-time Super League professionals in the gym as part of a television piece. Any viewers would have found it hard to tell which players were full-time professionals and which ones weren't.

When I arrived a few years later in Australia and at Manly Sea Eagles, they were approaching the peak of their footballing powers. Their Head Coach at the time was Des Hasler, himself a fitness-mad player before taking up the clipboard and someone who started as an S&C coach before circumstance led him to the hot seat. Under Des, the Sea Eagles were to pioneer many sports science initiatives in the NRL, leading to three Grand Final appearances between 2007 and 2011 where they won two of them. Hasler was dubbed by many in the media as the 'professor' or 'mad scientist' as the conjecture, and stories (and some lies) started to leak out about how the Sea Eagles were leading Rugby League's preparation race.

When I trekked 'out West' and to Penrith Panthers to keep the coaching flame burning, you can imagine how happy I was to hear an accent that wasn't too dissimilar to mine bellowing out in the gym. Carl Jennings, as Northern English as warm beer, was the head of S & C at Panthers under Head Coach Matt Elliott. These men well and truly brought me under their wing, and I was continually part of and privy to more discussions about preparation at the NRL level than I had ever been. I was becoming part of the furniture at the club that summer, so much so that when the team were asked to do conditioning games in training if the sides were unequal, this author was sometimes asked to make up the numbers. There were rumours that Coach Elliott rushed to the finance manager of the Panthers after seeing me play these games and asked that the club break the bank to sign me as their new front-row star. Nothing eventuated and everyone involved immediately and since, for some reason has denied it!

What is undeniable is Matt Elliott was always looking at new, cutting-edge ways to prepare elite players. Back in 1997, his Bradford Bulls team had steamrollered their way to their first Super League title which was only their third top-tier premiership in history and their first in almost two decades – decades that had been dominated mostly by the all-conquering Wigan sides. Elliott and Jennings worked to create one of the biggest sides I have ever seen, and they didn't lack skill, either. They won the competition by topping the table seven points clear of their nearest rival, scoring 153 more points and conceding 21 less than them, too.

By the end of the first decade of the 21st century, they had done some good things at Canberra Raiders and were now at the Panthers, a club that seemed to have lost its way somewhat since their own 2003 Premiership success and was on the brink of some much-needed change throughout the organisation.

Despite some of the rumoured unrest in and around the club in general, Elliott and the coaching staff were, by the time I was with them, very much connoisseurs of the game-based approach to skill development and conditioning, hence my world-class cameo in some of them.

I enjoyed a summer spending every day at Penrith Panthers headquarters before I started my first season at St Gregory's College, the job that was to transform my life (for the better). Spending so much time in close proximity to what was going on and helping out where I was needed cemented my belief that I was a 'games-based' coach too and that when I had a chance to run my own program from top to bottom, that's how I was going to go. I also knew I needed to lean very much on the sports science experts who were employed in the school. My experiences with Twisty, Manly and then Penrith were integral to setting me on this path and held me in good stead, but I wasn't an expert and never ran a conditioning game without taking on and deferring to the advice of experts in the field.

At St Gregory's I was faced with half a squad that were training at NRL clubs for most of the week and half that weren't getting that training. I set up two groups accordingly, one that did everything with us and the other that had to attend all training, but only had to partake in the field sessions that didn't contain small-sided conditioning games (one a week). This ended up being the second pre-season I ever led that didn't contain one 'traditional' fitness drill or shuttle (the first was at Sea Eagles). We just played either small-sided games for skill development and conditioning or 13v13 'scrimmage' games to learn how we wanted to play strategically. We also used teachers as strength coaches in the gym to develop programs with input from myself - inspired by the teachings of Twisty and what I had seen in those NRL environments.

I ventured up to Queensland very confident in the processes by now. The success of these methods was confirmed again at Ipswich, where we invested in GPS units and heart rate monitors to tell us exactly how hard the players were working, how many kilometres they were running and at what speeds, in real time, on I-Pads. By the third year of my time in Queensland, I had charts on my office wall that were mapping and monitoring everything the players were doing, so much so, that we could start to predict when we were at risk of overloading the players. This helped us to lower training intensities, accordingly.

Many of you reading will have never been exposed to some of the experiences I have, and I understand this. I have been part of enough environments as a coach, coach mentor or observer to know that our game is not resplendent with teams everywhere playing conditioning and skill games. An awful lot of it is either the exact opposite or game-based practice is only a small percentage of all the training routines out there. Games, by their nature, are variable and without GPS and heart rate monitors, they are very hard to measure. Coaches of all kinds tend to like to feel they have control of what their players are doing and players running in all sorts of directions with no markers on the ground highlighting the distance being travelled by players can be somewhat confusing.

I do strongly believe, however, that the era of 'four to six weeks of pre-season' (A.K.A not seeing a ball and just being run into the ground instead) followed by 'ball work' for a week or two before games start, should be well and truly confined to history. I would go as far as to say that if you are doing 'fitness' work with your squad and you have no real knowledge behind the choices you are taking in giving your players said work then you are taking a huge risk. In 2024 alone, I have heard several coaches explain, or I have seen with my own eyes, fitness sessions that were either a carbon copy of something the coach did as a player themselves several years before, something they were making up in the car on their way to training, or even worse, as the session unfolded. I think this speaks to a worrying culture in our game.

We have already looked at how the sport has evolved from a skills and tactical perspective but only briefly touched on the fitness and strength-related improvements. Since the last two decades of the 20th century, Rugby League training has been characterised as tough and uncompromising and that is nothing to be ashamed of. What is questionable, however, is the direction it has been taken in at times, by coaches that judge session quality on how many players vomit outrageously during and after it. The machismo that all of us have at some time or other seen, or maybe even displayed, is probably a significant side effect associated with playing and coaching an, at times, brutal sport such as Rugby League.

I do not think it is too hard to expect any coach operating at what is quarter time in the 21st century to do some research about some basic principles of safe conditioning for Rugby League Football.

An exercise designed to get maximal intensity in working repetitions on each occasion would have a higher rest figure than the duration of the work figure. For example, 1:1.5, 1:2 or 1:3 and so on. The activities then performed are categorised by fast, explosive actions that require complete recovery before being attempted again. A good example of this is a sprint.

Put in a very simplified manner, your players should be doing some endurance work in the earliest parts of preparation and the work must be periodised and tapered down before competition. Unfortunately, the first line of that last paragraph – ending with the word 'work' represents the only thing some coaches are aware of. They have some idea that they need to 'flog' the players (give them endurance) to make them 'fitter' but that's where the knowledge ends. I have seen so often coaches do this work off the top of their heads or by replicating drills or activities they did as players, all in the name of 'fitness'.

In this type of training, skill work is done after the fitness work. Often, players are too tired to concentrate after going through such an ordeal. Also, if we want to get into the nitty gritty of analysing the best way to teach skills and generate skill acquisition, I can promise you that, attempting to do skills after a 'flogging' of 15 to 45 minutes does not feature as a method in any academic studies!

This book is not a conditioning book and isn't attempting to be one, but it can guide you to some advice and ideas. On the Rugby League Coach YouTube channel, check out the playlists and look for the S&C one, or for more detailed advice head to rugbyleaguecoach.com.au and click on the S&C section. As always, you are advised to take all relevant precautions and seek appropriate medical advice before undertaking a fitness-related regime or directing others to follow one.

The one-percenters - developing your players physically beyond fitness work

Most of the coaches reading this book will coach a team twice a week. That's approximately five hours of 'contact time' as an absolute maximum.

In the offseason, that leaves the poor coach with concerns about their players' lifestyles with stress symptoms for a further 163 hours a week. During the season, add a game day period of up to five hours again. Only 158 hours to worry about what they are up to now. Let's imagine each player sleeps eight hours a night (absolute maximum) which leaves 102 hours of awake time.

No matter how well you train your players on the field, what they do before and after training and often, away from the observant eye of the coach on any given day is just as important as training when it comes to top performance. You can run the most perfect pre-season and in-season training regime in rugby league history but if the players in your care aren't doing everything right away from the training paddock, then each thing that player does that is not 'on the money' will detract from performance. The severity of that Ill-disciplined happening will determine if it is a small decrease in performance or instead, something bigger. It is better for the player to successfully carry out and maintain adherence to as many of the one-percenters – the things that can aid successful performance - as they can.

Obviously, the higher the level you coach at, the more resources you will have at your disposal, but there are several practical ways that, even with no budget or very little money available, coaches can instil small things that make a big difference. With that in mind, let's look at what could be done. The first two apply to training sessions, the rest of them, to the 102 hours the players are away from you.

In training - Warm-ups and cool-downs

As much as doing thorough warm-ups can impact technical and tactical coaching time, or indeed fitness or speed work, the importance of gradually warming the body up deliberately and for the appropriate amount of time should not be underestimated. Neither should a cool down in terms of the impact it can have on the next session.

In training - Speed, agility and quickness

Developing speed, agility and quickness (SAQ) successfully in your players requires complete and utter focus on it over a sustained number of training sessions. Where other activities apart from SAQ need to be undertaken in a session, the SAQ component should occur at the start of training, after a thorough warm-up. Doing it any later in the session risks fatiguing the muscles and therefore, the quality of the speed-related tasks is unlikely to be completed in a fashion that can generate the appropriate improvements.

Another important note about any speed-related activities – every repetition should be followed by a complete rest before the next repetition in order to target the appropriate energy systems.

Hydration

Water makes up approximately two-thirds of our bodies, so it stands to reason that it is rather important to us! Being hydrated when training and playing helps us to maintain an appropriate body temperature as it naturally rises when we are active. The inevitable perspiration from the physical activity associated with the game also speeds up fluid loss.

Lack of hydration can cause drops in concentration, response times, endurance levels and decision-making. It can also create a higher risk of injury - all things we coaches don't want our teams to suffer from.

How can the players (and therefore any human being) tell that they are dehydrated? Their urine (wee/pee/piss) isn't clear or like a straw/very pale, yellow colour. Advice on how much water to drink varies from a minimum of two litres a day to up to five litres, dependent on climate, humidity, activity and body mass considerations. There is also knowledge out there that air conditioners, heaters and larger artificial lights (found regularly in workspaces) can also be a reason to increase consumption levels.

Sip it, don't gulp it.

Diet

We are what we eat.

The end.

(*Note: If you want a diet sheet for your players or yourself, email me at admin@rugbyleaguecoach.com.au and I'll send it to you for free*).

Monitor players' strength training routines

In the last few decades, there has been a multitude of gyms and other fitness centres that popped up in so much of the Western world at least. Wherever I have travelled around the world, including beyond the Western one, it has not been hard to locate a gym if I wanted to use one. As a result of this trend and availability, many budding Rugby League players often go to gyms in their leisure time. This applies to children, teens and adults in many places where the sport is on offer.

We males, when in our teens and twenties in particular, often want to get a big chest, shoulders and arms, plus a six-pack so we can impress people on the beach with our shirt off. (FYI - I am still a work in progress but approaching my peak in my mid-40s). More and more, kids are being encouraged by their parents to hit the gym or do weight training before they hit their teens to thrive on a rugby league field. 'A' Grade and amateur players seem to be stronger and more athletic than ever in some of the more advanced geographical areas where the game is played. That's often a result of the activities they do in the gym away from their club training two nights a week.

The problem that occurs if these players are doing lots of upper body work but neglecting their bottom half is that, over time, that imbalance in the body can cause problems. Those who do lots of chest, shoulders and arms (and maybe even legs) but neglect the back of the body, can also have posture problems and bodily balance issues. All this eventual imbalance means that the rugby league player that is running around functionally out of balance, puts certain ligaments, tendons, joints and bones under certain types of pressure over a sustained period.

Therefore, it stands to reason that we coaches need to be aware as much as we can of what our players are doing in the gym and we need, wherever possible, to get appropriate advice from experts in the field in order to help our players as much as we can.

In my experience, players in any scenario who are doing resistance work, must be following a functional training program. That is training that will benefit them for Rugby League and duplicates some muscle movements found in the sport. It is also fundamental that players are doing what is appropriate for their age. Using school years as an example, players starting in high school (year 7) should ideally be commencing a six-year plan of resistance training, year 8's a five-year plan, year 9's a four-year plan and so on.

Unfortunately, what happens throughout much of the sport is that a player is passed from coach to coach as they grow through a system and there is little in the way of information exchange between coaching parties. Team coaches often notice trends in their newly adopted team through observing skill levels and tactical nous within a group, but less considered, very often, is what strength training programs the players have followed before arriving to work under a new coaching team. This can even happen at some of the higher levels, with efforts made by strength coaches to protect their knowledge and offerings.

If you can hire a strength coordinator for your team or club, you don't necessarily need to have a gym at your venue to ensure successful outcomes. Having someone co-ordinate the resistance training that is done by members of your club can be a great help as they can write programs for teams or individual players, amend any current programs that players are doing in their own time and coordinate the activities, performance and testing protocols for all grades.

Sports science development

Just because you don't have the budget available to spend money on sports science initiatives doesn't mean you can't get some initiatives going! One trick is to contact the local education establishments – the universities, colleges or schools. When approaching them, ask to speak to the Science or the Physical Education departments. These approaches could help you acquire some resources, be they human or tangible even if for a loan period.

Sports science and associated expertise can add value to your team in some of the following ways.

- Fitness and related testing

- Medical screening

- Dietary advice

- Sports related psychology

- Biomechanics training

- Player development plans/player welfare

Like with taking on anything new and shiny, the challenges for us coaches are that we don't get over-excited by sports science initiatives to the point where they take over the coaching environment or impact the confidence of the players. For example, if you have a player who is talented but arrived for pre-season overweight and unfit because of some external factors that neither they nor you can control and the player shows a great attitude from day one, too much fitness testing, skin fold testing and the like can expose the flaws for everyone to see. It can also destroy the confidence of a player.

As I write this paragraph, (December 2024), I am hearing testimony of an under 18's player who, told he was 'too small' by many coaches in 2024, hired a strength coach (who works at a State League Cup club by the way) on my recommendation. He has changed his diet completely and trained the house down in the gym, building 11kg of mass in a matter of months. He is still a very lean person. The coaches of the rep team he is trying to make have put him in the 'fit to play' club (it used to be known as fat club but the PC brigade doesn't like that anymore) due to *'not being fast enough'* at a fitness test, by a matter of seconds. He is a forward but they put him in the backs category for some reason when looking at fitness scores. The family don't feel like they know why this is the case and haven't, in their minds *'received a straight answer'*. The rep team tested their players on day one when they got together again a matter of weeks later and was tested again after the Christmas period.

A lot of the coach's decisions regarding options around these interventions should also be mindful of the existing culture of the team so that the risk of 'over-coaching' is avoided. Giving members of the team too much information and too many chances to fail too soon may be a symptom of suffering from paralysis by analysis. I'd imagine that's what's happening with the scenario explained in the last paragraph.

The mental aspects of the sport

As a society, we know more than ever about the importance of mental health (I delve into my own experiences around this topic in Part Three). As a coach, you're likely an amateur sports psychologist without even knowing it!

In the lead-up to a rugby league match, the way a player thinks and feels emotionally about the game will determine how they behave or play in the game. To achieve the goal of winning the match or playing a satisfactory role, a player must learn to develop coping strategies that reduce the internal tension and anxieties that accumulate during the week leading up to a game.

A coach often, subconsciously, will use psychological ploys to deal with such scenarios. For example, a coach may praise one player or berate another, depending on what they feel will be the best way to motivate each individual. A coach often sets a 'theme' for the training week, eg: *"It's going to be a tough one this week, guys"* and a lot of what the coach says or does will have an impact on the players in their care. Indeed, among the roles that are often linked with that of a coach are motivator, counsellor, friend, mentor, advisor, supporter, organiser and so much more. All this before we get to the X's and O's!

Keeping players focused

In a powerful example of the power of positive thinking, one of the first things former Liverpool FC Manager Jurgen Klopp said when arriving in Merseyside, UK to coach the round ball game, was that his new charges needed to turn from *"Doubter to Believer"*. He managed to coach the side to some very excellent outcomes during his tenure, a vast improvement on what had been achieved throughout several years before. More about Mr Klopp's coaching later.

In a possible example of positive thinking crossing into complacency, Brisbane Broncos won the two opening rounds of the 2020 NRL competition. One win was from a daunting trip to North Queensland but the other, at home against a South Sydney side destined to make the finals and coached by 'super coach' Wayne Bennett, would make observers froth at the prospects of this young and talented Brisbane side. Confidence was high and fans and the local media shared that positivity.

Yet while Souths would recalibrate to make the finals that season - including making the Grand Final the following year - Brisbane Broncos went into freefall. They would lose seventeen games, winning only one more all season. Destined for the dreaded Wooden Spoon (the faux award given to those finishing in the last position on the ladder), their embattled coach Anthony Seibold left the club after thirteen rounds.

The reason this time sticks out so much as a potential example of the importance of managing emotions within a sports team is that 2020 was a season like no other – it was the season impacted by the COVID-19 pandemic. Government restrictions on gatherings meant that teams, groups and crowds could not mingle together for the best part of two months from March to May of that year, forcing everyone including NRL players, into isolation at home. When restrictions started getting eased off it was announced a slightly reduced NRL season would resume.

The Broncos lost to the Parramatta Eels and then the Sydney Roosters on the resumption. Then, in Round 5, they were 18-0 up against Manly Sea Eagles at half time, having played excellently. They conspired to lose the match 20-18. If they had won that game then they would have probably won at least one of the next two, yet losing to Manly in such a fashion showed to many seasoned observers that there was some mental fragility there. A trip to Newcastle followed, and again, a disappointing performance was served up, and they lost. As a result, when it came to them playing unfancied neighbours Gold Coast Titans at home in round 7 (a game their fans and most observers expected them to win), they were seemingly more worried about losing than focused on winning. They smacked of a team that was shot mentally and lost the game heavily.

Of course, many other factors contribute to successful performance or otherwise, but it was very hard to pinpoint many other ways where the Broncos were getting it wrong. They had arguably the most talented roster in the competition and a side capable of finals football in the eyes of many. The isolation period during the government restrictions is the outlier. Alone with their thoughts, rather than being comforted and influenced by in-person group think and strong mentors, it was the most unique test of the mental strength of so many people in general, never mind those who did professional sports for a living. Did the young Broncos get complacent?

A STRENGTH AND CONDITIONING OVERVIEW

One of my favourite ever coaches to study is another round ball coach, Sir Alex Ferguson. His success speaks is unparalleled in British soccer. He has said in much of his writing and commentary on coaching and leadership that:

"Complacency is a disease"

Journalist James Cambridge, writing for the UK Express newspaper in 2016, wrote:

> SIR ALEX FERGUSON has claimed he was so successful at Manchester United because he eradicated complacency among his players.
>
> Ferguson spent 27 years with United, winning 38 major trophies including 13 Premier League titles.
>
> And the 74-year-old has revealed the secret to his success was ensuring none of his players ever got complacent.
>
> "The important part of being a successful team is to avoid complacency," Ferguson said at the World Business Forum in Milan.
>
> "It is a disease that has to be guarded against.
>
> "If we were winning at half-time, that was brought up – avoid it, it is a disease.
>
> "If you lose a goal, you lose the game – keep your foot on the pedal.
>
> "With complacency, you do not see it happening, you do not see where it is coming from.
>
> "But, when it hits you, you cannot get out of it, you can't eradicate it.
>
> "So that was an important part of how we constructed a winning mentality at Manchester United, to avoid complacency."

There are practical ways that coaches can help their players without studying for a degree in sports psychology. For example, working on controlling players' mindsets so that they focus on the tasks at hand rather than becoming overcome by emotion is one method. During the week of a big game, encouraging players to think about the key components of the game they have to focus on as a team or as individuals is a good way of doing this. Telling a team to focus on completing the first five attacking sets of a game and to follow it with a strong kick chase is a good way for them to settle into a game. Encouraging a player to take a carry of the ball early is a great way to help them shed some nerves quickly,

One of my big coaching initiatives is a focus on the importance of the 'next action' after a good or bad moment in a game. When the good things happen, teams that don't control their emotions can start getting too confident in their ability, believing that everything is going to go well, and this can lead to over-confidence and over-playing, a cause of unforced errors. Alternatively, errors can be compounded if players mentally dwell on an error. Making one error leads to another then another.

When studying games, I have found that tries tend to be scored after anything between two to five (or more in tough games) sets of sustained pressure at good levels of football. Tries don't just 'happen' for attacking sides, they have to be worked at. Occasionally, a team will need only one set but the vast majority of the time, they have to build pressure over a sustained period.

Staying in this 'grind' is essential for football teams and this can be hard, particularly for impatient youngsters who grow up on a diet of highlight reels of great tries on social media. What those clips often don't show is the hard work that has gone on beforehand to create the opportunity for that try!

I call these phases of the game, the 'battle'. The battle ends when one team scores a try, and a new battle begins with the resultant restart. Have you ever heard the phrase *"We have won the battle but lost the war"*? That's an idiom for winning a small victory but losing the larger one - a mental approach often used by the military. To win a game of Rugby League, you have to win more battles than the opponent. It's as simple as that.

The next time you watch a game, including games at NRL and Super League level, have a look at how many teams may get 10-0 or 12-0 up, only for it to become 10-10 or 12-12 or similar, moments later. Either this game you are watching is a nip-and-tuck affair between two teams that have low error rates and excellent attacks or, as is more likely, the team that got ahead, got so confident that they 'felt invincible' and tried too hard to get a third score, lost the ball somewhere near the halfway line and gave their opponents an avenue back into the game. An example of this from the NRL level is outlined in-depth in Chapter 11.

To be a ruthless football team, there needs to be a constant focus on the 'next action'. We are seeing efforts to deal with this happen at the professional level with teams getting together in a circle to 'slow breath' together and reset after scoring a try, but these physical efforts are futile if they are not coupled with a relentless focus by the players in that team of starting that whole process of winning another battle, and focusing on the merits of that battle alone, not what happened beforehand.

It pays to think about it in these simple terms. When a team concedes a try, they get a chance to gather under the sticks and have a debrief. This is a debrief that can last anything up to around four minutes. Four minutes to gather breath, reset and work out what went wrong. Those debriefs often start immediately as the ball is put down on the try line by the opposition. While the scorers are celebrating for a minute or more and a kicker is preparing for the conversion attempt, the vanquished are well into their inquiry and focusing on what is needed to turn the tide.

Constantly focusing on the 'next action' has to be practised very regularly and it has to be truly believed by players who have to commit to it. You will never truly know how well they are committing to it until you see the evidence play out on the field, in the subsequent battles. I coached one player who used to tap the studs on both his boots as a mental cue that what he had just done was over and what was to come was more important. Cricket batters have some excellent ways of focusing on the next action after each ball that they face. Watch a game of cricket and watch how each batter resets themselves after each delivery, whether they score from it or play a hideous shot. They will often follow the same routine, many walking away from the 'crease' and the stumps in order to turn back and start over anew.

Another strategy that can help players to always look at 'next action' is to encourage players to focus on the 'processes' that lead to a victory or title success and not the eventual 'outcomes. Outcomes are the result – the try that is scored or the match result at the end. Players who focus on outcomes tend to imagine themselves scoring a try or lifting the trophy at the end of the game and/or season. Those who focus on the 'process' focus on the various stages of how to get there and nothing else.

With every team I have successfully led to a grand final or a title win, at the start of the campaign, we have focused on nothing but 'winning a game' and the processes that lead to that outcome. By focusing on grabbing a win at some point, we are taking the pressure off each individual game, and we are also not looking at the prize at the end of the season, only trying to get our campaign up and running.

Quite often, the teams I have inherited have struggled beforehand and expectations outside our four walls were low. The competitions, unless a knockout cup, were round-robin at the start at least, so if we were to lose or draw our first game it would never be fatal. In longer campaigns, losing more than one game at the start isn't fatal either. Whatever we dished out in game one (or later) we just learned the lessons from it and made sure we were better the week after. I have been privy as either an insider or close outsider to so many campaigns that have been lost by coaches not handling any defeat in the right way.

That now brings me to one of the most commonly discussed things in rugby league circles, the coach who delivers a 'spray' to his or her team at half-time or full-time following a poor performance or a loss. There are so many commentators who like to say, that coaches *"only have one"* - meaning once a coach has lost their rag in the sheds, it loses its power if it happens again.

I prefer to mentor coaches to approach players as human beings who deserve respect. If your players are trying their unmentionables off, they don't deserve a tongue-lashing. It's a very tough sport we play and if they have gone out there and given their all, that's all you can ask. They deserve praise for that. If they lose, they need guidance on how to fix it.

Of course, there are exceptions! When my Poland side was preparing and playing in the 2018 Emerging Nations World Championships, they set a very high standard for each other. There was a high care factor in the group, and they pushed each other to greater heights. Until our second-round match versus Japan that is.

We were slightly ahead on the scoreboard at halftime against Japan, but the absolute crap the players were dishing out in the first half was nothing like what we had seen in the warm-up game or the round-one win. I could see that some players thought this international business was easy, they were lazy in thought and concentration, if not in physical endeavour. They also seemed a little comfortable and appeared to be acting arrogantly to me. These are all warning signs that the team is starting to drop into a complacent mindset – and complacency is a disease.

I gave the players both barrels at halftime. I significantly raised my voice, with the key being to criticise the 'acts' not the 'actors'. I didn't question any players' manhood, single anyone out or tell them they were awful human beings, instead,

I questioned rather vociferously what I had just witnessed in the first half and how this didn't represent what we had been doing up until that point. The players were shocked – they were leading on the scoreboard after all, and it was the first time that I had been angry with them. They learned at that moment that being ahead in the game alone wasn't good enough as I was preparing them for tougher tests ahead. I also made a point at the end of my energetic and assertive sermon to say to all the players *"love you all"* and we made sure we all shook hands and backslapped each other before we went out again. It was a far better performance in the second half, and I never had to raise my voice again.

I have also used this strategy many times in longer campaigns, indeed, there are too many to mention. The key lesson is to focus on the words you use as a coach, even if they are delivered in a louder manner. Avoid ranting and losing your mind. Don't disrespect anyone. But do give players and the group ways to improve and let them know what they've been doing wrong.

Have I done it perfectly every time in my coaching career? No. Will you? No. We are all a work in coaching progress. We are all just pushing along, trying to figure it out. But being aware of where we are in terms of the performance of this kind of coaching debrief at this juncture is key. It will help us refine it and get better as we get older and (hopefully) wiser.

Key Points from This Chapter

- The 'whole session is conditioning'. As soon as the players start warming up, their heart rates will start increasing and the process of conditioning begins

- If you are doing 'fitness' work with your squad and you have no real knowledge behind the choices you are taking in giving your players that work then you are taking a huge risk.

- Your players should be doing some endurance work in the earliest parts of preparation and the work must be periodised and tapered down prior to competition.

- What your players will do away from training is important

- Developing speed, agility and quickness (SAQ) successfully in your players requires complete and utter focus on it over a sustained number of training sessions

- Lack of hydration can cause drops in concentration, response times, endurance levels and decision- making. It can also create a higher risk of injury

- We are what we eat

- Focus on processes not outcomes

He made me feel like the best player in the world! – Se'e Kali

I was playing Rugby League and had made an Auckland rep side in New Zealand when I was introduced to Lee Addison by my coach Fita Hala, who is now with the Canterbury Bulldogs. Lee was in NZ scouting and was Head Coach at Ipswich State High School in Queensland.

I moved in 2014 to the school with some other boys to get coached by him. I have big memories of when I first moved over with some great players and people. The training was tough, and I found myself losing some kilos and getting fitter very quickly, but I'll be honest, in the first couple of weeks there, I was mucking around a lot and probably going with the flow a bit too much. Lee had me training in first grade until his patience with me snapped.

Lee's way of motivating me was unique but it worked a treat. I have since learned that he was upset that I wasn't putting in enough effort and he said to me:

"Being honest with you Se'e, we only asked you to come over to make the other overseas boys feel comfortable and you're doing a great job of it! You'll be a great reserve-grade player for us!"

Straight after the chat I rang my Mum and told her I wanted to come home *"right now"* and that I thought the coach was *"crazy and he doesn't like me"*. My mum told me to stick it out because I was already there in Australia.

From that moment, when we were doing Lee's favourite – 13v13 training - all my mates were on the first-grade side of the ball while I was on the reserve-grade side. My choices were to cry and run away from this or to act on my mum's advice and stick it out. I buckled down extra hard and eventually made the first-grade side again and I never left it after that!

In 2014, we went undefeated through the season and won the second division title and managed to get ourselves promoted to the 'Super 6' Langer Trophy. For me personally, Lee hooked me up with a local club where I played Under 18's (winning the comp) and also some A-grade. I also made the representative side for that area, the Metropolitan West team, to play in the Queensland Schools Championships. There was also a big article about me in the Courier Mail newspaper. I was on my way thanks to Lee's psychological ploy to motivate me and my mum's advice.

The key thing I learned from Lee Addison that year was about working hard in all areas of training and that included the gym. Doing so much training and including changing our bodies in the gym was a massive change from what we did in New Zealand. Rugby League had become a full-time thing for me and Addison kept me humble, by continually telling me when we were winning and getting accolades that *"Complacency is a disease"* and a constant quote of his that I always carry with me to this day - *"Don't fall in love with yourself"*.

To prepare for the 2015 season in the top division, Lee and the school leadership used me in a mentoring role to make phone calls from the school to any players who wanted to have a big year with us in 2015. They included Kalani Ili who eventually captained South Sydney Under 20's and Kiko Manu who, after joining us Ipswich High, went to Canterbury Bulldogs and made his NRL debut a few years later.

When 2015 arrived, Addison said to me *"Big Wuss - you're going to be our captain"*. (Big Wuss is our nickname for each other!) I was humbled and I feel for the first half of the year I grew in the role. But I made a mistake from a football perspective, but the decision I made ended up being one of the greatest life blessings too.

In our mid-season holiday camp, I broke the rules of the camp by asking Lee if I could go to the supermarket when really, I was going to see a girl. Addison caught me out and he was upset with me. He didn't go mad at me; he was just sad. The whole team also gave me the 'evils'. Lee had no option but to take the captaincy off me. That was the culture in the team that Lee created, and he delivered the news. You mess up, you deal with the consequences. We had a very tight relationship as captain and coach, but he still told me straight and I respected that. He also never treated me any differently after it, I just wasn't his captain anymore. I appreciated that too. He didn't disown me.

At the end of that year, just before I left school, I got my partner pregnant. Lee Addison was the first person I told outside of family and he gave me nothing but support and care and still does to this day. That's the biggest thing with the Big Wuss you see, he's all about the relationship he has with his players. He's not just a coach but also like a big brother or a father figure to all of us. He didn't and doesn't care if we made it in the game or not. His coaching and mentoring were all about being a genuine bloke and having a great relationship with teammates and staff. This was all massive to me and showed that he cared about you the person not just the player.

I even got to meet his dad after our first 'Super 6' game and I saw first-hand the close father-and-son relationship he has with his old man. His Dad, so nervous about his son's teams, constantly walked around the field chain-smoking when we were playing because he wanted his boys' team (us) to do so well.

That's another thing I carry with me to this day. I am a current NRL agent, and I am in that space, working with talented players with a potential in Rugby League and it's all come into my life because of Lee who helped me become a mentor when I was 16, 17 and 18 years of age. I want to open doors and get players opportunities, but just like my old coach was with me, I am honest with them at all times.

That's the biggest thing about the Big Wuss, he never really 'beat around the bush'. He even loved players who were in our C grade. It was about the character you showed, not just how you played, He also told us all to work hard for each other first and foremost and not to worry about our individual highlight reels.

I was never one of the best players in New Zealand. When Lee found me, I was in the 'development' rep side which meant I wasn't in the first-choice teams. But when I came to play under him at Ipswich, he made me feel like the best player in the world and took me to higher levels and I did get some NRL club interest. I carry that now when I meet people, I take them for who they are. Unbelievably, I am now in my 11th year in Australia and Lee has passed so much down to me that I can give to my kids. For generations of my family moving forward, we can say to the kids, it's all because of the Big Wuss, the Pommy Man who got this Big Wuss Kiwi and brought him to Kangaroo land to help him chase his dreams.

Se'e Kali is an NRL Player Agent

10

Recruitment and Watching Players

"They lack experience".

So said much of the same media that had also regularly told us the Brisbane Broncos of 2020 and 2021 had a premiership-capable roster.

They were indeed a young squad and once again, I use Alex Ferguson as a guide. He has said several times that a team needs to be a three-way split between young players with their best years ahead, players at their peak and players who are at the experienced end of the scale and that you move on the experienced ones before they get past their used by date.

Although a soccer man, Ferguson's formula is very straightforward and makes sense for any team measure in any team sport. It's a fair measure to use when assessing how the Broncos had got this balance all wrong in those years.

The words the Broncos fans often used to explain their approach was that they were *"building a squad for the future"*. Their coach at the start of 2020, Anthony Seibold, regularly referred to his side as the *"youngest in the competition"*. Ben Ikin, a former Bronco, Origin star and media pundit who would eventually play his own off-field role at the Broncos referred to their skipper, Alex Glenn, as the *'accidental captain'* in a Fox Sports article dated June 5th, 2020.

In the important 'spine' positions, namely hooker, halves and the full-back position, the Broncos previously had players that Ikin described as having *"experience, combination and a good understanding of the clubs' history and culture, traits the coach seemingly didn't value."* They were replaced by players who were a lot less experienced and very early in their careers. Ikin closed his article with thoughts that he couldn't *"quite figure out if the coach is the victim of a broken system or part of the problem."*

On the NRL 360 show on Fox Sports in 2019, he said:

"The senior list management at that club for a while now has been deplorable.

"There are many holes in that roster in key positions to the point now where they are going to go into the market late to try and find themselves a playmaker for next year, in a squad that's out of balance, that's got too much strike and not enough game management.

"And they've left a leadership hole."

The legendary coach Jack Gibson coined the phrase *"The best coaches are the best recruiters".* In some of my own coaching jobs I have had zero chance to recruit players due to one reason or another, but in others, I have had ample opportunity to do so. It is an element of sports administration I have studied and practised for at least half the time I have been a coach.

It is also one of the murkiest areas of sports administration and one of the most cutthroat areas to work in at certain times. It is also hugely time-consuming. A lot of time can be wasted talking to potential prospects who are testing the market and trying to drive up their worth.

As professional, semi-professional (anybody who pays players) or strong amateur clubs scramble for a signature, they often stroke an ego with compliments and talk about future prospects to their prey. Some operators are excellent at being honest and curbing expectations and excitement at this stage, but others (in the form of their desperate recruitment personnel) are not. There are plenty of questionable approaches out there and even if you are full of ethics, transparency, candour and fairness in your recruitment practice, there will be others who will accuse you of not being like that, particularly if they lose out on a player or two to you.

For those of you who coach teenage, young adult and adult players, you may have to deal with player agents as well. The amount of player agents has increased exponentially in the game since the 'Super League War' in the 1990s, which drove player market values up around much of the Rugby League world.

Player agents now gather en-masse at carnivals and tournaments in an attempt to sign the next up-and-coming talents. Just like the old-fashioned and well-coined persona, 'the used car salesman', the 'player agent' or 'player-manager' can also have a huge job ahead of them in gaining the trust of parents and players and often come across in the same way as would a salesperson trying to sell said used vehicles.

Many around the world are excellent, ethical operators but some of them are, unfortunately, a different kettle of fish. So many of them fill the kids and their family's heads full of promises, full of praise and sometimes, frankly, full of shit - all so they can get their catch, the client

I have all sorts of experiences, mostly good but some not as good when it comes to the recruitment game. So many in fact, that I could write a book all about those tales! The idea of this particular book though, is to give you some practical advice on how you can develop your coaching and therefore, in this chapter, how to develop your own recruitment strategies.

Get the right people on the bus

I do not know who coined the phrase, to 'get the right people on the bus' but I do know that I have heard it numerous times from leaders of all kinds and no doubt you have, too. The bus in question, you would hope, is a one-way journey to success!

There is no doubt that human resources are often the most important resource in many industries. In a people-focused industry and pastime like playing, coaching and administering Rugby League, humans are hugely important.

Teams can be brought down quickly by poor attitudes, toxicity amongst team members and mercenary attitudes towards positions and promotions. On the field, results can be impacted by selfish players who lack discipline, lack concentration, lack desire, lack care and lack togetherness. When I think back to any grand finals that any of my teams have won at any level, adult or teenage, there have been some traits that stand out when I compare those teams with others. They contained players with:

- Utter determination
- Fighting spirit
- Selflessness – they put the team first
- Huge levels of mental fortitude
- A never-say-die attitude

Also, they:

- Were equally as keen to defend as they were to attack
- Could defend very well for long periods
- Were consistent
- Were happy to do things that made them feel uncomfortable
- Were disciplined, in most if not all aspects of their life
- Had humility
- Were extremely fit
- Were all good people

Melbourne Storm is one of the most successful NRL clubs and, indeed, one of the most successful sporting clubs in Australian sport over the last quarter of a century. They are said to have a 'no dickhead' policy at their club (not sure that's the official policy title but you get my point) and do more background checks on any players they are interested in than any other club I have had the pleasure to deal with. I remember one of their recruitment managers calling me about a player I had coached in my first-grade schoolboy side eight years earlier! I was asked a multitude of questions about everything apart from his footballing ability! I can also promise you that everyone I speak to in the game who has dealt with Melbourne in that realm says they've had similar experiences.

In my experience, the connection between being a good person and being good at Rugby League is strong. In the schoolboy programs, I ran for twelve years or the rep systems I was in prior, every one of those players who were successful in achieving some of the highest accolades in the game were very good people off the field and remain so to this day. Any adult representative teams I have coached have also followed a very similar pattern.

Use the wisdom of crowds

Quite often when recruiting, I will ask my current players who they hate playing against and who they respect from other competitions they have played in. I can easily form a list of players to watch from that. I also talk to people in the game either in person or on the phone and ask a very simple question:

"Who are the best players in/for (insert context)?"

Never underestimate other people and what they can see. Sometimes even the 'untrained eye' is the most valuable because their technical knowledge is, or is close to, zero, so they just see instead...well, who knows what they see! It could be valuable though.

If you go up to the side of the field as a latecomer to the match and ask three or more people who the best player or two on the field are, when the answer is obvious, you'll probably get your answer unanimously and unequivocally. If they've been around that team for a while, you'll hear about a lot of those that aren't 'blue chip' too.

'Blue chip' players are not hard to find in most contexts - that's why they're blue chip! They tend to do amazing things once, twice or a few more times in a game (dependent on their role). I remember coaching my team in 2017 against a side that had former Gold Coast Titan and now New Zealand Warrior Tanah Boyd in the halves and a man who is now a human wrecking ball for Gold Coast Titans and Queensland, the gigantic David Fifita, in the back row. It was hard to escape the feeling that the final score was Lee's team 10 v Boyd and Fifita 18, as the former kicked us into submission and steered his team around the park with the precision of an orchestral conductor while the latter was a younger version of the wrecking ball we now know, who ran in two tries from the halfway line while seemingly giving the impression that it was all too easy for him.

What's harder to do is find the talent that stands out a little less and sometimes, not at all. Let's look at some examples of what some watchers sometimes miss:

- The **middle forward** who doesn't make many (or any) breaks, but they always dominate the collision. They make great metres, mostly accumulatively and consistently. They get behind the ball after a kick return consistently, they take carries in most, if not all sets and don't ever shirk that work. They run good lines and the players tackling them are finding life very difficult. They get very quick play the balls, consistently.

- The **hooker** that passes so efficiently from the base of the ruck that you hardly notice they are there because those running off the ruck are making such good inroads. When they run, they may not electrify the audience, but they make comfortable metres, maximising the space they are given. When they do run, they get very quick play the balls, consistently.

- The **edge forward** that continually runs lines that appear to the casual observer to be decoy runs as the ball passes in front or behind them. They can make good decisions so if the players outside them are in a better position, they'll pass the ball selflessly rather than run themselves. When carrying the ball, they get very quick play the balls, consistently.

- The **halves** that manage the game so well, you're thinking *"This side is well organised'"* yet it's all the other players that are scoring the points, making the breaks and getting on the highlights reel.

- The **outside backs** that make comfortable and consistent metres when advancing the ball and are error-free. They are also good at passing to someone else in better positions than them. Instead of trying to run outside a defender when super close to the sideline, they will turn inside to ensure a quick play the ball and more plays for their team, rather than giving possession away. They get very quick play the balls, consistently.

You may also notice in these examples speed of play the ball was mentioned a lot and I didn't mention defence once! I did it on purpose. And that is the perfect segue to the next two points...

Offence is only 50% of the game

So many observers don't even LOOK at a player's defence! Yet, if all things are equal, defence is 50% of the game! Not looking at defence is absolutely crazy! Crazier still, several first-grade players in both the NRL and Super League have very questionable defensive ability. There are some VERY high-profile players in regular headlines for their attacking efforts in recent years, yet an analysis of their defensive ability would make you wonder how they made first grade and why the opposition isn't running at them constantly.

When looking at players, which players ***don't*** miss tackles? Which players dominate collisions when they tackle? Which players can move laterally easily, meaning they can't easily be stepped by an opponent? Which players don't tire in defence and constantly work? Which players scramble to cover for others' missing tackles? Which players chase kicks energetically or chase down runaway opponents when others decide it's too hard? Which players don't do many tackles, not because they're not trying to, but because the opponents don't want to run at them? Which outside backs are just as good in defence as they are in offence? Which wings and fullbacks catch high kicks and field low ones comfortably?

When Ipswich State High School won the national title in 2022, I said to the coaching staff (and they agreed) that for the first time in the school's history, they had the right mix of 'blue chip' players and others that did all the things mentioned in this section and the last.

The importance of the 'contact line'

When an attacker carries the ball into the defensive line, the exact moment the contact is made by one, two or more defenders, I refer to as the contact line. When people ask me about the top thing I look for in a player, **dominance of the contact line in both attack and defence** is often my answer.

A quick play the ball is a highly valued trait in the list of things that good players do consistently. A play the ball is part of what we in rugby league call 'the ruck' and for many years, the ruck in Rugby League has been described in various ways that all essentially amount to it being the centre of the football universe. As a result, winning it more often than not is seen as essential for successful teams. Individuals winning the contact line in attack and defence is a huge contributor to that on most occasions.

If your team is full of players who win most of the contact lines they're involved in, you're going to be very hard to beat. When coaching, I never watch a game from any other position than from the sideline, either on ground level or elevated and as close to being in line with the halfway line as possible for this exact reason. If my players are winning the contact lines, I know we are building a great foundation for the rest of the game. As a result, if I am recruiting for my team or my organisation, I take a serious look at the players' ability in the contact line. If they are young and therefore not physically mature or if a player has some technical deficiency in their approach to the collision (for example, tackle technique), the assessment of the player then comes down to how willing they appear to be to go into the contact.

Make lists

Write. Log things. List names. Put them in positional columns or age group columns. Indeed, put them in whatever kinds of columns make sense to you. Just log everything you've seen when you are scouting players, including when and where you saw them, the number they were wearing and the like. If you see names repeatedly on the lists, you know you've got someone to target. Let me show you a hypothetical example using a method I have seen and used many times before.

We will start with a table:

	A	B	C	D	E	Total
1.	X	X	X	X	X	5
2.						
3.			X		X	2*
4.						
5.						
6.	X					1
7.						
8.	X	X	X		X	4*
9.						
10						
11						
12						
13	X		X	X		3

The numbers on the left represent the football team we are watching, and the letters at the top, represent the scout who is watching the team in any given week, so in this case, five different scouts over five weeks. The * indicates that there may be some anomaly, such as if a different player wore that jersey in one of the weeks. or there is a problem such as injury, suspension or if signed by someone else.

As you look down each column, you can see which players the scout's thought were worth looking further into. Their choices are marked by an 'X' on each occasion. As you look across from the numbers on the left, you can see how many 'votes' each player received with the total confirmed in the column on the furthest right.

Using this table, we can then compare what has been found with how many vacancies we have in our team, how much we have left in our budget or to see if someone in the position we have been looking to fill has been identified.

Based on vacancies or budget available, if there are five spots or more up for grabs, then all players with a mark would receive consideration and those with three or more marks should probably be signed. Four vacancies would mean that number 6 would not be considered if the vacancies needed filling urgently because he or she was the least popular player. Three vacancies mean the top three players get selected, two vacancies equals the top two and one vacancy would see us prioritising the most popular player (number 1) over all others.

If we are looking only for a Fullback, we have found one worth signing. The same if we are looking for a Prop or a Lock, although there is a * next to the Prop that we have to check out. If we are looking for a Centre, again, we have something to check out and because there are only two positive marks next to this person's name, we should probably look further at their gameplay. When it comes to Wings, a Half Back or a Second Row forward, we have not found anything worth consideration yet.

Don't just watch the big games

Players often choose teams to play for based solely on geography, friends who already play in the team or if they're young, where their parents are happy to take them. Players with great ability aren't necessarily going to be at the top team in the top division or even in representative teams.

The team that's bottom of the ladder might have the best player in the competition playing for them. The teams at the top of the ladder may have more quality players playing for them but sometimes, a group's whole output can outweigh the sum of its parts.

Lazy recruiters just go to the big games, talk to other recruiters to share and steal information from them and target the players that everyone else is targeting. Smart recruiters know that there are some good players there but only need to see them enough to ensure they're a good fit for the organisation, then they head out to where no one else is bothering to look.

Stars of recent years can be overvalued so operate in the here and now, not on reputation. Big players can sometimes be overvalued and small players can be undervalued. Halves and outside backs can be overvalued, forwards can be undervalued. Here are some other things to consider:

- Think about what they could be in a year, two years, three years and so on
- How much do they do of the stuff that people would rather not do?
- Have they got a fighting spirit?
- Are they tough?
- Identify and abandon sight prejudices such as size, headgear, background, running style etc
- Will they fit into the team?
- Make sure you have the core players in the core positions.
- Don't underestimate experience

When the Manly Sea Eagles won the 2008 Premiership during my time at the club, they did it comfortably in the final. It was also Steve Menzies' last game for the club.

The legendary backrower was one of the most senior players in the team that season and when he left, not only did his line running and ball-carrying ability leave the room, but his calm leadership did too. In 2009, Manly didn't reach anywhere near the heights they did in the previous season, and it would take two more seasons for them to win the competition again.

I remember in 2009 there were a few factors, but I felt (and one of the senior coaching staff also felt) that losing Menzies' leadership skills was one of those big factors.

Players like Menzies were or are not natural leaders to the casual observer, but they often lead without a title. They lead with a combination of giving an example to follow and subtle words at the right time - whether it be at a key stage in training or with younger or less confident players during relaxed moments in and around training environments. On the field, when it's time to stay calm in a game situation, such as under the sticks when tries are conceded, when you've got to close a game out or when you've just defended three sets on your line successfully, your experienced heads are the ones that can keep players focused and calm.

When clubs are deciding who to let go, they tend to look at age and physical decline as key factors. They often undervalue what's going on between the ears and the years and years of information that the player has processed and that frowned upon word to the 'new breed' - experience. Because our game is obsessed with physicality over everything, the golden leadership trait of experience is way down the list all too often.

Beware of this if you are a coach. If you're a fan, watch for the leadership and experience value leaving your club during this off-season. Look what happened when Souths Rabbitohs let Adam Reynolds go to the Broncos. Souths left the top four and the Broncos replaced them! (For one season at least).

Key Points from This Chapter

- Your squad should be a three-way split between young players with their best years ahead, players in their peak and players who are at the experienced end of the scale

- Have a 'no dickhead' policy

- Use the wisdom of crowds

- Look at the defence of a player as much as the offence

- Don't underestimate experience

"My development as a coach was transformative" – By Josh Bretherton

I will always be hugely thankful for what Lee did for me as a coach. He completely changed my views towards coaching. From the time I spent with him I developed a passion for coaching, and it sent me down a path (one I did not plan on) which has ended up becoming a big part of my life over many years. I have had some incredible experiences coaching and developed so many strong relationships with great people. As well as myself, Lee has mentored many coaches and more importantly, I know that Lee has had a significant impact on the lives of many young people too.

He shared his extensive knowledge endlessly and spent lots of time with me and other developing coaches to ensure we learned constantly. The things I have learned from him have been invaluable in terms of my own pathway as a coach. He was obsessive in his application and led a coaching culture of constant growth, which was brilliant. The coaching I did with Lee built the fundamental practices I use every day and has been so important for me and the programs I have been involved in.

Lee came to us with a laser-like focus to create a performance-based and elite program. When learning from Lee, he brought his wealth of knowledge and a history of working at NRL clubs and schools with great Rugby League history like St Gregory's. He implemented formalised structures that were best practice models from some very successful Rugby League environments, including a program wide game plan which meant that from the top to the bottom of the program, everyone plays to the same patterns, calls things by the same name and uses shared coaching cues. This is a simple and obvious thing, but it had a huge impact on player development.

Working with Lee changed my mind set and helped me prepare myself to work in performance environments. Getting to work with elite players daily and being a part of a program that has played a role in so many people's development is a very rare experience that I have enjoyed hugely. It's a journey and experience I think about all the time.

My development as a coach under Lee was transformative. In our first years coaching together, I was definitely growing and learning at a very rapid rate, and it was a steep learning curve for me. When I started as an assistant to him, I was a very young coach who would try and fill gaps and roles wherever I felt I could and was genuinely happy to play any role and learn anything I could. Things such as planning and delivering a football curriculum and how to identify players were not in my skill set at the time and it took me years to develop and grow in confidence with these skills. All the way through this process, Lee was supportive, seemed to know the journey I was going through and was happy to take on bigger working loads while I developed confidence and knowledge.

As a coach under Lee, I developed and learned fundamentals across a variety of areas. If I had to identify three main things I have made a focus of my coaching after watching him for many years; they would be:

1. Organisation; Planning and preparation is priority.

2. Analytical mindset; Constant reflection on team, player, coach and personal performance.

3. The importance of strong relationships between coaches and players.

I'm a whole lot better organisationally these days, I reflect more critically, and I keep better notes, but I wouldn't say I've reached Lee's level yet. He was obsessive in how he would journal things, reflect and keep notes on all kinds of things and this is what I believe makes him so good at what he does.

I developed hugely in terms of seeing the game in a more complex manner. I used to view the game through a very basic filter whereas now I am a lot better at understanding the nuances of it. Also, I now truly understand the importance of relationships when it comes to coaching. It's not that I didn't have that ability, because I am a teacher, and I think that's a strength of mine. I have always valued the relationships I had with my students, athletes, colleagues and peers. What working with Lee made me realise though is that it is a very valuable a tool when it comes to coaching players in a football team. I was a coach more worried about X's and O's and making sure we got those right, whereas true coaching is a combination of both.

These fundamentals are really important as far as the development of players is concerned. It's extremely useful when a player arrives at the top grade of any system if they have developed alongside team with the same calls and training methods that they have practiced over and over again. It makes a huge difference to a players' confidence in knowing what to do when the pressure is on. But most of all they gain strength from the quality of the relationships they have with the people around them. Relationship is key.

Lee has been a foundation piece of my Rugby League coaching journey. I am thankful for the time we got to work together and his support and guidance. I have greatly enjoyed the path that I have followed because coaching is a gift, whether working with beginners who are passing for the first time, through to elite players there is so much joy in coaching.

Josh Bretherton has been Director of Rugby League at Ipswich State High School since 2018. He is also the coach of one of the two Queensland Under 15's Schoolboy sides that compete annually in the National Championship. Prior to this, he was Lee Addison's Assistant Coach at the school and with Ipswich Diggers.

11
Analysing the Game

In 2012, I took part in the Brisbane version of the 'High Performance Rugby League Coaching Course' run by the NRL. To many of us with a lengthy history involved in the game, it was historically or colloquially known as the 'Level 3' coaching course.

Part of the assessment to be completed was an analysis of the 2012 Parramatta Eels. Here, we were asked to place ourselves in a hypothetical position of being the incumbent Parra coach taking over at the start of the 2013 season. I had a chance to study the Eels in-depth and formally log some of those thoughts. This chapter is an edited version of some of the submissions I made in December 2012. It needs to be noted here that this was purely based on my opinions as an 'outsider looking in'. It was not one of the deepest analyses I have ever done of a team but it's one that I had written up! All technical or tactical points mentioned are relevant in this modern day.

To generate as full a picture as possible of the performance level of the Eels at the time, its context and to compile the information for the assessment, I went through the following processes:

The process

Stage 1 – Gathering Information

- Interviewed a former long-term employee of the club, Matt Cameron, for a general overview of the club.

- Obtained footage (both TV and 'Eagle Cam') of Parramatta between NRL Rounds 1 and 8 in 2012.

- Gathered external statistics from various sources, such as foxsports.com.au, NRL Match Centre, NRL Stats and a variety of other sources.

Stage 2 – Studying footage to gather further information

- Watched Rounds 2 and 3 of the Eels 2012 premiership campaign for general trends without stopping and starting the recording and duly noted down any key occurrences for further research.

- Studied Eels' Rounds 2 to 8 in depth, putting the footage through Sports Performer Analysis software, and judging the team performance based on the Key Performance Indicators (KPIs) I have used as benchmarks with teams I have previously coached. Tagged and edited the footage accordingly.

- Studied all offence 'exit' sets continuously followed by the same with 'good ball', looking for key trends and deficiencies as well as strengths and opportunities.

- Conducted further study of the Eels' situational offence, for example, error trends and analysis

- Studied all defence sets continuously, splitting the field into opposition 'exit' and 'good ball' sets looking for key trends and deficiencies, as well as strengths and opportunities.

- Conducted further study of the Eels situational defence, for example, left side defensive performance as opposed to the right side.

- Watched and studied two randomly selected games between Rounds 9 and 26 to establish further trends and (hopefully) confirm those previously noted.

Stage 3 – using the information gathered to outline the performance level of the Eels

Where was Parramatta at as a team? What can we conclude from our study of Eels footage and associated statistics using the following subheadings?

- Technical and tactical skill analysis (attack and defence)

- Physical skills/competence and the impact on tactical and technical skills (decision-making and execution)

- Playing roster – analysis

- Psychological factors – resilience, motivation, arousal, maturity

- Social and cultural implications. Team harmony, conflict, background, attitudes, values etc

Stage 4 – Further research to improve the performance level of the Eels

What do experts in football and sports science believe can be done to improve the Eels? What does the literature in these fields suggest? Ideas were collected and presented using the following subheadings:

- Technical and tactical Skills (attack and defence)

- Physical skills/competence for a positive impact on tactical and technical skills (decision-making and execution)

- Playing roster – recruitment

- Psychological factors – resilience, motivation, arousal, maturity

- Social and cultural implications, team harmony, conflict, background, attitudes, values etc

Results of the analysis

Now you have seen the overview of the full study (it contained 108 pages!) I have just included the start of my answers to Stages 2 and 3 of the study here.

I watched Rounds 2 and 3 of the Eels 2012 premiership campaign for 'general trends' without stopping and starting the recordings and duly noted down any key occurrences for further research.

When looking at the Eels, I tried to answer some questions such as:

How did the Eels defend? 'Up and out' or 'up and in'?

Were there any obvious patterns to their attack?

Who were the key players?

In simple terms, my first watch aimed to see how they were coached to play. I found the best way to do this was to watch the game as a whole, getting a feel for the game and, if I felt it relevant, making note of some of the TV commentary.

When I next looked at the games, I went from Rounds 1 to 8 and looked at them from an analysis perspective, with a view to finding elements of individual, unit and team play that could be improved on. The games were analysed using the 'Sports Performer' analysis software.

I felt that choosing Rounds 1 to 8 would give me the best indication of the work that was done in pre-season before the weekly grind of football started to impact in terms of injuries, fatigue and representative football. Covering these rounds also gives time for combinations to grow and patterns to emerge. I would hazard a guess that a team pushing for premiership glory would be hoping to get as many wins as possible in the first 8 rounds and would plan accordingly for this.

Technical and tactical skill analysis (attack and defence)

After casually watching Rounds 2 and 3 as planned, I eventually ended up studying Rounds 2 to 8 of the Parramatta Eels 2012 season after technical problems prevented me from doing an in-depth study of Round 1.

Within this report, I have effectively 'diarised' my thoughts. As a result, the written report of the Round 2 match v New Zealand Warriors includes the most detail. This forms the initial basis of my general thoughts on the Eels with subsequent reports acknowledging the evolution of my analysis and the evolution of trends in the Eels' play over the almost two-month period between Monday 12th March and Sunday 29th April 2012, which also included an international and representative weekend break.

As a coach, I have a series of Key Performance Indicators (KPIs) I have developed with teams that strong performance in correlates strongly with strong performance on the field. I encourage the team and players to concentrate on 'process' rather than 'outcomes.' The KPIs therefore can also be classed as a series of 'process goals.'

I have applied my usual KPIs to Eels' Rounds 2 to 8. They are as follows:

- Completion rate (80% target)

- Defence rucks lost score (less than 20% target)

- SSS Score (60% target)

- Fail to deal with kick score (zero target)

- Piggybacks / defensive penalties (less than four target)

- Field position gifts

- Total tackle cost

- Line breaks against (zero target)

- Turn hips, jump out or pinch in (zero target)

- Offloads conceded

- Quality kick score

- Go forward score (target 65%)

Explanations of KPI's

SSS Score

'SSS' stands for 'Shoulder, 'S' Shape body and studs' in the ground when performing a tackle. As this form of tackling may not be part of the analysed teams' tactical plan, I was often content to tag a tackle as SSS if shoulder contact had been made in the collision. A percentage of SSS tackles was then produced for statistical purposes.

Field Position Gifts

When a team has the football, an ideal scenario would be to complete the set and end with a try or otherwise end up with good field position. If the team drops the ball before the opposition try line and before the end of their set, they have, in essence, given their opposition a 'field position gift' and there is a tackle cost involved. For example, if Parramatta drops the ball on the 3rd tackle on the 50-metre line, the field position gift is classed as '3 tackles at 50 metres'. Other field position gifts may come in the form of the opposition forcing a repeat set.

Total tackle cost

The tackle cost is totalled up at the end of the game, between those given from field position gifts, but also piggyback penalties. For example, if five penalties are given away on tackle 3 then the 'piggyback tackle cost' would be 15. This is then added to the total of the field position gift tackle cost. This gives the team an indication of how many tackles they could have had in offence rather than defence.

Turn hips, jump out or pinch in

With teams I coach, I tend to use a predominantly 'up and out' defensive system, which means anyone leaving the line early or turning hips in towards the attacker too early (prior to 1.25 metres away from the ball) causes disruption in the defensive system.

Go forward score

If a Parramatta player gets up and plays the ball with some members of the defence still retreating or not in position at marker, then this is classed as 'go forward'. Alternatively, if the defence and markers are set, this is classed as 'no go forward' and feedback is given in the form of a percentage.

Average metres conceded on exit

The metres the opposition gains from catching or retrieving our kick (or another form of restart) until they kick or give away their last tackle is recorded. To be classed as an exit set for statistical purposes, the first three tackles of the set must be completed in the opposition half. This statistic gives us an indication as to how they are managing the 'arm wrestle' element of games.

Average metres gained on exit

This statistic uses the same criteria as above but refers to our metres gained from the Parra half.

The KPIs in context

It is important to realise that these KPIs relate to what I would look for as coach of the team and don't necessarily equate to a judgement on the players' ability to carry out the instruction of the then Eels coach Stephen Kearney.

Throughout this report, I have attempted to outline what I believe the Parramatta players might have been asked to do as part of their plan. That said, I believe these KPIs are important for the hypothetical situation of myself coming in as coach because they immediately give a yardstick to the directors, the team and the coaching staff. It indicates where we are hypothetically headed and how far we are away from reaching those goals.

The match Parramatta v NZ Warriors

Prior to this game, the Warriors had only ever won 3 matches in 12 attempts at Parramatta Stadium. Nathan Hindmarsh was a late withdrawal from the game after spending that Saturday in hospital with a virus. Jarryd Hayne returned from a knee injury but still appeared to be playing with a slight limp. Hayne left the field under medical supervision after 15 minutes of play.

Having studied this match in the depth that I have, it is ironic that I believe the one major issue confronting Parramatta Eels after this first match was staring everyone in the face. There are times when I believe Rugby League coaching is overloaded by analysis of the 'X's and O's' and also by (sometimes) overloading players when it comes to the physical aspects of the sport. I believe that, after this game, if the coach of Parramatta Eels was only allowed or able to address three areas, then I suggest they should have been:

- Game Sense

- Hold the Ball

- Limit Piggyback Penalties

To back this up, after exactly ***7 minutes and 30 seconds*** of play, the Eels were 8 points to nil ahead after scoring two tries. They got there by doing the following:

- Completing 5 from 5 attacking sets

- Playing to a clear plan

- Playing to 'edges' in good ball

- Using their creative talents at the right time (playing 'what was in front' late in the tackle count)

Then, from ***9 minutes 57 seconds***, the following occurs:

Joseph Paulo executes a 'tip on' almost exactly on the centre spot of the field. It's a poorly executed tip-on. Joseph opens his hips up and telegraphs the pass to Tim Mannah, meaning in that split-second moment the two NZ defenders can hang off Paulo and the oncoming Mannah rather than commit to a tackle on either player. The other issue is that by 'opening up' his body, Paulo is closing off the opportunity of a 'dummy and go' himself through the defensive line. His body is facing the touchline rather than the try line.

By doing this, Paulo has limited the number of variables or 'stimuli' thrown at the defensive unit. I believe this is a huge part of the game of Rugby League. The hole that Mannah is attempting to run into quickly closes up and as a result, he is simultaneously 'half tackled' at the point he caught the ball. This may seem a trivial point, yet if we consider that Mannah is running onto the ball at full speed into a space which he was expecting to be somewhat bigger than it was, then this gives him very little time to react to the 'new' situation. Rather than steaming through a hole, Mannah is now partially tackled by a Warriors player.

Once again, let's place ourselves in Mannah's shoes and try to imagine the mindset he is in during that particular moment. Mannah has attacked the ball like a man intent on making a break. There are numerous examples in the NRL of this play producing breaks and half breaks. Indeed, Matthew Groat of Wests

Tigers executed the play against the Eels later on in Round 8 which resulted in a big line break for his teammate. The chances of a well-executed tip on play producing a break or significant half-break are seen as high in Rugby League circles.

As Mannah catches the ball, he is simultaneously tackled. He now has to consider an alternative to running through the gap. The alternative he chooses is to attempt to offload the ball. There is, however, only a split second for Mannah to make that choice. Option 1 (run through the gap) has now been deleted. We could broadly categorise that his other options were to take the tackle to play the ball quickly (option 2) or turn to offload (option 3.)

The offload is poor, goes to ground, and the opposition gains possession. We have our first 'field position gift' of the game (56 metres) at a cost of 2 tackles.

By **10 minutes and 32 seconds**, Parramatta have conceded a 3rd tackle penalty. This is now our second field position gift scenario to examine: a gift of 16 metres (by the time the kick for touch has been completed) at a defensive cost of 3 tackles.

To put this into different terms, the Eels initially gave the Warriors only 56 metres to travel in 6 tackles. After 3 tackles were completed, the Eels then gave the Warriors a further 6 attempts with only 16 metres to travel to their try line. In essence, the Warriors have now been given nine tackles to travel 56 metres.

The mental and physical cost here to Parramatta is of massive importance and the mental boost to NZ Warriors is enormous. The opposition has allowed them the opportunity to cover only half the football field to score. On top of that, they have accrued 40 of the required 56 metres via three tackles and a penalty won. (We need to consider here the proximity of the Warriors to the Eels try line when they took the penalty touch finder – 29 metres. The NZ Warrior's number 6 didn't put much power into the kick at all. He didn't need to.)

By **11 minutes and 35 seconds**, the Warriors have scored a try. It took them three tackles, which means they didn't need all six tackles available to them. The kick is also converted.

I would argue that in the space of **one minute and 38 seconds**, the landscape of this game changed dramatically, or, to coin a commentary phrase, the pendulum has swung.

During this one-minute, 38-second period, Eels dropped possession, gave away a penalty and allowed the Warriors to score through midfield. The issues I believe this exposes are:

- Paulo and Mannah are not accustomed to performing the tip-on play in a pressure situation. (Paulo encountered similar problems throughout the other analysed games)

- The Eels have failed to sustain pressure against the opposition, and they have given the Warriors an opportunity to get back into the game.

- The Eels compound this error by conceding a penalty on the back of it. (A problem that plagues them all through the eight analysed games)

- NZ Warriors have gone from feeling 'under the pump' in a game they were losing 8-0 in, to having a new lease of life and a chance to redeem themselves.

- The Warriors then score a try, 3 tackles in, through the middle of the Parramatta defence. This is in contrast to the two tries the Eels scored out wide, which were not converted.

I feel this is a huge period of play in the context of the Parramatta Eels season.

There are other developments in the game which point to Parramatta not handling the 'mental side' of the game too well. They visibly run harder, more dynamically, better and take more chances after a try is scored. They seem to give in a little once the going gets a little tough in the match (for example, the error compounded by penalty.) They also lack patience in certain areas of the game and seem to want to score off every good ball set rather than building pressure and waiting for the opposition to crack. They often seem to want to create the opening there and then, rather than wait to pounce on the opening.

Their poor kick chase is also an example of a '1% er' where they let themselves down. They often let the opposition out easily from their in-goal. Games of Rugby League can be split into broad categories – things players enjoy doing such as carrying, passing and kicking the footy, as well as other things that some players don't enjoy doing, such as defending and getting onside. Chasing a kick and applying defensive pressure are two of those elements of the game that can often fall into the latter domain rather than the former.

This kind of approach often gives the impression to the naked eye viewer that the Eels look unfit and tired in crucial areas of the game. I would argue that, without seeing their fitness test statistics, a huge part of their issue is mental. How else can they look so fresh when things are going well and so flat when things aren't?

I think, quite often, the following negative cycle occurs with Parramatta:

- *Poor previous*
- *Poor reaction*
- *Body reacts*
- *Player reverts to type under pressure*
- *Base fitness and skill levels tested*

Let's now delve deeper into each of these:

Poor previous - The player or players fail to execute a task. E.g.: the Paulo/Mannah tip on and offload, resulting in a negative impact for the team and a field position gift at a tackle cost.

Poor reaction - The player or players then, often keen to make amends for the earlier error then push the boundaries too far either in attempting a skill such as a harder tackle or by testing the boundaries of the rules, thus giving away a penalty.

In his book *'Critical Moments During Competition'* Roland A. Carlstedt highlights that:

"Theory of Critical Moment (TCM) proposes that psychological factors are most crucial to performance during specifically delineated periods of competition and explains how select personality, behavioural and psychophysiological measures influence sports performance when it counts the most"

Body reacts - Once the body starts to react to the negative happenings, the second part of the cycle kicks in. Coaches and therefore players, have the opportunity to recognise these stressors and prepare accordingly for them in training.

I believe this 'negative on negative' situation causes the human body to react adversely as a result of the negative mindset situation. Jonan Lehrer states in *Choke – The Secret to Performing Under Pressure'* that (in the context of pressure in sporting situations):

"...we assume that the brain areas that are working harder are recruiting more oxygen and other important nutrients such as glucose. We also assume that when a particular area of the brain needs more oxygen and glucose, the body's vascular system will shunt more blood to that part of the brain to satisfy its needs."

As a result, we can possibly assume that some of the blood leaves the 'athletic' parts of the body, such as the legs and arms, as it cannot leave vital organs such as the lungs and heart. This shunting of blood from limbs such as legs and arms could possibly have a negative effect on the way they move and the speed and the way they react to the brains' instructions.

Player reverts to type under pressure - It is a common thought that 'practice makes perfect' and, the '10,000-hour rule' championed by the likes of Istvan Balyi has attempted to quantify what is needed to become an expert on a particular skill or discipline. According to Lehrer, this also coincides with the *"power law of practice (which) predicts a straight-line relationship between functions of practice time and performance."*

Paul Fitts (1964) describes a three-stage model where performers go through a cognitive, associative and autonomous stage of learning. Reaching the elite 'autonomous' stage *"requires extensive practice"* so that *"the learner can perform the skill with minimal mental effort and few errors"*, according to Fitts.

If we are to concur with this theory, then we might argue that if Eels' performance of certain skills and tasks changes so dramatically in the course of the context of the scoreboard or game situation, then some players of theirs may be only at the associative stage in their learning of certain things they are being asked to execute. Under this pressure, they will go back to what they know best, which will be the initiation of a cognitive, associative or autonomous skill set, which, as a result, will impact the level and standard of execution.

Base fitness and skill levels tested - I believe this is the key stage which determines how well a side is coached, or alternatively, how far down the line of knowing their roles they are, assuming there is a direct link between repetition and performance under pressure.

If we accept that blood is shunted away from the 'athletic' areas of the body and at the same time, players are only at the 'associative' stage of skill development then it could be safe to argue that the base skill level and fitness level of the athlete is tested.

Using this model, it could be argued that you can only measure an athlete or a team when they are under pressure. In summary, I believe Parramatta Eels were very poor under pressure throughout the monitored games and the opposition often exploited that.

Parramatta Offence

Exit

In this game v NZ Warriors:

- Eels seemed to take some exit sets across the field, which basically meant a play the ball in the middle of the field on tackle 2 or 3, followed by a further one or two pass play that saw a play the ball on or near the far scrum line from where they started their set. The last play before the kick often comes back to the centre of the field. I believe this set may have been called 'Chain'.

- Another version of their exit sets saw them get quickly to their nearest scrum line via a plus-one play on tackle 1 or 2, before embarking on a series of tip-on plays across the field.

- If neither of the above sets were used, then it appears their sets were directly targeted at halves, particularly evident on a couple of occasions in the 2nd half when prop Mannah switched from the open to the blind side of the ruck to be tackled by a smaller Warriors player.

The above set construction gave the impression that Eels coach Stephen Kearney had instructed his team to move the Warriors around, to attempt to tire their large forwards for as much of the game as possible. This was further evidenced when, in one example, Eels hooker Keating picked something out by pointing to what he seemingly perceived to be a lazy NZ forward. This plan has merit as it is a known fact that bigger forwards struggle with lateral movement and by working them over, there will inevitably be disruptions in the NZ defensive line as they have had to work so much. This fragmented defensive line is likely what caught Keatings' eye on this occasion.

That said, I do not think the Eels executed it exceptionally well. They sometimes went sideways (plus one) when they would have had more success from being more direct. There is more than one way to move the big pack around – sideways and backwards being two of them. As coach, I would have interchanged the sets, sometimes one of each, sometimes, two or three so that the shock level stays there for the opposition. Instead, the statistics show that the Eels only ran out of dummy half 11 times, the dummy half run being the most direct way of going forward. It was evident that there was a bit more space 'through' the Warriors in the second half with one significant set from exit on 51 minutes.

Keating was, however, one source of added variety around the ruck. He often jumped out in a lateral manner, feigning inside balls before hitting an outside runner, or hitting the second runner with an inside ball. Ben Roberts often got involved over the halfway line, often carrying out a plus-one play or a 'block' play.

The Eels play was full of 'overs' lines of run, tip-ons with open hips (as discussed earlier) and in general, they seemed to struggle with go forward, a result no doubt, of the emphasis on lateral play at times over direct play. This is also supported by our internal stats showing the lowest 'go forward' score of the study as well as the second lowest 'average metres gained on exit' score.

Poore, Moi Moi and Taniela were the best at acquiring go-forward for the Eels, ably supported by the sharp and impressive Keating at hooker. I was less impressed with the performance of Tim Mannah. He is a wholehearted performer who has a happy knack of landing on his front more often than not but today was not his day. That said, I also believe that he is being used wrongly, as his second stint when the opposition's defensive line was more fragmented and fatigued showed. As he is not the largest prop and therefore, reasonably mobile, I would have used Mannah as the 'second' hit-up forward after a more dominating and/or larger runner such as Moi Moi, and I would also consider using Mannah off the bench in the latter part of half one and half two to exploit his mobility and his ability to find the floor.

In the first few sets, the Eels had field balance or shape by tackle 2 of each set (an equal number of bodies spread from touchline to touchline). It was clear this was something that they were coached to do although this changed and became less and less prevalent throughout the game. Once again, I believe this links into the negativity cycle and the theories of skill acquisition, directly related to how these players were coached.

Good Ball

I could sum up my opinions of the 2012 Eels good ball in one simple line - If they moved the ball, they tended to score or go close to doing so, but they didn't do it enough.

In fact, they hardly moved the ball more than two passes in this game, and it inspired me to create a new statistic on how many times they did. It was a mere four times throughout the game. On these line shots, they tend to be too flat.

Overall, I feel they have poor decision-making in good ball, poor structure, poor direction and poor ability to read defensive numbers. On the first good ball set they had, if they had shifted the ball a play earlier, they would have caught the Warriors short on the left. Eels often take one hit up too many. Some notes on their good ball sets were as follows:

- 3 plays to the middle (launch pad) from the right, a play to the left edge, and a line shot going back (which was often too flat).

- Plus-one to far scrum line, then an extra hit up, 3rd tackle Sandow at the line, 4th tackle Roberts has a spontaneous play but missed a chance to target space.

- Three hit-ups to the middle, Keating scoots back on play 4 to Roberts who tips on, to score on the short side. (This was an example of spontaneous 'play what you see' football on play 4 working).

- Two hit-ups to one scrum line, Sandow shifts the ball back to Roberts who moves it to the opposite scrum line. Eels play back and then on the last tackle; Hayne has a play on the short side.

- 2 into near scrum line, then there is a 'long-long-short' shift - 4th play looks like what may be an attempt at spontaneous play against a broken defence

We could potentially summarise the majority of Eels' good ball play in this game as a lot of 'plus ones' with much launched from the middle (or past post) of the field after 3 'settlers'. It is sometimes unclear if they are attempting to target the scrum line area in terms of trying to open up the field for the next play, or if they are targeting the opposition halves defending '3 in.' Shaun Johnson of the Warriors, in particular, seemed to be tackling a lot.

Roberts played predominantly left side whilst Sandow played predominantly right side. A common problem was their decision-making – namely going short with passes when they should have passed long in particular. The irony is that the Eels had a perfect start, scoring two tries from targeting edges, yet they always seemed to be looking to play through the Warriors after that. Was this a poorly prescribed plan or an example of reverting to type under pressure?

When they did execute sets well, with a plan for all 6 tackles – it worked. On **67 minutes 49 seconds**, Sandow scored on tackle 4 because Parra worked the Warriors over, with a good mix of lateral movement leading to go forward and Sandow exploited the fragmented space.

On **76 minutes** if they were targeting Johnson in defence it finally worked – he missed a tackle which led to a try.

Now, a note on some NRL side's obsession with 'spotting' opposition players. In the games I analysed, players who got heavily spotted didn't often miss tackles, and if they did, it was late in the game. Granted, there was sometimes a quick play the ball on the back of a player being tackled by a 'spot' but, is this not less effective than targeting space when space is available?

Parramatta Defence

The Eels show signs of tiring quickly, and their line speed and discipline appear very average under pressure.

The ***marker system*** appears to be a 'split marker' system with defenders eventually both moving the same way to tie in with the defensive line. Sometimes, the first marker will jump - particularly in the opposition's red zone. I would describe the Eels marker play as inconsistent.

Their ***defensive style*** is 'up and in' and, early on, defenders B and C would rush up, turning hips in significantly. This seemed to change **10 minutes** into the game as A defenders became more mobile, no doubt a correction from coach Kearney. This was also referred to by commentator Laurie Daley around the **29 minutes 30 seconds** mark in the Fox TV footage.

Eels defend 'thick to thin' with the winger furthest from the play the ball significantly detached from the rest of the defensive line (often permanently stationed between his scrum line and 10-metre line). The far side centre sits on the outside shoulder of his opposite number. In the opposition exit area, the thick element is more compressed, and the thin element comes in a touch, apart from the winger.

When the opposition shifts the ball or there is potential for the shift, the 3rd defender in (Sandow or Roberts) rushes out to attempt to disrupt the flow of the opposition movement. If the Eels have any opposition movement 'covered; they will hold their defensive line, then retreat. Their edge defence already concerns me, with edge defenders seeming to misread the situation on 5 occasions, leading to breaks or worse, tries. 'Up and in' seems a problem for this group – particularly with young outside backs who misread situations and thus create an uneven line regularly.

Their collisions are often made chest first, indicated by an SSS score of 49% which, as discussed earlier, is probably a result of a lenient approach to the SSS concept as it appears not to be part of the Eels methodology. I feel better tackle techniques could improve this, along with defenders adding to their 'peel off' time from the tackle, with often the 2nd or 3rd man in jumping up quickly.

Added to this, the tackles are often passive due to the spacings associated with a spread, up and in defence. In this context, the low 'rucks lost' score of 33% is indicative of what a good coach of defensive control Steven Kearney is. The term I believe Parra once used is 'catch' – they catch their opponent before he lands on the ground, to ensure a slow play the ball. When it goes wrong, however, it can be slightly catastrophic, with 'dead marines' common. Tim Mannah was a common 'dead marine.'

The team operate a 'pendulum' back three defence system although they did look shaky dealing with two kicks. They are also not a great kick-pressure team, with the 'C' defender the one who often has this responsibility alone.

Of concern is the defence of Ben Roberts, particularly with regard to passive tackles on his left shoulder – a problem which led to a try. The Eels it seems are guaranteed to concede when it comes to defending back-to-back sets. This is a mental issue and shows a lack of fighting spirit.

Of occasional concern was the defensive 'split' which was not always equal, whilst the NZ offload increase in the 2nd half, led to tries. I feel that Parra has real problems defending in 'chaos' situations.

Key Points from This Chapter

The stages of analysis used are:
- Gathering Information

- Studying footage to gather further information

- Use the information gathered to outline the performance level of the team

- Further research with a view to improving the performance level of the team

"I'd given up the thought of us winning anything" – By John Kiernan

I started volunteering at St Gregory's College in the late 1980s. The school was huge in the schoolboy Rugby League world at the time and has won more titles than any other in Australia. In the 1990s when we at our best football wise, I got a job there.

I worked as a trainer under all the coaches that came through, at a golden time for the school as we were sweeping all before us, more often than not and breaking records that still haven't been broken. I was working at the school when it was at its peak. I opened up and ran the gym and trained so many players that became household names. Well-known names include Trent Barrett, Jason Taylor, Ryan Hoffman, Beau Scott, Chris Lawrence, Jimmy Smith, Russell Richardson and plenty of others who played NRL such as Peter Cusack, Matt Seers, Robbie Mears, Simon Bonetti, Daniel Heckenburg, Wayne Evans, Tim Horan, John Minto, Mick Francis, Peter Driscoll and Michael Howell.

Most of our sides in the 1990s were crammed with players who went on to the NRL or very high levels and we also had so many New South Wales and Australian Schoolboy reps. The school won four out of five national titles between 1989 and 1993.

The following decade saw things gradually change at the College, as different Principals had different priorities to Rugby League. We did well in the early 2000s getting to two finals, winning one, but things dropped alarmingly after that. They also brought Rugby Union into the school, which meant we weren't just focused in one direction anymore. As a result, our performance as a League school gradually declined and we didn't win anything at all for years.

The man who I always thought was the best head coach I'd ever worked with at St Gregory's was the late Peter Mulholland. He went on to coach Perth Western Reds, Paris St Germain and was also the recruitment boss at Penrith Panthers, Canterbury Bulldogs, Newcastle Knights and Canberra

Raiders. He was the coach of our great sides in the golden years of 1989 to 1993 and was widely thought of as the greatest schoolboy coach in history, not just at Greg's but in Australia.

I didn't think we would see a coach of that calibre again and, in the later years of the 2000s I'd given up the thought of us winning anything as things had dropped that much. A sign that I wasn't very confident was that, in the middle of 2009 I'd booked a holiday and some leave for the middle of the following year- 2010.

Lee Addison turned up in 2010 and I kept telling him how good things used to be and that he didn't have much to work with. He would never listen to it though! All he would talk about is how he was going to straighten them out. He never once complained about the squad he had or the restrictions he had to lead the program under.

At the time, I had been around that school for almost twenty-three years at the time and I felt very qualified to offer this opinion- it was the weakest squad I'd seen at the school and Lee had, at the start, one class player who was obviously going to go on to NRL and the rest were lads who would work their guts out, but weren't of the same class talentwise. I wasn't the only one saying this too. Peter Mulholland and others from the NRL clubs had very similar opinions – that the new coach didn't have much to work with.

As Lee got to work, I gradually started to wonder if I'd made the right decision for my wife Mary and I to head to the States for a mid-year holiday. I could see things were changing. He got the players in the gym in the mornings, and I could see how hard they worked on the programs he had given them. When I saw Lee in action on the training field, I knew the lads had a real coach who was going to get the best out of them.

They started the season with the toughest fixture possible –Patrician Brothers Blacktown away – and duly won and they kept winning. Four of the boys also got selected for the New South Wales Catholic Schools Rep side, matching the number who made it in 2009, when we had a lot more talent at the school. In 2008 we hadn't got any NSW reps at Under 18's, 2007 we'd got one in and in 2006 we'd got three in and one of those was

Chris Lawrence, the future Wests Tiger! So, it was the best return for us in a while!

When in the States, I was getting messages galore that we'd won some big National Cup games. Yet the big moment came when Lee himself rang me as we just got home, they'd won the Sydney Premiership for the first time in years. I was in shock! Lads also started getting offers from NRL clubs all of a sudden.

In 2011, Lee's boys became back-to-back Premiers for the first time at the school since...the 1990s! They also got four players in the NSW Catholic squad again. They also went even better in the National Cup and got to the Catholic State Grand Final. He had definitely brought the good times back and the school was a force again.

My opinion is that Lee Addison is up there with Peter Mulholland as the best coach I witnessed at St Gregory's in the almost thirty years I worked there. I always told Lee that he'd arrived at the school too late and if he had the opportunities and some of the squads available to him that a lot of the previous coaches had, he would have done even better. Mulholland had the cattle, but Lee in comparison didn't and improved so many players, squeezing every last bit of ability out of them.

When he got the chance to start his own program up in Queensland, I was very happy for him. Even though I was going to miss hanging out with him at school I thought he'd made the right decision. I think it was about two years later that his new school went further than St Gregs in the National Cup!

Our friendship didn't stop when he moved to Queensland, in fact it went the other way - we speak every week, catch up regularly and are great friends.

John 'JK' Kiernan is very well known and hugely respected at St Gregory's for the work he did training the players during some of the greatest days in the schools' football history. Until he retired in 2016, players trained in 'JK's Gym' at the college. He had served the school for over 25 years.

12
Look After Yourself, Coach

The flame that burns twice as bright burns for half as long.

Like in all workplaces or if juggling a series of tasks, coaching at any level can cause occupational burnout amongst its exponents. Often leading to exhaustion and physical and mental symptoms such as those associated with so many illnesses, burnout is the physical and psychological reaction to the high stress and pressure that comes with being a coach. This can happen to the local volunteer coach as much as it can happen to the career coaches.

If you're a junior club or community coach, the pressure that can come from parents or game day spectators often makes volunteer coaches second guess why they bother. These people often 'befriend' the coach to try and curry favour for their child to be picked before turning on the coach as soon as something doesn't go their way. Some parents or spectators don't even bother with the befriending part of the relationship with the coach. Instead, they stand off from them, seemingly premeditating that they will likely disagree with the coach's tactics or team choices. It's as if some spectators have 'criticise coach' as a default setting.

For coaches moving up in the coaching world or those already 'up there', the pressure to get results can be crippling. I remember starting my professional coaching career in Australia on zero wins from three games. My Dad had flown over to Australia to support and take pride in his son, a coach at one of the NRL's leading clubs, and here I was, coach of a team that was winless when they shouldn't have been. I remember being unable to relax and constantly looking at the footage of the team playing, planning training and writing team lists over and over again, analysing everything I could. I could also tell the Manly Sea Eagles weren't happy with the results this Pommy coach they'd taken a risk on was producing.

During my time in a professional job in England two decades ago, the club I was working at was so unorganised and training attendance was often poor, as the financial structures for the contracted players meant that they were not sanctioned for missing training. I had walked into this job late – the season was about to start, and I accepted the position without finding out the real story at the club. The Head Coach of the club was a loose cannon, and the players and other coaches seemed to mirror their leader. It transpired that the previous coach of the Under 21's side I was now coach of had walked out on the eve of the season and I now knew why. The drive to the club was a long one, particularly when I was driving to a place where I was putting fires out rather than coaching footy. With three months of the season to go, I was already looking for the exit door as I felt down and seriously unmotivated, which is a crippling feeling for me. If I cannot see the point in something, it's only a sense of duty or a commitment to something that keeps me going. To top things off, my family was going through one tragedy after another, and my head and heart were elsewhere. They ended up sacking me with two games to go because I left a session with my assistants while I was in the hospital with my terminally ill mother. It was an awful time, and when it was over, I felt relieved.

This chapter is very light on advice because I am not a medical doctor or a trained psychologist. When it comes to the words in this chapter I am on the same level as you. This chapter is designed for you to self-reflect on your own journey. Where I can offer advice is in highlighting the potential pitfalls and giving validation to those coaching 'stressors' you may be suffering. The other advantage I have is that I have been doing this coaching thing for over a quarter of a century, so I can now predict so many problems before they arise when I am working in a club or similar.

Younger or less experienced coaches haven't had the same time on the circuit as I have and they tend to go into coaching jobs full of energy, full of ideas, full of passion and with no interest in club politics, negative thoughts or toxicity. Yet there are some clubs out there where the politics, negativity and toxicity will find you whether you like it or not. I can predict many of the pitfalls that can come a coach's way and have become more and more adept at steering clear of such environments altogether.

To talk further about burnout as a coaching issue, I have chosen to use a high-profile Soccer coach as an example. This is the most significant case of coaching burnout I have seen in recent years, and it was even more of a shock because the coach was doing great things at the time when he decided to jump ship from his job. Even though we are using a Soccer story, please stay with me as there are several important lessons in this that can instantly be applied to coaching Rugby League.

The departure of Liverpool FC Manager Jurgen Klopp at the end of the 2023/24 English Premier League season sent reverberations around several worlds when the news was released Friday, 26th January 2024, four months before the end of the campaign.

Firstly, it's worth noting that the English tend to call their Head Coach a 'Manager'. The role of a Manager at an English Premier League club the size of Liverpool is akin to that of a CEO in industry. In this case, the manager is the CEO of the football department, so to speak, with many support staff under their watch and a portfolio crammed with varying work commitments. The work on the training ground and on match day is arguably the easiest bit.

When it comes to Klopp, we are talking about one of the world's top football managers – a managerial heavyweight. Most commentators list the German manager as one of the top three, four or five in the world game. A high-end operator who has also had significant success where others have failed.

It is quite reasonable to assume that due to his success in the job and the way he approached it, that Klopp and his staff created the modern incarnation of Liverpool rather than the club itself being the making of Klopp and his staff. Prior to his arrival in 2015, the three decades or so earlier can easily be described as a series of fluctuating fortunes, periods of decline and near misses at the club. There were trophies but the much-coveted Premiership (champions of England) title had eluded them since 1990.

In Klopp's nine years, Liverpool ended their league title drought and won a European Champions League and four other trophies, including a World Club title. They were there or thereabouts when the titles were decided for the majority of Klopp's tenure, too.

What is even more impressive about his time at the club is that he did not have the same financial resources at his disposal as some of the other big clubs in England and Europe. His off-field staff had to work extra hard to recruit the right personnel at a lower price than some competitors. There are several examples of less heralded players signing for Liverpool and thriving during his reign.

As he announced his impending departure, Klopp spoke of *"Running out of energy"*. He told the BBC:

"Resources are not endless,

"With all the responsibility you have in this job, you have to be top of your game.

"I've been doing this (for) 24 years now. I always invested everything I had. I realised my resources are not endless and I prefer to pack everything into this season and then have a break or stop or whatever. We're not young rabbits anymore and we don't jump as high as we did.

"I still think it's the right thing to do. I don't take these things lightly.

"What we've built is an incredibly strong structure. It's one of the reasons I can leave.

"I have to explain a little bit that maybe the job I do people see from the outside, I'm on the touchline and in training sessions and stuff like this, but the majority of all the things happen around these kinds of things. That means a season starts and you plan pretty much the next season already.

"When we sat there together talking about potential signings, the next summer camp and can we go wherever the thought came up, 'I am not sure I am here then anymore' and I was surprised myself by that. I obviously start thinking about it.

"It didn't start [then], but of course last season was kind of a super-difficult season and there were moments when at other clubs probably the decision would have been, 'Come on, thank you very much for everything but probably we should split here, or end it here.' That didn't happen here, obviously.

"For me, it was super, super, super-important that I can help to bring this team back onto the rails. It was all I was thinking about".

Is the organisation working for you?

Let's look first at the issue of coaching and working on a project that needs some hard work and heavy lifting. This could be in the form of taking over a failing club or team where you can see the potential. An analogy might be buying a house where you can see the potential, but you know it needs a lot of work to just be habitable versus moving into a fully furnished and pristine, ready-to-go home.

Klopp probably moved into a 'Liverpool house' in between the two. If it was a home, it was habitable, but some elements of it were old and tired, some needed renovation or repair, most things needed severe freshening up, rooms had to be re-organised, and one or two extensions and a swimming pool would undoubtedly bring significantly added value.

In business terms, the club was 350 million pounds in debt in 2010-2011. Klopp joined in October 2015. When he left, they were listed as the seventh richest club in the world and success on the field or otherwise has a huge impact on that. Klopp did not just add those extensions and that swimming pool; he added significant value.

Klopp walked into a very different organisation than his main competitor over that decade, namely Pep Guardiola, manager of Manchester City FC. Guardiola walked into a club tailor-made for him. (It is well documented that for years, the club was preparing the club holistically, and they saw Guardiola as the perfect final ingredient), Klopp found a club that was still trying to rediscover its identity.

The previous Liverpool manager, Brendan Rodgers was sacked with the team in 10th position in the league. Also, news of recruitment committees (that weren't common in the game) was doing the rounds, some big-name players had left Liverpool, and their replacements didn't meet the mark. The recruitment was under fire.

As Klopp arrived in town, Liverpool, as previously mentioned, was working on a tighter budget than other clubs when it came to player recruitment. High-flying Manchester City and their own heavyweight boss Guardiola had what seemed to be an endless amount of money available to recruit players.

Things were in place at City, and 'Pep' essentially just had to bring the coaching expertise. Alternatively (and it appears obvious to me), Klopp had something of a rebuilding job to do on and off the field. Have you ever had to, or do you need to fix problems on and off the field as a coach at a Rugby League club?

It is always easier to arrive in an organisation where the philosophies reflect those of yourself, where you can focus on your 'core job' of coaching and 'value add' rather than being distracted by the associated 'white noise'.

As a coach, it's far easier to work in a well-resourced and supportive club where you can totally focus on football, coaching (core job) and fostering positive relations with players and club colleagues (value add) rather than dealing with lots of negative player behaviour, toxic club politics and working in a club where support and resources are inconsistent. (White noise).

If you work in a very busy pub or bar and there is only one other staff member with you, you can only just about do your core job (serving drinks) and can only briefly do the value add of striking up a conversation with customers or clearing their empty glasses from their tables. The chances are that if the establishment is understaffed there is likely plenty of white noise coming from those who own or operate the place, too.

We can apply these thoughts to almost any occupation or pastime. It's hard to be productive if you're always reacting to something that brings extra distraction to your day, or tasks take much longer because you lack the resources to make it easier.

Sometimes, a leader is so good that they make the organisation perform significantly better than they have shown in previous times despite limitations. I'd put Klopp in that category.

Think about your own coaching job; how much is in place for YOUR creativity and value add to thrive, or how much of it needs some heavy lifting just to get to that point? And how much are you able to focus on your 'core job' and 'value add' rather than the 'white noise'?

The flame that burns twice as bright burns for half as long

The second intriguing element of the Klopp departure was that he is a very, very passionate person. He wears his heart on his sleeve. He is also deeply intelligent. Pep Guardiola is the same. It is said both think about the game and the job non-stop and both have felt the need to take 'sabbaticals' from their careers in the past.

Guardiola went on a year-long sabbatical in 2012/13 to 're-charge his batteries' after achieving amazing things at Spanish giants FC Barcelona. He lived in relative anonymity in New York, spent time learning a new language and spent lots of time playing chess with a world champion!

After leaving Dortmund in 2015, Klopp went on a significant break before Liverpool came calling, and he is on a break from coaching now.

In his press conference and interviews announcing his departure date, Klopp referred to himself as 'old' on at least two occasions. He was only 56 and looked as fit as a fiddle. He also said he wouldn't miss doing *"Nine press conferences a week".*

A body language expert, Darren Stanton told the Daily Mail in the UK that:

"Klopp looks like a very tired and burned-out man.

"His voice was lower in tone, volume and pitch, which shows someone tired, not just physically, but mentally.

"It will take him many months for him to re-find his strength and his time at Liverpool has taken its toll on him.

"It's come to a point where he has to decide between his health or his job.

" Klopp's non-verbal communication was in line with what he was saying, which tells us everything that Klopp said was the truth.

"The sad micro-expressions we see on his face, head-bowed and mouth-dropped, are all consistent with what he is saying.

"It's a combination of real sadness and disappointment that he has no other option to leave.

"He strokes his own legs a lot, which is a gesture of self-reassurance, like giving himself a hug to say 'This is the right thing to do'.

"He showed a lot of courage to present himself in the open during the video, showing his full body and not sat behind a desk or something - this shows there is a lot of honesty in what he says."

Now, neither Darren Stanton nor this author are medical doctors, and this needs to be made abundantly clear at this juncture. But it looks like Stanton and I were both looking at another human and thinking that he looked and sounded worn out. While Liverpool is or was not in any way a struggling or failing organisation, there was an economic and market reality to their position in comparison to their closest rivals that created some of the 'white noise'.

Jurgen Klopp added an incredible amount of value and did his core job exceptionally well while dealing with that white noise. He had to work extra hard to get Liverpool up to the same level as Manchester City. The last decade, in particular, had been a very intriguing time as the two battled it out for supremacy in England, Europe and the World. In those wider geographical contexts, its honours even, but in the English Premier League, Manchester City were the undisputed kings overall, and Liverpool pipped them to the title only once in Klopp's time. In one season, Liverpool achieved more points than they ever had in their history but still finished second to their rivals from Manchester, who broke the national points record!

Guardiola worked at clubs for three and four seasons previously but has stayed a lot longer in Manchester. After four seasons at Barcelona, he needed a 'sabbatical'. His time at Barcelona is when his '24 hours a day' approach to the job became common knowledge. He also won a vast array of trophies in that time and took the team to amazing heights, and quickly. They are heights the club has only briefly reached again in his absence.

His time and success at Manchester City seemed on the surface to be a little more stable and 'organic' (as organic as a team full of multi-million earning superstars can be). It seemed like a sustainable growth model in action at City during the Klopp-Guardiola era.

It's obvious 'Pep' has learned how to manage himself better with age and experience, but the number of resources around him compared to his time at Barcelona must also be telling. The Director of Football and Chief Executive of the club for most of his tenure have been two of his long-time colleagues and friends. The owners of the club supported him when things didn't perfectly go to plan (namely, not winning the coveted European title until the end of his 7th season). The trust between the front office, ownership and coach is clearly evident. When things faltered, the sky didn't cave in. They also (basically) improved year on year in Europe before taking out the hallowed prize in 2023.

Jurgen Klopp also spoke of the trust he has for the ownership at Liverpool and those around him off the field, but there was an element of 'the sky caving in' during the previous campaign to the one where he decided enough was enough. Liverpool finished fifth in the English Premier League, and for big periods of the 2022/23 season, it looked like it would be worse than that. In 2020/21 they also finished third a year after being the Champions.

In Europe, the ups and downs were even more noticeable. They were runners-up in 2017/18 and then European Champions in 2018/19. But they were bundled out in the round of 16 in 2019/20 and the quarterfinals in 2020/21.

They were runners-up again in 2021/22 but a year later failed to get past the round of 16 again.

This 'boom and (sort of) bust' process in the super competitive European competition and relative low point in the previous domestic campaign lends support to the theory that the Manchester City organisation had a few more strategic ducks in a row than Liverpool. Any season failure at Liverpool could not be pinned on the coach.

It is worth noting that Manchester City are the exception rather than the norm. If Liverpool is Pepsi or Burger King/Hungry Jacks, then Man City are Coca Cola or McDonald's.

None of us coach in clubs as big and high profile as these, and many of us have coached or do coach in organisations that don't function smoothly at all times, if at all. And even though many of us won't have an obsessive media or worldwide fan base and their extreme emotions to deal with, all stress and emotion attached to the coaching job is relative. We spend more time with some of our club colleagues than we do with much of our family and in our homes, so understanding these things is crucial. Mental health, in general, is crucial.

Other managers and coaches in sport have worked in such conditions for longer than Klopp. Sir Alex Ferguson inherited a relative mess and had to do a huge rebuilding job at Manchester United (arguably the most well-known club on the planet) for almost four years before the trophies started rolling in constantly. He managed Manchester United for a quarter of a century and seemed to have arguments with a multitude of opponents, officials and media outlets along the way!

In the NFL, Bill Belichick left the New England Patriots after 24 (mostly) highly successful seasons. Wayne Bennett has done a quarter of a century all up at the once-all-conquering Brisbane Broncos in the National Rugby League (NRL), and his coaching flame shows no sign of getting extinguished soon. With a draft system for recruitment of players in the NFL and a restrictive salary cap in the NRL, you could argue coaches in these competitions have to do more rebuilding than most. Also, certainly in the case of the NFL, the off-field commitments, profile and demands would be very comparable to those in English football. In context, the NRL is a pressured environment.

What is clear is that Belichick and Bennett are FAR less demonstrative and outwardly passionate on game days and in media interviews than Jurgen Klopp and Pep Guardiola. While both are great students of their respective sports, both Belichick and Bennett give the impression that they can switch off from the game and the job when it matters and give little attention or content to the media.

This isn't a foolproof example, but it does show how, outwardly at least, four different coaches seem to deal with what look like very similar things.

We are all different. We all react differently to different challenges and jobs.

Klopp spoke very passionately in his first-ever unveiling as Liverpool manager, he is reportedly a highly demanding and no-nonsense boss with huge love for his players and staff around him. His football has sometimes been described as 'heavy metal' and you could imagine much of his coaching and management style reflects that. He certainly stirred the emotions of everyone at the club too. It was a great ride if you were connected with the club.

But if Stanton was right, then Klopp was really worn out – that is not a good thing. I am big on this because I have recognised this in myself, before and so have friends and family.

One coaching job I did for five years took an awful lot of heavy lifting and, despite the amazing success that was achieved, I was mentally exhausted and knew my time was up. For four of those five years, I was also one of the last to leave the workplace each day. I was obsessed. In my final year, I adapted and took home some work instead or left it until 'tomorrow'. In my next job, which lasted four years, I also kept up those same habits and had things more 'in control.'

Guess what? Performance never dipped at all over those nine years, whether I was obsessed or not! In fact, great things happened!

An obsession is not healthy, it never is.

To many, Jurgen Klopp had a dream job. One of the most sought-after in the world! In any industry yet he felt compelled to leave, at a time when things were going great.

The flame that burns twice as bright definitely burns for half as long. If you leave a light on permanently at home, you'll be replacing the bulb sooner than if you turned it off when you didn't need it. Klopp has been one of the brightest flames and light bulbs I have ever seen.

How's your coaching flame and how can you keep it flickering?

I am not a medical expert nor a psychologist, so this chapter has been short of advice. Your coaching 'stressors' could come in ways that seem so trivial to other people. Stress is relative and perception is reality.

The only wisdom I feel I can offer is for you to look after yourself and always consider what impact coaching is having on you and your family at any time. If it ever gets too much, remember, it is only a game. Also here are some quotes that may help:

"I've missed more than 9000 shots in my career. I've lost almost 300 games. 26 times, I've been trusted to take the game winning shot and missed. I've failed over and over and over again in my life. And that is why I succeed." **Michael Jordan**

"Life is 10% what happens to you and 90% how you react to it." **Charles R. Swindoll**

"You have to find that balance between taking care of your body, taking care of your mind, and taking care of your soul". **LeBron James**

"Your struggles develop your strengths. When you go through hardships and decide not to surrender, that is strength" **Arnold Schwarzenegger**

Key Points from This Chapter

- The flame that burns twice as bright burns for half as long

- There are some clubs out there where the politics, negativity and toxicity will find you whether you like it or not

- Do your homework before joining a club or taking on a team

- We are all different. We all react differently to different challenges and jobs

- Your coaching 'stressors' could come in ways that seem so trivial to other people. Stress is relative and perception is reality.

"Some of my fondest memories in the game" – By Taylor Brown

Lee Addison has been a main catalyst for not only my Rugby League success but commentary and my life in general.

I met Lee at St Gregory's College in 2010, when he took up the role as Head Coach of the First XIII Rugby League team. Throughout this time, Lee pushed me both physically and mentally to turn my football from that of a park footballer into a New South Wales Schoolboy, National Youth League and Queensland Cup representative over a span of ten years. His attention to detail throughout my time at St Greg's was not only applicable to myself, but to the whole of our squad, turning many players into the best version of themselves through hard work and honesty to each other. Not only was this period of my life instrumental in how I approached challenges and opportunities moving forward, but it was also some of the fondest memories I have in the game.

Since my time playing the game has slowed and regressed with age, commentating opportunities have arisen and Lee has not only supported me, but actively contributed to this endeavour. After caveats appearing on his *"The Rugby League Coach Podcast"*, Lee and I formulated many successful podcasts together including *"Queensland League Scene"* (which was also a TV show) and *"Around the Town with Taylor Brown"*. The overall majority of these podcasts and decisions derived from advice or ideas from Lee, thinking of ways to propel my media career forward and put my thoughts and opinions to the masses to gain more experience and time behind a microphone, and to procure a further outreach of my name and reputation. A chapter we continue to write together to this day.

Although this book delves deeply into Lee's dedication to Rugby League and coaching in general, it is my belief that Lee's qualities shine through in all aspects of his life. For the last three years, whilst Lee and I seem to speak every other day, he has been a sounding board for Rugby League, commentary, and life itself.

Life throws challenges at everyone so we always confide in each other and Lee has become a very dear friend and trusted advisor through the good and the bad, whatever the subject matter may be. A confidant and pillar of support that has never wavered, and a man that has always had my best interests at heart.

Taylor Brown has played for Canterbury Bulldogs, St George Illawarra and Redcliffe Dolphins. He played in the 2011 St Gregory's College Premiership win and represented New South Wales Combined Catholic Colleges in the same year. He now commentates on the Queensland Cup and other Statewide competitions on behalf of the Queensland Rugby League.

13

Coaching in the 21st Century

If you're a male and a talented and experienced Rugby League coach in New South Wales or Queensland, in some towns and cities in New Zealand or the North of England, let me tell you a way to get some amazing coaching experiences to challenge and grow you hugely, but they will also elevate your status as a coach in a heartbeat.

If you're a coach in those places who has only coached males, leaving to coach in Victoria, South Australia or Western Australia, with the level of knowledge and background you have, gives you every chance of attaining a higher position a lot quicker.

If you're Australian and go to England or France, it's almost 'pick your job' time and seems to have been that way for decades! My job prospects in UK coaching circles went up in no time at all after spending some time in the land down under. I was the same coach and person, only a couple of years more experienced, but apparently, I could now be considered for head coach positions at clubs where before leaving, I'd be lucky to get the under 15's.

Other ways for male coaches to challenge themselves are to switch from coaching the males to coaching in the female game or to coaching either gender overseas.

Ladies – the female game is proudly yours, and it's growing rapidly, so opportunities abound for you to spread your coaching wings in that realm. Women's and girls' Rugby League is one of the fastest-growing sports in Australia and one of the fastest-growing female sports in the world. If men can get a fair shot at securing jobs in the female arm of the game, then it is only fair that equal opportunities come the way of the ladies, too. Maybe one day, a lady can be seen in the coaching box of a (male) NRL or Super League team. There are precedents in the sporting world. In America, Jen Welter became the first female coaching intern in the NFL, whilst my former University classmate Hannah Dingley became the first woman to manage a professional men's football team in England in 2023.

It is thought over 70 countries play Rugby League globally, so sometimes, it seems there is a new world order coming into the game. They are all bringing new stars, freshness and new train of thought to the game and how it should be played without the historical 'baggage' we sometimes find in the heartland regions.

There is nothing like a Rugby League World Cup to help create dreams for people all around the world. Every nation in the world that plays Rugby League wants to be at the big event one day. Nations such as Greece, Jamaica, Lebanon and others are just on the fringe of bursting through to the top table, Samoa and Tonga, one could argue, already have. They are all bringing new stars, freshness and new train of thought to the game and how it should be played.

There is also nothing like a failure or failure to qualify for the tournament itself to bring into sharp focus the performance of the established 'old' nations. Nations such as Wales, Scotland and Ireland have had previous successes stretching back over more than two decades, and by their previous lofty standards, recent World Cups have been failures. There are new nations ready to take over.

Coaching in any of these 'new' areas of the game brings out different skills in the experienced coach. In the heartlands, unless you're coaching infants, rarely does it occur where you have to tell a new player to *"put the ball on the floor and roll it behind you with the foot"* when they've been tackled. Instead, they can just mimic their mates in the team who have known how to play the ball since the womb because their parents and grandparents played the game too.

In the heartlands, it's easier to turn your coaching to tactics and strategy because most players know where to run and know that they need to retreat back to the referee after each tackle in defence. In new areas of the game, they may not know that much when they start.

I got exposed to this different style and challenge coaching-wise before I got my very first coaching job. When at university, our team was a mix of heartland players like me and those who'd travelled from different parts of the country to study and decided to try a new sport. They were from places where the game wasn't played at all, and if they had played Rugby, it was Union, where the 'breakdown' is very different when a tackle is completed.

What I saw working really well during my student days was the peer mentoring coming from the more experienced players in the direction of the new breed on an almost constant basis. This powerful type of coaching intervention was something I tapped into almost immediately when I started my own journey as a coach.

The following pages outline what I believe are the essential steps to help 'new' organisations get themselves to the top echelons of whatever area of the sport they want to reach, be it a women's state league team wanting to reach NRLW, a club in far-flung places wanting to reach the state leagues, or clubs or similar wanting to be the dominant force above their fellow 'new' entrants to the sport.

I will now outline some basic coaching and organisational principles for working in 'new' territories using the example of international Rugby League and how an emerging nation with plans to make a full World Cup can go about their business. Feel free to substitute any reference to a nation or World Cup to whatever realm you are considering or currently operating in to get ideas on how to grow the game where you are. Rather than repeat, *"You can also apply this to..."* at each stage of the writing, please view the rest of this chapter with an open mind as to what circumstances it can be applied to when reading the content. There are so many different places where the game is played in the 21st Century that trying to cover them all is nigh on impossible.

Reasonable goals for an emerging Rugby League nation could be described as follows:

- Attain a World Cup place
- Maintain their World Cup place in future tournaments
- Thrive in World Cups, achieving unprecedented success

I talk as someone who has worked in international and domestic rugby league development for well over 20 years. I talk as someone who was on the support staff as Ireland Men reached the heights in the 2008 World Cup, was Assistant Coach of the USA for the 2011 World Cup qualifiers and the 2013 Cup itself, and coached Poland for six undefeated test matches in 2018/19. As you already know, I also got two schools in Australia to the top of the sport over here in Australia, when they started with nothing, or next to nothing, and now one of the things I do is consult for nations on how to grow the sport and have done several trips overseas to aid such processes.

I dedicate my life to helping players, coaches and nations become better versions of themselves, and I've got quite a lot of ideas that I think you'll like on how emerging nations need to go about things. This could also apply to a 'new' nation or a nation or organisation that is established but has 'lost its way'.

I approach emerging nations' development from two directions – the bottom and the top, using a method I call the sandwich model. The model talks about getting your top team firing as soon as possible but also how to develop the future, so your nation doesn't follow the other 'one-hit wonders' of previous World Cups or Emerging Nations World Cups. It approaches it from a 'performance' angle but also hopes to create many subsequent benefits to the corporate and consumer world as offshoots (but someone else can worry about all that).

Who are you? Creating your own Rugby League identity

Countries where the game is played (or about to be played) I have a message for you.

You are not Australia.

Australia might be the current World Champions, and indeed, they've been on 'top of the world' for almost the whole existence of the international game (in our lifetimes at least). But trying to copy carte blanche what happens in Australia has not worked for so many nations that have tried to usurp those pesky Kangaroos. One of the best examples of this is England, where the game was born in the late 1800's! Great Britain or England sides of the past were renowned for playing flowing football with tough forwards, diminutive halves and exciting outside backs, yet found themselves copying the Australian way of completions and attrition when the Ashes tests of 1982 onwards started to show a wider schism than ever. Whilst the English were busy playing catch up, the Aussies were always one, two or more steps ahead and developing the blueprint that so many have tried to follow since. But with very little success!

Why copying doesn't work

Australia is a nation of 26 million people, where they have played the game since the early 1900s, where climate, economy and traditions are conducive to such activities and where many kids get a Steeden put in their hands before they reach primary school. For a Rugby League nation (or similar) that hopes to one day reach a World Cup (or equivalent), it is a case of dreaming about growing the game in that area and wishing every kid played Rugby League. Unlike Australia, the sport hasn't been played en masse in that 'new' place for more than a century; there are few, none or next to no bespoke Rugby League facilities available and the only shape of ball the kids in that area played with before reaching primary school was spherical.

You have to approach things in a completely different way – it stands to reason! Every emerging nation I've visited as a coach (and indeed some established nations) has seen us training on parts of a hockey field or on synthetic soccer fields more often than not.

There's the way you play and your 'identity' to consider in a new territory. Using cricket as an example, traditionally, the English way of playing cricket was 'sensible' and 'patient', yet the Aussies, India and others would see that as 'boring' and score more runs in one hour than England would in a day. They would attack the ball and throw caution to the wind! (Eventually, England changed all that with the 'Bazball' concept – a great example of lateral thinking under a coach from overseas). In Rugby League, it might be that you play with flair or relentless fundamentals. Your defence may be highly aggressive or calm and composed.

The key questions when considering this are:

- What are the overwhelming traits of those in your nation/area?

- What sporting or cultural values will the players already know and embrace?

- How can you work with your culture, not against it?

The Rugby League cultural differences between Australia and England give us over a century of evidence to work with. Aussies don't think anything of playing and training all day in searing heat, smothering themselves in sunscreen, wearing hats and training gear that is light and breathable. Players in parts of Europe will have to get out and get it done before the winter snow arrives or spend most of their time ploughing through thick mud whilst wearing several layers of clothing.

As a coach who grew up and started this stuff in England before travelling around the world to coach, I've got some other insights into what happens in various parts because of the weather, too. In England, when you call the players in for a team chat, they sprint. In Australia, their default is to walk in. Why? It's freezing in England most of the time and roasting hot in Australia most of the time.

In terms of approach, in England, we are fans of 'taking it' to the opposition. Soccer is a game played by people a lot smaller than us and many of them like to fall around and feign injury. In England, they call the game 'Rugby'; in Australia they call it 'Football' and they consider it a game of football. Pre-match preparation for a physical battle in Rugby or a game of Football creates very different images in the mind and also in the pre-match changing rooms of England and Australia.

On a 2019 visit to Argentina, I got ready to take a session at one of the top universities over there, scheduled for a 10:30 am start. I was ready with the cones and balls at 10:15 am. At 10:30 am, I was still stood there, whistle in hand, waiting for the group to turn up.

All the squad eventually arrived by 10:55 am! I asked the tutor why this was, and he told me, *"That's how it's done everywhere, and that's it!"*. It's the Argentinian way, apparently, and there was diddly squat this coach could do about it.

In France, there was historically a culture in that they did many things to make it tough for visiting opponents. I've yet to visit France and not have poor directions to a training or match venue, and even the officiating is interesting. Once, I was part of a team that was officially told kick-off was at 6 pm.   As we finished our high-octane warm-up in the southern French evening sun, our opponents started slowly meandering in for the 7 pm kick-off time. No wonder we were 30-0 down at halftime! In the second half, after our coach had settled us all down, we got the game back to 30-24 with seven minutes to go. We were on a roll and doing everything right until....'(insert final whistle sound)'.... game over. The ref had called the game rather early!

I could continue with these anecdotes, but that would take me away from the main point of this chapter. When developing your team for World Cup or equivalent glory – be yourselves! And be proud to be that!

The sandwich model

Juniors in any nation can only be inspired to make a World Cup if they have some heroes to emulate NOW. Too many times in Rugby League, a nation has done well in any given World Cup, only to fall by the wayside in the following years. It's because they didn't plan for ***what came after*** the tournament.

World Cups happen every four years, so the journey to success doesn't stop. The key to the sandwich model approach is that, just like making a sandwich, there is something on the 'top and bottom'. What this means for player development is having a 'two-pronged' approach – with both a short and long-term focus acting in parallel. In a sandwich, this is the two slices of bread. You can't make a real sandwich with one piece of bread – it will be a pale imitation. If you don't have both slices of bread, the sandwich falls apart and is only half of what it could have been.

Many people need to see the dream before they can believe the dream.

As a child, the chances are that you watched a sporting event or team and thought ,*"I want to play in that/for them"*. It may have been slightly different if your parents didn't let you watch that sporting event and instead, chose to explain what it might look like for you in ten years when you were old enough to choose your own viewing habits. It would have remained a concept for you, and no matter how much your parents said, *"You'll love it, just be patient"*, it still would have been harder for you to picture what it 'looks like' before you actually saw it for yourself.

Sounds obvious, right? Unfortunately, too many very well-intentioned long-term junior development programs in Rugby League fail because the 'end game' is not in sight. They focus only on a 'bottom-up' approach, and juniors invariably drift off to other pastimes with more instant fulfilment. The other mistake most commonly made is that they focus only on the 'top' and sometimes don't even look 'down' at the juniors. Or if they do, it falls well short of its intended goals. This is common in the heartland especially.

There have been so many World Cup and Emerging Nations World Cup performers over the years that have had great tournament showings, yet they have essentially been a 'flash in the pan' or have never been bettered or matched for decades after.

My point for now is that you need to go into developing your program from the top and bottom, seniors and juniors, or apply what I call the 'sandwich model'. When Wales made the semi-finals of the World Cup (twice) and Ireland and the USA made the quarter-final of theirs, you can almost guarantee that there were kids in each respective country watching a TV set, dreaming of doing that themselves one day. They could *see* the dream. It wasn't just a distant concept. When we don't have this tangible thing in our weaponry, we risk kids and adults drifting off to the other code, where they ***do*** have a tangible international product that floating fans can see, feel and be part of in some way.

Delivery

So now we have established we are going with a sandwich model, how do we go about delivering that? At both juniors and seniors?

Most organisations start their journey by assembling a senior team. That's a logical first step so as to get something happening straight away.

We will now look at how to best go about that process to get to and then WIN the BIG games. It looks first at how to recruit players from around the world before going into detail about how to coach and manage the group for the big games.

Any Rugby League nation has at its disposal two sets of people:

1) Those who were born there

2) Those who have parents or grandparents who were born there. (I dare say that is an awful lot of people)

We then have this sub-category:

Do they already play rugby league?

This is when it gets too difficult for some in the game because the numbers dwindle quite significantly at this sub-categorised point. Instead, we are going to see what we can do with those in Rugby League first. We're not giving up without a fight.

When I got the Poland job six weeks out from the 2018 Emerging Nations World Trophy tournament, I was lucky that I had a man called Shane Young, who was like a dog with a bone when it comes to finding players of Polish heritage. During my first phone call, it was clear we had something like six to eight players with a combined age of about 300! Many of them were retired. I only met my full team for the first time five days out from the start of the competition. But the key thing is we had a full squad. Shane had worked recruitment wonders. We ended up winning the Emerging Nations Trophy and being undefeated. I can promise you that without Shane's tenacity, we wouldn't have been so successful.

Organisations or nations have got to leave **no stone unturned** in pursuit of every player that can represent them and is already in the League ecosystem. It's an awful lot easier to do this now in the social media age, and the governing bodies are also quite good at storing the eligibility details of players on their books. Back in the Polish days, I remember buying copies of the Rugby League Week magazine and looking for players who had Polish-sounding surnames. Don't just look at the professional ranks either – there are some rather good amateurs knocking around, too.

And of course, there's also one other big thing...... Rugby Union. Let's not kid ourselves that Union has everything all sorted. Each country that plays Union will still have players who are missing out on their own pathway, such as players 21, 22, and 23, when a squad of 20 has been picked. Many of them love to try the other code if they think they can achieve something special in it, and the skills are very transferable. Union and League players have things two things in common:

1) They love to run in possession of an oval-shaped ball
2) They love to tackle

This provides an absolute gold mine to tap into in some places.

The most challenging decision for nations

It's an issue that splits many in the international game. It's an almost universal stumbling block to development and also a bone of contention when it comes to selecting the representative or national side. The issue of mixing 'domestic' or 'local' players with those of 'heritage' or 'outsiders' is an issue we see at all levels of the game. From international to state to regional.

There are so many conflicting but well-meaning opinions on this, that it is often hard to get a consensus on the best way forward, yet below, I outline a method of solving this issue. I would like to start with some honest truths about the scenario. (Sorry if at times it sounds somewhat blunt).

- The 'heritage issue' applies to the vast majority of nations ranked 9th and below in the men's rankings and can also apply to Tonga (4th), Samoa (5th) and Fiji (7th) at the time of writing.
- Quality players from traditional heartlands with heritage links to a nation (or similar) will improve the quality of your team significantly.
- Players with only domestic league experience in many nations or non-traditional rugby league areas may have the physical attributes required to play the game but will most likely lack the experience and rugby league 'IQ' to allow for satisfactory performance if 'heritage' players aren't included to 'shore up' the team.

Next, I outline a method of solving this issue.

How not to do it

A perfect 'test case' for the 'pro heritage' theory is the clear downward trajectory of the USA National Side from 2011 to 2022. In 2011, they qualified successfully for the 2013 World Cup in what was dubbed 'third time lucky' (The Guardian) after two previously failed qualification attempts. What had happened previously was a steady growth of the domestic game, which meant some people from established RL areas visited the states to play or coach. Some indeed stayed there to become residents or citizens.

The 2011 squad was a mix of 'domestic' and 'heritage' players. Both groups of players brought a wide range of abilities, ranging from NRL players Joseph Paulo and Matt Peterson to domestic players who had never played outside of the USA. Once qualified for the 2013 showpiece, needless to say, even more established stars put their hands up for selection. The slant of the squad was undoubtedly leaned more towards heritage than domestic.

The USA Tomahawks reached the 2013 Quarter Finals, and we were undoubtedly the 'success story' of the tournament. To coin a marketing phrase at the time - we 'Shocked the World'. Some in mainland USA were angered by the amount of heritage players included in that squad, and after some political upheaval which ultimately favoured a new approach, the 2017 World Cup squad was almost a complete reversal of 2013, with only a very small sprinkling of heritage players in there. The USA finished bottom of a relatively weak Group D, losing all three games, scoring only twelve points and conceding 168. This was the worst record of any team in that tournament.

It was to get worse. They didn't even qualify for the 2022 tournament, and instead, Jamaica, a team that the USA had fended off in previous years, had now overtaken them.

Imagine that instead of political sparring, some would have put energies into growing the next generation after 2013. Imagine instead of an (almost) blanket ban on heritage players; they came up with something somewhere in the middle. A compromise?

It's a small world we live in now. So many of us are of mixed heritage, including myself. Many of the Samoan players who reached the 2022 World Cup final were born in Australia or NZ but identify strongly as Samoan. In many cases, they speak both English and Samoan in the home and their parents were born in the homeland. Try telling those players that they should have missed out because they are not 'domestic' players in Samoa!

The disbanding of the USA team I was coaching in the 2013 World Cup and 2011 Qualifiers, as explained earlier, is a perfect 'test case' of what can happen if heritage players are cast as the devil.

Fast tracking developing, domestic players does not work. Watching a boxing match, the job of a boxer looks relatively straightforward, doesn't it? They just punch each other, don't they? Or is it a nuanced sport with skill, dexterity, ring craft and where much more is needed to succeed?

It's the latter, and Rugby League is the same.

Let's take the most 'simple looking' of all positions – prop. I once had a player (domestic from an emerging nation as it happens) try and tell me how simple the role of a prop is if you had the physical and mental attributes. I conceded that, yes, it was 'relatively' simple compared to other positions on the field. But then I proceeded to break down all the components of it to him, including line of run, advantage line running, type of carry, body positioning, when and where to run, and so on and so forth. Props work in the smallest space and with the smallest margins on the field. They have to fight extra hard to get any advantage they can in a very congested and unforgiving area of the field. One poor body position into a collision and, to put it bluntly, you can be put on your arse.

It's why props in the NRL and Super League peak in their 'later' years – they take some time to learn these nuances and to become more 'streetwise' (just like heavyweight boxers). In Australia, many professionals were once kids who played this game from age six. Their siblings play, and their parents and grandparents have also played. They got to the top of their profession in a very congested market. A market where there are more participants in one age group in one junior area than in the whole of some emerging nations or regions combined.

This difference in experience and exposure to intense Rugby League environs throughout life is even noticeable between the nations that run the two biggest competitions in the world! There is a huge difference in the quality of the mid-range Australian and British professional players. A reason so many that are surplus to requirements in the Australian game can flourish in the UK game.

The quality then drops a few notches further when you get to the French, New Zealand and Papua New Guinean domestic competitions. Yes, their best performers may be playing in Australia and the UK, but these are rusted-on League-playing nations that have decades and decades of playing our game behind them.

To expect a team selected primarily from the domestic competition of an emerging nation to compete with the season professionals or amateurs from established nations is like putting a toddler up against Oleksandr Usyk (World Heavyweight Boxing Champion).

Peer coaching

My Poland side was preparing to play the Czech Republic in Lodz in September 2019. With 100% domestic players used in matches before this one, Poland had never won a test match on home soil. I, along with players Nathan, Stephen, Liam, Rob and Chippie, flew from Australia to participate in this test match. One born and bred Pole, Wojtek, was fluent in English as well as Polish and Rob, born and bred in Australia to Polish parents, was fluent in both languages too. Some of the domestic players could speak some English, others couldn't speak much. Chippie had played a bit of Queensland Cup, Liam had been a decent player in the past but was well retired now, and the others were park footballers or retired park footballers.

Without enough experience to fill certain positions on the field, I threw convention out of the window and formed the side instead around the ability to speak two languages. In other words, the bilingual players were placed in the defensive line and attacking shape next to players who were a) inexperienced in the game and b) could only truly understand Polish. We played with one halfback (Nathan) and had two attacking pods on either side of him, again, a mix of experience and inexperience. We also had a middle pod made up of a mixture of playing backgrounds. My water runners were programmed to talk to the ones who could understand them, too! Damo, an Aussie, just spoke to those experienced players whilst Chris (bilingual) relayed all messages to everyone else.

We won convincingly. But that's only half the story. Throughout that training week, the experienced players in each pod were treated as 'assistant coaches' even though they were players. That meant Chippie (left pod), Liam (right pod), and Wojtek (middle pod) took a very lead role in coaching individuals in the nuances of their roles. I had learnt many years before, starting with those university days, that the value of a teammate offering a player advice is huge. Peer coaching if you like. I believe it is hugely powerful when facilitated and coordinated by the coach, as it was in this case.

Experienced heritage players don't just bring on-field benefits, they bring off-field benefits in the bucketload. There should be transparent and open avenues for both heritage and domestic players to get into your squads.

Whoever coaches your 'new', national or rep side will likely need to bring together an interesting mix of professionals and amateurs, athletic and less athletic, experienced and less experienced people. Get a full-time professional club coach, and there's every chance they have never coached anyone in the community or amateur game before, never mind someone who is still learning the absolute basics. Get an amateur or lower grade coach, and there's every chance they'll have never worked with players of the calibre of the professionals in your squad. You need a specialist – someone who has seen as many levels of the game as possible. Someone who knows how to talk to your players and has empathy for any possible limitations of players' abilities. I can give you several examples of this very process working at the very level in question.

Find their why

We were in Philadelphia preparing for the first qualifier against South Africa in 2011 when coach Matthew Elliott got up in front of the players, assembled in a relatively small room and proclaimed:

"Everyone in this room is now a brother. That's non-negotiable".

Quite a bold statement/request, considering many of the people in the room were complete strangers to each other. But it worked. Everyone bonded. We had found our 'why' – each other.

In 2013, Steve Johnson, the team manager and the person wholly responsible for assembling the team and sorting all logistics, demanded that every player and staff member learn the words to Star Spangled Banner, the American national anthem. It was our 'why'. We were representing a proud nation, even if, in the case of some of the staff, me included, it wasn't 'ours'. Steve Johnson himself was the glue that kept the group together. He may not have known it at the time or even to this day, but towards the end of the trip, a few players, upset at not getting picked for much game time were homesick and were starting to share their potentially negative thoughts privately with those they trusted, on a confidential basis. They didn't want to air their laundry amongst the group because they didn't want to create any instability and ultimately, they didn't want to wreck things for 'Johnno' who they knew had worked tirelessly. Johnno had become their 'why'.

In 2018, after my full squad had met and convened the night before, only one hour before our warm-up match and five days before our Emerging Nations World Cup campaign kicked off, I sat the Polish players and staff in a circle in our camp venue and asked one simple question:

"What does playing for Poland mean to you?"

Everybody in the room had to answer from the heart to everyone in the group, and no one was to leave.

What unfolded was the most powerful and emotional few hours in a team environment I have ever witnessed first-hand. Thirty grown men in various states of tears, stunned silence or laughter. Poland, of course, was a nation invaded in World War Two, and many of our players were sons or grandsons of those who fled Nazi persecution. Indeed, there was one story of a player whose qualification was in doubt until the last minute because his parent was born in a POW site that, at the time, was occupied by Germany even though it was originally Polish land.

I truly believe that the fact all the players essentially 'bared their soul' to each other meant that this was the moment we won the Emerging Nations World Trophy undefeated. I think just after that meeting the players knew it too. We had well and truly found our 'why'.

Coaching the team

"So Lee, we've potentially got ... players in Poland, ...and some in the USA, and you've got lads in England and Australia keen to play."

So said Team Manager Shane Young just after my appointment, a mere six weeks before the Emerging Nations. Then he started to list the players from that crew who had been retired for a year or two. I was starting to think I might have to dust the boots off myself! To cut a long story short, what I had (eventually) was a squad of players of very different levels of ability, background and experience, the oldest one 37 and the youngest 17. And they were spread all over the world!

Luckily for me, I had literally just launched a new website dedicated to the sport. As a result, it was not too much of a mental shift to set up a Poland RL page on the site for somewhere the players could access everything they needed to know prior to the tournament.

The page contained......

• Tactical videos and diagrams outlining what sets and plays we would use during the tournament. The idea was that they arrived having done their own 'video sessions' showing them what they needed to know.
• Bespoke training plans for players based on their level of performance and current level of fitness and strength (advanced and intermediate) with explanatory videos
• Player & staff pre-tournament messages from around the world, where they reached out directly to each other
• The team training plans for before and during the tournament
• Dietary advice for the players

I would not be lying if I said that I thought that this page online had done 60-70% of the coaching for me prior to the tournament. This was evidenced in the warm-up game against Hungary, where the players carried out something resembling the game plan, having only all met each other one hour before kick-off.

It is relatively easy these days to communicate with a group of players via the plethora of technological sharing options available to us. The page was perfect as it allows PDFs and videos all in one place and for a specific web address to be made. It did not require players to subscribe to any external service – they just used their allocated password to access the site.

They're not all professionals - less is more

One of the biggest challenges facing coaches of emerging nations is the vast range of talent in the squad they inherit. Most such teams can contain a mix of professionals, amateurs and domestic players from the country in question. Professional players can come from NRL, Super League, State or Championship level, and the amateurs can come from the Australian park or amateur level anywhere. The reality for the coach is that they will be inheriting a group with varying fitness and strength levels, not to mention skill and 'footy IQ'. The domestic players may struggle with footy IQ, depending on the nation in question.

I must credit Matthew Elliott with giving me some of the biggest lessons in this realm. I was taken with Matt to the USA when I was working with him at Penrith Panthers, where he was Head Coach. He had already been a successful Head Coach at Bradford Bulls and Canberra Raiders, so when I got the chance to join him at Penrith, I just jumped at it. Being in close quarters to him at Panthers, I saw him as intense and very detailed in his preparation. When I got the invite to join him with the USA, I was expecting to have to bring my coaching 'A game', and I thought he would bring his intense A game too.

The reality is that he brought his A game, but a very different kind of A game. One that, at the time, I wasn't mentally prepared for. Matt simplified the whole coaching program for the 2011 qualifiers and mandated that we would not train for longer than 90 minutes a day. At the time I remember thinking it was a huge risk and that he'd lost his mind! It wasn't. It was a genius act. We won both qualifiers by the exact same score-line of 40-4, and we were in the World Cup!

The program took into account that it was the end of a long domestic season for every player, regardless of their playing level. It recognised that players had made some huge sacrifices to get on the trip. Sacrifices such as missing work pay or self-funding their trip, plus the personal sacrifices needed to get to a fitness and strength level required prior to the tournament.

The program also allowed the players plenty of free time. We had a midtrip 'bonding night' without curfew, and there were plenty of team trips around

Philadelphia and New York. The result was a super happy camp that all moved in the same direction to achieve the goal of reaching the World Cup.

Two years later, Matt had the NZ Warriors job, so handed the USA mantle over to Terry Matterson, who got the USA job one week before the 2013 World Cup! The team met for the first time in the departure lounge at Heathrow Airport as we prepared to head to France for a warm-up game. Again, simplicity was the key, and we beat France against all odds. Just like his predecessor, Terry didn't set a heavy workload for the players and there was nothing overly technical in the whole preparation. Terry was himself an assistant coach at the time with the North Queensland Cowboys, so it was clear he was adapting to suit the situation at hand.

I put all these learnings into my own international coaching environments, and I have chronicled that in other pages here. This kind of coaching job must be delivered with such considerations in mind!

From the outside looking in, I feel I have seen this balance handled somewhat poorly, with a representative team full of professionals!

Prior to their 2024 first-test defeat to England, Samoa's coach was claiming his side *"had only had six sessions together"* beforehand. Six sessions are a lifetime in terms of preparation for full-time players with a common goal, such as representing their heritage!

It's more than enough to get professionals moving in the same direction! If a coach can't get their team humming in six sessions, then they're complicating the coaching process.

Don't be a one-hit wonder

To make or only succeed at one tournament or competition is like scoring a try on the field and messing up the next three try-scoring chances. It's like making that sandwich with one piece of bread again – it's only half the job. We don't have to look back far to see teams who've succeeded at one World Cup and failed at the rest. Or teams that made one and then failed to make another through normal qualification methods. Look deeper, and there are even more cases of 'one hit wonders', namely successful emerging nations in the various tournaments over the years that have drifted off, never to be heard of since.

It's clear they only looked at the 'here and now' or the top of the sandwich.

To sustain a new Rugby League nation or project, there needs to be as much a focus on the future as there is on the 'now'. You can either run these focuses concurrently or in separate phases of time. Focusing on the 'now' means looking at the next 2-3 years. It might be a World Cup or Emerging Nations World Cup cycle. Approaches here are designed to make sure the Test Match ranking is at least maintained, if not bettered. It also seeks to ensure that the nation is well prepared for the Emerging Nations World Cup or any potential World Cup Qualifiers. It focuses mostly on the senior team, allowing building blocks to be formulated ahead of the next phase.

Use experienced players as development coaches first

When meeting for international or representative matches or camps in non-rugby league areas, this is an ideal opportunity for players to conduct introductory Rugby League clinics to local schools in the area visited. This, in essence, could be the 'first phase' of any long-term player development plan and is definitely cost-effective. Although not wanting to interrupt too much training or match preparation, players will most likely be enthused by the opportunity to experience 'spreading the gospel'.

Clinics should be delivered with clear goals in mind and with a coordinated approach. Every goal connected with growing the game in the area or nation should be focused on 'growing the base'. Numerous studies and amounts of evidence show that the bigger the base, the better the top-end product will be, be it administratively, supporter base or performance-based.

Suggested initial goals for each individual attending the clinics could be:

- They fall in love with Rugby League
- Create a want for participants to play Rugby League
- Create a desire for participants to watch more Rugby League

One of the ideal goals for these clinics from a high-performance and long-term development perspective is for talent identification to take place. If this is the case, then it is suggested that a delivery curriculum is followed in order to highlight skills and traits where you can find suitable athletes/players. It is suggested that in the first phase, details of the best players are collected so that they can be invited to follow-up activities in the short term and also to what is suggested in the next step outlined below.

Developing the future

From the database of players collected, if possible, it is a good idea to bring them into high-performance camps. The stages of this crucial phase of this plan are as follows:

- From recruitment, two squads are picked, making a combined total of approximately 40 players in each age group or combined age group

- The squads spend two to five days in a residential or non-residential 'high performance' camp where they receive intense, high-performance coaching with a view to selecting a representative squad for each age group, that either plays meaningful fixtures or is a 'merit' side for that particular year.

- It is suggested that the first camp starts at the earliest available time to allow all skills learned by players and coaches to be passed down to lower levels as soon as possible.

It is also suggested that all lower-level clubs or teams are encouraged to play according to the principles (and maybe strategies) of the national or representative side, particularly in terms of core and unit skills. This will ensure that:

- All players are playing to principles that will become second nature

- Allows there to be a way of playing that goes from grassroots upwards and from the top team, down

- Means that when players get to a representative level, they have a 'head start' and already have a good understanding of training content

The benefits are enormous

As a coach I have experienced all the feelings associated with qualifying for World Cups, winning World Cup matches against all odds, Emerging Nations World Cups success and coaching teams that are in developmental areas.

The emotions that were felt at such times are beyond words. They run deeper than anything else I have experienced in the game. The joy I see in peoples' faces when they discover our game and the strength of the passion the game brings out in people new to it are special things to witness. When that transmits into on-field success, it's something else again. The interest conducting such programs attracts and the joy it brings to people in the host town, city or country in particular when you are successful. Quite simply, the benefits of doing this properly are enormous.

There are a couple of 'viral' videos out there – one of me teaching a player how to play the ball properly via a Spanish interpreter and another of me with an amateur 'translator' who was eventually mocked on television by one of the biggest comedians in Argentina! They still bring giggles to those who were around for the filming and bind us for life.

There's a new Rugby League world emerging out there, and we need to help it as much as we can.

Key Points from This Chapter

- Consider challenging yourself as a coach by working in developing areas of the game, including emerging nations and the ever-expanding women's game.

- Coaching in any of these 'new' areas of the game brings out different skills in the experienced Rugby League coach who will have to focus more on the fundamentals of coaching

- A sandwich model of development approaches long term growth from the top and the bottom

- Peer coaching is very powerful in emerging RL areas

Wojciech Sieczkowski, PhD.

I'm a Pole who found and fell in love with Rugby League in Ireland! How often does that happen?

I had no background in the game as I'd only played Union before. I learned the basics of this new sport by watching my mates play! These include basics like passing the ball backwards and tackling, the same things you were asked to do in Union. But the play the ball and the two-man and three-man tackles and retreating ten metres in defence were all new to me. Big thanks to Richard Egan for explaining those basics to me.

When I bulked up, I was moved to the second row, but I didn't fully understand why I was asked to play on the edge. In fairness, I was pretty told to run in a straight line and not pass the ball. I was a very good tackler and didn't shy of those direct runs at the highest speed I could muster. I was clocking around 12 seconds for the 100 metres and weighing around 110-115 kg back then.

In 2016, I was getting towards the end of my career (or so I thought). I played a game back in my home country of Poland. We lost badly to the British Teachers squad. Our defence wasn't structured and the coaches weren't able to give any meaningful advice. I thought my playing career was slowly drifting away.

Two years later, when I heard of the Australian branch of Poland Rugby League being formed, I was skeptical at first. But it soon became apparent that things were happening, and there was talk of an Emerging Nations World Championships (ENWC) potentially in 2018 and that certainly appealed to me. The opportunity to play in the ENWC was tempting, given that they called for players, especially those of us born in Poland.

When coach Lee Addison gave the green light on my selection, I was on cloud nine. But this also meant a lot of hard work for anyone selected before we all met at the tournament. The brilliant news was Lee Addison provided us with clear-cut instructions online, including manuals, videos and strength and conditioning plans – all the things I wish I had available in the ten years prior! It was amazing. I now understood the rucks, the edge, the structure for props, what halves had to do and how those teams worked together on the field.

Having arrived at Sydney Airport, I met the lads at the camp which was being held a few days before the tournament. The energy was enormous and the vibe amongst the group was fantastic.

Lee is not only great at explaining the rules of the game and building game plans in a short period of time (The ENWC was confirmed and organised at the last minute), but he is a genius at gelling the team.

One rule he brought in was that we weren't allowed to scratch our balls! If you know men, we are pretty good at that. If we got caught by Lee or a teammate, we had to do ten push-ups, even if it was in the middle of training. Needless to say, everyone did scratch theirs at some point and we all did plenty of push-ups. It was hilarious!

The biggest memory though was when Lee sat us down at a roundtable and asked everyone to share their story and roots connecting them to Poland. He also asked us to describe what it meant to represent the country they were born in, or where their parents or grandparents were born.

No words can describe the emotions and the spirit in that room. That day will stay as one of the best memories of my lifetime and no doubt those of everyone else in the room.

The ENWC was held in Sydney and the company I worked for had offices in North Sydney, allowing me to work for the three weeks of the tournament. I had the pleasure of crossing the famous Harbour Bridge every day!

I got one cap in the tournament. I could understand this because there were some fantastic players in our team who had great experience, some of them professional experience. I got injured in my first appearance, but I was tackling everything and doing ok I was definitely blessed to have this opportunity. Although seriously happy that we won the tournament, appetite grew with eating and I probably lost contact with reality a bit and was quite disappointed instead of happy overall, to be fair.

I was fighting hard to get that second cap, so I made a pledge with Lee after the tournament. I watched every video on his site, then lost weight again to get myself down to 112 kg and got seriously fitter. I also watched every game I could, and I was understanding it all better now. I took it upon myself to organise a tour, contacting teams around Europe and my team played Harderwijk from Holland and Madrid from Spain, somewhere in Germany. I also played in a Nines tournament for Exiles in Dublin.

All of this was to prepare for the proposed September 2019 international period where several of the previous year's ENWC squad travelled to Poland. Coach Lee was accompanied by Steve, Chippie, Nathan, Liam, Rob and Alex plus staff members Damo and Shane.

When selected, this for me, was an extension of the ENWC. I absolutely gave it my all. I also was able to translate between the languages as half the team were made of domestic players and the rest were of Polish heritage.

Once again, credit goes to Lee for pulling this off and gelling the team together. He once again asked the Australian based lads to share their story with locals and I had the honour of translating. No one even dared to consider for a second that they were playing with anything other than 100% Polak's.

Then it came to the night of team selection, and I was in the team to play the Czechs. We had a simple but very well-structured and, most importantly widely understood game plan. We converted one half to a third prop and only had a couple of plays to remember.

The following day I received a phone call from Lee. The senior players had a vote and I was unequivocally voted team captain.

No words can describe what this meant.

The lesson is to never give up and work hard. After thinking my career was drifting off in 2016, I was now Poland's captain of a strong, organised squad in 2019. Without the instructions and guidance from Lee and what videos and other teaching resources I found on his website, none of this would have been possible.

The test match was tough and of course, I broke some ribs in the first tackle! I didn't tell anyone, and I just knew I was going to play the full game no matter what. I didn't care. I had a good game. We had a good game, and we won the test. The game was live-streamed so the lads back in Australia watched, all our families watched and there were plenty in attendance. It was awesome.

The following year in Poland, with this momentum, we organised a four-team domestic competition. I was able to pass on what I learned to players who were mostly Amateur Union lads trying League out. They grasped a basic understanding of League quickly as I had a ready recipe. My team Tryton Warszawa - won the competition! This was another great adventure with amazing memories.

2024 was the year I officially retired after saying to everyone around me that I was going to for years! One of the reasons I kept delaying my retirement was that I simply wanted to take advantage of everything I learned about the game so late in life. I'm very proud that one of my protégées who I was able to pass on to the love of the Greatest Game of All (and my basic understanding of it based on Lee's coaching) was able to build and win the Polish domestic competition in 2024 with his team.

In Poland, as I guess happens in most emerging nations, one must organise, build, play, coach and do what seems to be everything on and off the field, on their own. It is very draining and difficult. And then, of course, the inevitable off-field politics kick in and leave something of a sour taste.

2023 was the last Tryton Warszawa played because the administration of the game in Poland is weak, and they have squandered all chances to lift the profile of the game on the back of the huge momentum from the ENWC in 2018 and our success in 2019. For reasons unbeknownst to those, like me, who wanted to build something more.

For me, that's all irrelevant now. The beautiful memories of the ENWC in 2018 The Test Match in Poland in 2019 and the domestic title win in 2020 are memories that have been a reward for all the sacrifices that have been made. Lee Addison was the biggest factor in all this, and I will be forever thankful.

Wojciech 'Tek' Sieczkowski was born and raised in Poland and played Rugby Union since 1998. He started playing Rugby League in Limerick, Ireland at the age of 26. After playing for Treaty City Titans and Dublin City Exiles for several seasons, he returned home to Poland. Tek played for the Poland national side in the 2018 Emerging Nations World Championships and captained his country in the 2019 Test Match versus the Czech Republic in Lodz, Poland. He has won domestic titles in his home country as a captain/coach and has also helped administer the game in the country until 2024.

Part Three

The Coach's Calling...

"You need to get yourself to a doctor or Hospital immediately, Lee. You're at great risk."

So said the nurse on the other end of the NHS Direct phone line, which I'd called because, as I'd told her:

"I don't want to live, but I don't want to die either".

On hearing these words, the nurse sent me straight to see a medical specialist and I was soon diagnosed with Depression. Back in the early 2000s, a man being open about being 'depressed' wasn't as common as it is a quarter of a century on. In the lead-up to that NHS phone call, I'd been partying as much as I could and working when I had to. Burning the candle at both ends, as it's known. One day, I got home from a night out on the drink at 7 am, had a shit, shower and a shave and reported for work at 9 am. I drank seven nights a week, at least one bottle of wine a night if I wasn't going out on the town. I was in my early 20s and was in freefall. Bored with my life direction, I decided to drink and party constantly.

It got to the stage that I wasn't enjoying anything, not even watching my beloved Rugby League, Manchester City or the England Cricket team. I was so bored and depressed with life, only having a beer made me feel happy and I soon got bored of that too after six months of drinking everything in sight.

There was only one thing I could truly focus on that made me forget everything I was going through. Coaching. Coaching – and the sport of Rugby League - saved me. It's the only thing I could focus on happily without feeling anxious or downright depressed.

Once diagnosed, I studied and read about depression. It was at this point the penny started to drop. There was a reason I was feeling as I was. Once I took the medication I needed to help, armed with my newly acquired knowledge of my condition, in no time, I started to rebuild my life again.

Once diagnosed with Depression, it's always lurking there in the background, ready to strike. Every day, even a quarter of a century on, I have to take steps to ensure what's going on between my ears is mostly positive rather than negative. I still love a beer with my friends and family, but too much of it often brings on those negative and anxious thoughts again. I know when to knock the drinking on the head now and have put very strong restrictions on myself to ensure I never fall down a mental hole again. I also only have a beer now if I feel I have earned it.

There have been times when life circumstances have seriously tested my resolve in this regard, but what that episode at the start of the Millennium taught me was that the answer is ***never*** at the bottom of the glass or bottle. Instead, I learnt as much as I could about the workings of the mind, so much so that I chart back to the start of any mental strength I possess or my ability to help players mentally on a football field (or off it), back to these times. I don't regret what happened at all; I think it made me so much stronger as a person and as a coach.

To get out of any stupor, the answer for me has been to focus on projects. Coaching people and trying to enrich lives has given me so much to aim for and lots of fulfilment. Having a plan, a strategy and approach that started in my head and eventually ends up playing out in physical form on a football field, or in others achieving things they never previously thought possible has been a gift and a thrill that has given me direction in life.

All I have ever wanted to do while on this journey was read coaching books or study coaching methods so I could improve. The Rugby League Coaching Magazine (RLCM) used to be a great source of knowledge. I would say however, I found the lack of books on coaching my sport very frustrating. My bookshelves are full of coaches and coaching stories from other sports, with only a small section dedicated to our game.

In 2018 I was so fed up with the lack of support and resources available to coaches of Rugby League that I took a leap of faith to set up an online coaching resource for coaches and players all around the world. I wanted to share my coaching experience and knowledge with as many people as possible and decided I was no longer going to keep any coaching 'secrets' from other coaches.

The site became the biggest offering of its kind at the start of 2020 after I inherited all the RLCM content that formed so much of my coaching philosophy and added all issues and digital offerings to my website! The main site was soon joined by a second site, dedicated to allowing coaches to take 'Courses' and a YouTube channel, giving access to coaching resources for free. This book is a natural extension of those offerings and my way of giving as much as I can to coaches in our game.

I have also spent plenty of time coaching players or mentoring coaches in all sorts of ways in person or online. All this has provided a welcome 'next stage' of my coaching journey, which, at the time of writing, is in its 27th year, 18 of them coaching in Australia.

One of the biggest reasons I decided to chance my arm in Australia and move to the other side of the world with two heavy bags, a laptop and a one-way ticket was that my family had suffered some devastation over two years as we lost three members of our family to Motor Neurone Disease. In the blink of an eye, my gran in her early 70s, my uncle (49) and my mother (48) were taken in one of the most horrific ways, and the diagnoses in such close proximity to each other caused medical people to delve deeper. It turns out that that side of my family is in the 10% that suffer from the 'familial' form of the disease – in other words, it's running through our family.

Rugby League people will be familiar with the bravery of former Leeds Rhinos half Rob Burrow in taking on the disease that eventually overcame him at age 41. You will also be familiar with the amazing fund-raising endeavours of his best friend, British Rugby League legend Kevin Sinfield. Two decades ago, when my family were dealing with it, a lot less was known about the disease, and it didn't seem to be on the public radar. I cannot begin to put into words how much I appreciate Rob and Kevin for what they have done to bring it to the public consciousness.

Back when I left for Australia, we were unpacking the fact that generations of our family had probably died from MND and not what they were diagnosed with at the time. Some in my family think that my way of dealing with the grief was to escape for a bit, with travelling to the other side of the world being a very extreme example of my retreating into a male 'cave'.

What is true is that the fear of falling into a depression again played on my mind, and I wasn't going to sit still wondering about life's direction if I was destined to die in my late 40s like so many members of my family. I also believe that I was so much stronger for what I had gone through before I was first diagnosed. It was then I learnt that knowledge of the workings of the mind was a huge blessing when dealing with severe setbacks.

Not long after my Ma died, I was at Rugby Football League Regional Camp (the ones I have told you about already). We had an absolute whale of a time at that camp, as staff as many rallied around to help me escape the grief. I also did, what I believe to this day, to be some of the best coaching I have ever done that week. Coaching was helping me escape again. Despite being racked with grief, I could still escape through coaching footy, and it took on an even deeper life meaning for me.

Then one night, I was sitting with my dad watching some shit Friday night English television and he asked, out of the blue:

"Why don't you have a go at coaching in Australia, lad?"

I didn't need to be asked twice. I managed to cobble together enough money for a one-way ticket, resigned from my job on the Monday and prepared to make the leap in the weeks to come. Upon leaving, I thought I'd worry about my return to the UK a little later and that I'd be here for a year or two, a maximum of four. Well, here I am two decades later, and I have not decided what I'm doing yet!

I do think this coaching thing has been something of a calling for me. I am simply following my calling. I coached my first-ever team in 1999 when I had only just left my teenage years. Back then, my university team couldn't find a coach, and the organisers thought they'd ask this opinionated, brash, impatient, forthright and determined captain of the side if I would coach the team that season. I thought they were crazy and duly informed them of that initial assessment. I had no desire whatsoever to coach and planned to leave the conversation, wishing them well for the season ahead. Instead, I left the spontaneous meeting promising to coach 'one session next Monday'.

Since that fateful discussion, I think I have coached, when it's all averaged out, at least three times a week for all of my life since. That discussion led to the University side having a winning season, where we got promoted to the top division, and we had a bloody good time whilst we did it. In one of the many team bonding sessions of that season, one of the deeper thinkers in the team told me over a pint one day:

"You should look into coaching as a career, Lee."

I initially thought this guy was also crazy until I gave it some deeper (and sober) thought. I was by now 21 years old, so the common thought was that I had to focus on playing again. I'd achieved some things as a player but always seemed to be slightly off where I wanted to be, even though I'd done things that the majority only dream of. I have, however, never been one to follow the crowd and when a few coaching opportunities started popping up here there and everywhere, it became apparent that I could forge something of a coaching career by my mid-20s.

It is a career that has taken me all around the world including NRL clubs and World Cups plus the schoolboy job at St Gregory's that changed my life for the better. Fate and luck also seemed to play its hand again as there was a very prominent news article that led to me getting that key role in the schoolboy game.

St Gregory's was the traditional big fish in schoolboy footy. From the 1960's to the early Noughties, the school had produced so many professional players and several NRL coaches. The list of past students includes the 'Coach of the Century' Jack Gibson and the multi-premiership winning coaches Tim Sheens and Trent Robinson.

The reality was that Rugby League had gradually fallen down the list of school priorities over the years. The change was such that Sydney's Daily Telegraph newspaper felt compelled to splash its back page with a story about Rugby League offerings at the school in 2009.

This article forced a group of very concerned parents, past staff and current stakeholders (including Canterbury Bankstown and Wests Tigers NRL clubs) to form a committee to change things. My name was linked quickly with the role. I met with the headmaster and the 'concerned parents and stakeholders' committee and without much delay at all they anointed me as their next coach. The committee were also quick to tell me what a tough coaching gig this was going to be. I was also told multiple times that it would take at least three years to rebuild the team to one that could compete with the Pats Blacktown's of this world.

As you know from reading this book, it took six months!

All the experiences and the lessons I have learned and much of what I have shared with you in this book almost never occurred. It seems fate played its hand again.

Just over three years before arriving at St Gregory's was the day I left the North of England to chase my coaching dream down under. Back then, I was due to take a domestic flight to London to connect with a different international company who were to fly me to Sydney to embark on my new adventure.

It was late morning at the airport and my domestic flight was due to leave in two hours. I was well ahead of schedule. I am the kind of person who likes to 'plane watch' when I am at an airport, so I took my customary position overlooking the tarmac. Although today was going to be anything but customary as there was far more action on the tarmac.

It was so windy and wet that planes were struggling to land. Many of them were doing a 'touch and go' where the attempted landing has to be aborted last minute, and they go straight back up towards the sky to try again. The TVs in the terminal were showing news of winds of up to 99mph causing havoc in England's green and pleasant land. I looked up at the departures monitor and my 35-minute-long flight to London had been delayed until 2:30 pm, which wasn't a problem because my flight to Sydney was leaving at 8 pm that night.

When it got to 1:30 pm the flight was delayed a further hour to 3:30 pm so now I started to get a little nervous. I called my father and he hadn't even got home yet. A normal 25-minute drive home from the airport was taking hours as cars tumbled and crashed in the weather, causing huge jams. The local news was showing a tree had broken and landed on the train tracks on the one line that left the airport - so getting a train to London was not an option either.

I called Gordon. Gordon, a Londoner and also my best mate's uncle that is. I had met him three years earlier at my mates' wedding and I remembered he worked at Heathrow Airport. I told Gordon all about my problems and he said not to worry, he would talk to the counter staff at the check-in area of my international flight and, as he'd already done about thirty years as a staff member at the airport, I was very confident I was in good hands.

We finally boarded the plane at 3 pm for a 3:30 pm departure but the door didn't shut quickly because one or two people had got themselves inebriated somewhere in the airport, with their bags already on the plane. This meant a 3:30 pm departure now became a 4:15 pm one. The drunk duo never arrived. Instead, ground staff dragged their bags off the plane, and we were good to go at 4:15 pm. We started to taxi out, and then, all of a sudden, someone pressed the call button and asked for help. The medical team ran on, tended to this person and then carried them off. Their bags also needed to be located and taken off the plane. It was now 6 pm.

We set off for London at 6:40 pm. The 35-minute flight time became a 50-minute flight. The wind delaying the approach into London Heathrow. I knew I was toast if I wanted to fly to Sydney at 8 pm.

I rang Gordon as soon as we landed, and he told me not to rush. When I met him in the terminal, he delivered the devastating news that the airline companies don't conveniently leave a seat on the next flight for you if you miss it. You are classed simply as a 'no show'. Also, the next flight wasn't for another 24 hours.

This was not good. I had $5000 Australian to get into the country. I couldn't eat into that for a new flight as they wouldn't let me into Australia. Gordon said I could stay with him that night and suggested I shouldn't panic and that we'd look at it again in the morning. He took me to a pub to eat and to drown my sorrows for the evening. On the night when I was due to be taking off to sunnier climes to chase my ambitions in coaching, I was stuck in a pub in wet and windy Staines, the home of Sacha Baron Cohen's comedy character Ali G.

I probably drank more Guinness than I should have that night (I had an excuse, right?) so slept very well. As I woke up, Gordon had just returned from his morning walk. He urged me to get ready as we had to go down the canal to go and see someone at their home. This someone happened to be some European big wig of the plane company I was due to be flying with the night before!

Gordon has never admitted it to this day, but I could swear this was a set-up. Sat in his study, Mr. Big Wig swiveled towards me in his office chair and asked why I was heading to Australia. I told him I was going to the Manly Warringah region of Sydney to coach Rugby League. I made myself sound like Wayne Bennett or Vince Lombardi there and then, which led him to his next question:

"Can I find out about you online?"

I didn't have a clue but answered *"YES!"* emphatically and rather hopefully. Much to my relief, when he googled me, a solitary article popped up. A paper had done a feature about me a couple of weeks earlier and there I was in all my glory on the PC in Mr. Big Wig's study. He preceded to tell me of his love of the game and how he liked watching it on a Friday night. He told me and Gordon to wait a second.

Next, his chair swiveled towards me again and he gave me some amazing news. I was on the flight that night at 8 pm and he'd also upgraded me. He also told me it wouldn't cost me an extra penny. Thank you, Mr. Big Wig.

A few hours later, Gordon and I headed to the airport. I slapped my two bags on the carousel when the lady at the check-in desk said to me:

"Welcome to our airline Mr. Addison but sorry to say, your bags are 35 kilograms over the limit and if you want these bags to travel with you today, you need to pay a further 300 pounds as per your booking conditions."

I'd flown to London by purchasing extra baggage but didn't think I'd need to do that for my Sydney flight. A quick calculation in my head worked out that at the exchange rate at the time, I now needed to fork out over $800 Australian and thus another risk to the exact $5000 I had in the bank to enter Australia. I thought *"I'm never destined to do this"*.

Enter Gordon to save the day for the umpteenth time. He turned on the charm and then showed the lady his Heathrow Airport security card and pass. The lady replied with, *"Oh, you're Gordon?"* as if he was some kind of deity she'd finally met. Her demeanour changed in the presence of the great man, and she waved my bags through as if they were 15 kilograms underweight and at no extra cost. I was free to finally make my way to Australia. As if to remind me of Staines and Ali G, the plane actually flew over Kazakhstan and I wondered if Sacha Baron Cohen's next character, Borat was down there!

These coincidences, timings and fate interventions seem to have been an intriguing side story to my coaching journey. My first coaching 'break' came when I was appointed as one of two Assistant Coaches to England Students, the Head Coach being a young Richard Agar. Agar went on to coach Hull FC, Wakefield Trinity, Leeds Rhinos, France and is currently the NZ Warriors

Assistant Coach. The idea back then was that he would mentor both of us young pups to, maybe one day, take the top job. Within weeks and before a training session even happened, Agar picked up a professional coaching job and had to vacate the role. Left with no other option as we were running out of time, it was down to myself and the other young assistant, Matt, to become 'joint coaches' of the side ahead of a match against Scotland Students and a two-match trip to play the British Armed Forces in Germany.

The second key moment was when Matt and I both applied for a lead administration role in the game. Was I to be a career administrator or a coach? Those doing the interviews were going to dictate my fate with their decision. I'd done a bit of both, but the administration role was a full-time job and coaching paid zip, so I knew which one I wanted at the time!

Matt got the administration job which left me alone with the England Students side. My old coach John Kain was alongside me in a support role but was happy to let me run the show. Within the following twelve months, I remained an unbeaten England Students coach, including being the coach of the side that got its first-ever win over Antipodean opposition, and I'd been selected as an Assistant to Great Britain Students under another old coach of mine, Vinny Webb. We toured Australia in a trip that was to plant a seed in my mind for the future and on returning, I got asked to assist an England Ladies side in a trip to Russia! In that year, I got to travel to Scotland, Germany, Australia and Russia doing the thing I loved and also well and truly caught the coaching bug for life! My mind was made up! Coaching had called me!

Several sliding door moments led to me being appointed at Manly Sea Eagles almost immediately upon my arrival to live in Australia four years later. When I had my own team to coach, however, we couldn't have had a worse start. Played three. Lost three.

It was common knowledge at the club that if Noel 'Crusher' Cleal came to join you in the coaching box, you were being watched. In Crushers' words, they had taken a 'bold move' in signing off the first coaching appointment at the club from the UK since Mal Reilly did some lower-grade coaching back in the day. They'd taken a punt on this unknown Pommy, and it wasn't looking good.

For our Round 4 game against Canberra Raiders, Crusher took his seat right next to me in the coaching box a few minutes before kick-off. It was fair to say we needed to win this one, and I had to 'coach well. We won that game by over 40 points and Crusher was apparently very happy with everything he saw and heard unfold. I never looked back.

Politics had meant that I didn't get the gig I wanted at Penrith initially and had to take up a coaching role with the Western Sydney Academy of Sport team (a mixture of Parramatta and Penrith juniors) to prove my worth and do my time. It just so happened that the Chief Executive Officer of the Western Sydney Academy of Sport also happened to be part of the 'concerned parents and stakeholders' committee that wanted to improve the footy output of St Gregory's!

My move to Queensland to continue the school program work up there was all started by a phone call 'out of the blue' that had come about because someone else in the Ipswich area had my CV and decided to hand it over to the Deputy Principal of the school. The DP was attending his one and only local Rugby League committee meeting to explain why he was kicking off a program and searching for a suitable Head Coach.

The 2013 World Cup was held in the UK and our team, the United States were stationed in a hotel a full 150 metres away from my uncle and aunt's house! Out of all the hotels allocated to the sixteen teams throughout the UK, we were stationed near Uncle Wayne and Auntie Jenny's! This was my first visit home to England since leaving and this proximity to family meant I could occasionally escape the gluten-free meals the players had to eat and it also meant I didn't need to queue up for the hotel washing machines and instead, could sub-contract that particular job to the family!

When I was with Poland in 2018, I introduced a call which was used to tell the team to *'keep doing what we are doing as it's working'*. The call was 'Wendy'. The players loved this, and that is all you need to know! This book is not the place to go into detail, except to say the Wendy in question was a mythical, made-up person, and no Wendy's were harmed or disrespected in the making of this team. In the build-up to the 2019 tour to play the Czechs in Poland, there had been so much arranged and rearranged that I was not willing to commit the time or finances to it and neither were many players. A lot was up in the air.

Four weeks before the trip, I received a call from Stephen Kolodziej, a player with the team who was also a committee member. Steve said he could get a sponsor for me and some of the players to go if I committed. He also added that some of the players were waiting on my position and were only going if I did.

It was at the moment that I think Steve was about to give up on me that a car drove past and slid into a nearby parking spot. The number plate - "W3NDY". The universe had spoken, and I decided there and then I was going to Poland. The trip was amazing, it was a golden time.

I hope that in reading this book, you may have got some inspiration or a light bulb moment that will help you on your own coaching journey or life. If getting a copy of this book changes at least one coaching life or life in general for the better, then it has done its job.

Reading books has been such a huge part of my coaching journey and life in general. I told some people recently that I actually believe everything good and significant that has happened in my life has revolved around reading or something I have read.

My bookshelves are full of all sorts and the tales in the written word of Sir Alex Ferguson, Brian Clough, Bill Shankly, Bob Paisley, Jose Mourinho, Arsene Wenger, Jurgen Klopp, Pep Guardiola, John Wooden, 'Bear' Bryant, Bill Belichick (and so many more) have had a huge bearing on me as a coach. I read them all because I decided coaching is my calling. I dedicated my life to coaching because it is my calling.

Maybe coaching is your calling too?

Thanks so much for reading right to the end. I'd love you to keep in touch. I publish The Rugby League Coach Podcast every Monday (You can listen on Apple, Spotify or many other places) and you are invited to send me an email to admin@rugbyleaguecoach.com.au to send your questions or just say hello.

I love your work

Lee

www.ingramcontent.com/pod-product-compliance
Lightning Source LLC
Chambersburg PA
CBHW060549080526
44585CB00013B/495